The Frontiers
of Science & Faith

Examining
Questions
from the
Big Bang
to the End
of the
Universe

John Jefferson Davis

InterVarsity Press
Downers Grove, Illinois

InterVarsity Press
P.O. Box 1400, Downers Grove, IL 60515-1426
World Wide Web: www.ivpress.com
E-mail: mail@ivpress.com

InterVarsity Press® is the book-publishing division of InterVarsity Christian Fellowship/USA®, a student movement active on campus at hundreds of universities, colleges and schools of nursing in the United States of America, and a member movement of the International Fellowship of Evangelical Students. For information about local and regional activities, write Public Relations Dept., InterVarsity Christian Fellowship/USA, 6400 Schroeder Rd., P.O. Box 7895, Madison, WI 53707-7895, or visit the IVCF website at <www.ivcf.org>.

Cover photograph: D. Robert, SPL/Photo Researchers Inc.
ISBN 0-8308-2664-5
Printed in the United States of America ∞

Library of Congress Cataloging-in-Publication Data

Davis, John Jefferson.
    Frontiers of science and faith: examining questions from the big bang to the end of the universe/John Jefferson Davis.
      p. cm.
    Includes bibliographical references.
    ISBN 0-8308-2664-5 (pbk.: alk. paper)
    1. Religion and science. I. Title.

BL240.3 .D38 2002
261.5'5—dc21

                                                      2001051793

| P | 23 | 22 | 21 | 20 | 19 | 18 | 17 | 16 | 15 | 14 | 13 | 12 | 11 | 10 | 9 | 8 | 7 | 6 | 5 | 4 | 3 | 2 | 1 |
| Y | 21 | 20 | 19 | 18 | 17 | 16 | 15 | 14 | 13 | 12 | 11 | 10 | 09 | 08 | 07 | 06 | 05 | 04 | 03 | 02 |

Contents

Acknowledgments _____ 6

Preface _____ 7

1 Genesis 1:1 & Big Bang Cosmology _____ 11

2 Quantum Indeterminacy & the Omniscience of God _____ 37

3 The "Copenhagen" Interpretation of Quantum Mechanics
& "Delayed-Choice" Experiments: New Perspectives
on the Doctrine of Predestination_____ 57

4 Theological Reflections on Chaos Theory _____ 71

5 Does Gödel's Proof Have Theological Implications? _____ 89

6 Artificial Intelligence & the Christian Understanding of Personhood _____ 103

7 Is "Progressive Creation" Still a Helpful Concept? Reflections on Creation,
Evolution & Bernard Ramm's *Christian View of Science and Scripture*_____ 113

8 The Anthropic Principle—or "Designer Universe"? _____ 129

9 The Search for Extraterrestrial Intelligence & the
Christian Doctrine of Redemption _____ 141

10 Cosmic Endgame: Theological Reflections on Recent Scientific
Speculations on the Ultimate Fate of the Universe _____ 159

Epilogue _____ 175

Bibliography _____ 178

Subject and Name Index_____ 196

Scripture Index _____ 200

Acknowledgments

Chapter two, "Quantum Indeterminacy and the Omniscience of God," originally appeared in *Science and Christian Belief* 9 (April 1997): 129-44.

Chapter four, "Theological Reflections on Chaos Theory," originally appeared in *Perspectives on Science and Christian Faith* 49, no. 2 (1997): 75-84.

Chapter seven, "Is 'Progressive Creation' Still a Helpful Concept?" originally appeared in *Perspectives on Science and Christian Faith* 50, no. 4 (1998): 250-59.

Chapter nine, "The Search for Extraterrestrial Intelligence and the Christian Doctrine of Redemption," originally appeared in *Science and Christian Belief* 9 (April 1997): 21-34.

Chapter ten, "Cosmic Endgame," originally appeared in *Science and Christian Belief* 11 (April 1999): 15-28.

Preface

In his *Scientists as Theologians* John Polkinghorne issued an "open invitation" for theologians to become more involved in the science-religion conversation. The present work is, in part, a response to that invitation. This collection of essays is based on research for my course Frontiers of Science and Faith, taught at Gordon-Conwell Theological Seminary, which was a 1994-1995 winner in the John Templeton Foundation's science and religion model course program. Participating in the Templeton Foundation's program reignited old interests in questions of theology and the natural sciences that dated back to my undergraduate days as a physics major at Duke University in the late 1960s. Most of the essays in this book were written during a sabbatical leave spent in Cambridge, England.

The purpose of this book is to reflect theologically on certain cutting-edge issues in modern science. A basic presupposition of these essays is that the results of modern science, properly understood, are no threat to Christian faith. Christian faith and scientific method are understood to be *complementary* ways of knowing God's creative work, each having its distinctive ways of knowing, methods and areas of validity. I also believe that a number of the areas of scientific research that are explored here point to the limitations of the scientific method for answering humanity's deepest existential questions, and call for a new opening of the conversation between the scientific and religious communities.

Chapter one, "Genesis 1:1 and Big Bang Cosmology," reviews recent biblical scholarship relating to the opening words of Genesis and current scientific discussions of the "big bang." It is argued that Genesis 1:1 does indeed refer to a real beginning of the universe in time and is consistent with scientific understandings of the universe's beginning.

Chapter two, "Quantum Indeterminacy and the Omniscience of God," explores the question, does quantum indeterminacy in nature require a revision of or abandonment of classical theism's understanding of the omniscience of God? The proposal of Arthur Peacocke for a "self-limited omniscience" on the part of God is examined, and it is concluded that quantum physics does not require an abandoning of the traditional notion of divine omniscience.

Chapter three, "The 'Copenhagen' Interpretation of Quantum Mechanics and 'Delayed-Choice' Experiments: New Perspectives on the Doctrine of Predestination," explores possible implications of recent experiments in quantum physics that seem to indicate that the "past" is not fully determined until the experimental measurements are completed. It is suggested that these experiments provided a framework for understanding the doctrine of predestination in a more dynamic way.

Chapter four, "Theological Reflections on Chaos Theory," begins with a survey of the main features and historical origins of the branch of physics now known as chaos theory. It is argued that chaos theory provides new ways of understanding the role of chance in God's providential interaction with the world.

Chapter five raises the question "Does Gödel's Proof Have Theological Implications?" A brief sketch of the life of logician Kurt Gödel is presented, and the salient points of his celebrated "incompleteness theorem" are discussed. I argue that Gödel's proof does not provide a warrant for epistemological relativism but does imply that the notion of truth cannot and should not be reduced to the notion of provability.

Chapter six, "Artificial Intelligence and the Christian Understanding of Personhood," argues that the progress of artificial intelligence research programs challenges Christian theologians to recover relational (as opposed to primarily functional) understandings of the person, and likewise challenges scientists in this field to reflect more critically on the ethical dimensions of their work. The scientific method cannot supply the moral framework needed to address the ethical questions posed by artificial intelligence research.

Chapter seven, "Is 'Progressive Creation' Still a Helpful Concept?" reviews scientific and theological developments since the 1954 publication of Bernard Ramm's *Christian View of Science and Scripture*. I conclude that Ramm's concept of "progressive creation," in which God is understood to have created through a variety of means over long periods of time, is still a helpful way of relating the biblical texts concerning origins to the history of life on earth.

Chapter eight, "The Anthropic Principle—or 'Designer Universe'?" examines discussions of the "anthropic principle," a term often used to call attention to the fact that the existence of life in the universe is sensitively dependent on the remarkably "fine-tuned" values of fundamental constants in physics and cosmology. The evidence of such fine-tuning, I suggest, is better explained by the hypothesis of intelligent design than by appeals to an "anthropic principle" or to multiple universes.

Chapter nine, "The Search for Extraterrestrial Intelligence and the Christian Doctrine of Redemption," examines the history of Christian and pre-Christian speculation on the question of intelligent beings elsewhere in the universe. I then argue that Paul's Christology and soteriology expressed in Colossians 1:19-20 are sufficiently comprehensive to account for the redemption of any such beings anywhere in the universe, if in fact such beings exist and are in need of redemption.

Chapter ten, "Cosmic Endgame: Theological Reflections on Recent Scientific Speculations on the Ultimate Fate of the Universe," interacts with scientific scenarios developed by physicists Freeman Dyson, Frank Barrow and John Tipler. It is contended that these scenarios do not succeed in escaping the "thermodynamic pessimism" of the nineteenth century and its predictions of the final "heat death" of the universe. The essay concludes that ultimate hope for humanity cannot be found in the laws of physics alone but must be derived from divine revelation.

I wish to thank my friends and colleagues Perry Phillips and Tony Castro for their helpful discussions of many of the issues in this book, as well as my students and colleagues at Gordon-Conwell, who have helped with their insights and suggestions. I also wish to thank the editors of *Science and Christian Belief* and *Perspectives on Science and Christian Faith* for permission to reprint several of the articles that are contained in this volume.

1

Genesis 1:1 & Big Bang Cosmology

W hen historians of science look back on the 1970s and '80s," stated physicist Heinz Pagels, "they will report that for the first time scientists constructed rational mathematical models based on the laws of physics which described the creation of the universe out of nothing."[1] These new theories in "quantum cosmology" attempt to combine elements of general relativity, quantum mechanics, and elementary particle physics in order to extrapolate the known laws of nature back to the initial "big bang," the moment of the creation of the universe itself.[2]

Genesis 1:1 states that "in the beginning God created the heavens and the

---

[1]Heinz R. Pagels, *Perfect Symmetry: The Search for the Beginning of Time* (London: Michael Joseph, 1985), p. 349.

[2]For an accessible discussion of recent trends in cosmology and elementary particle physics, including "theories of everything" which are attempting to unify the four fundamental forces of nature in one comprehensive theory, see John Horgan, "Particle Metaphysics," *Scientific American* 270, no. 2 (February 1994): 70-78.

earth." Do the biblical account of creation and modern cosmologies agree that the universe had a singular beginning, that the universe was "created out of nothing"? If there is such a convergence, what is its nature, and what, if any, is its theological significance? This chapter aims to explore these questions by examining biblical scholarship on Genesis1:1 and current big bang cosmologies. Conclusions on such issues are by no means obvious, since, as subsequent discussion will show, the idea of a true beginning of the universe is contested both in recent biblical scholarship and modern physics.

Some Preliminary Considerations

Before examining these trends in biblical interpretation and scientific cosmology, we need to take note of two perspectives that, for different reasons, would consider the questions we are exploring as either illegitimate or not worthwhile. Jewish scholar Nahum Sarna has stated that it is a "naive and futile exercise" to attempt to correlate the biblical creation accounts and the findings of modern science. Any such correspondences—say, on the concept of a true beginning of the universe in time—would be nothing more than mere coincidence.[3] Sarna's comments reflect what might be termed a "two realms" approach to such matters—the view that science and faith represent such dissimilar realms of discourse that no direct correlation or comparison is either possible or worthwhile.

"Two realms" approaches are exemplified in twentieth-century Protestant theology by Rudolf Bultmann and Paul Tillich. According to Bultmann, while it is the case that the Bible uses objective language to speak of God's acts, such language is not to be understood by the modern reader in terms of modern scientific theories about external events in an impersonal world; rather, they must be translated into the "existential" language of human self-understanding.[4] For Paul Tillich, the doctrine of creation is not the story of an event that took place "once upon a time." Rather than describing an event, the doctrine of creation is the "basic description of the relation between God and the world"; it is the symbolic and metaphorical

---

[3]Nahum Sarna, *Understanding Genesis* (New York: Schocken, 1970), p. 3. Similarly, Willem Drees, *Beyond the Big Bang: Quantum Cosmologies and God* (La Salle, Ill.: Open Court, 1990), pp. 36, 40, is reluctant to see parallels between Genesis 1 and the big bang because the scientific and biblical have such different purposes.

[4]For example, in *Jesus Christ and Mythology* (New York: Charles Scribner's Sons, 1958), p. 69, Rudolf Bultmann states that the affirmation that God is Creator can "only be a personal confession that I understand myself to be a creature which owes its existence to God."

expression of a timeless truth.[5]

While such "two realms" approaches may have the apparent advantage of avoiding conflicts between science and religion, they have the grave defect of drawing the lines too sharply between these two areas of human experience. While the biblical writers and modern scientists clearly have markedly differing languages, methods and purposes, they all are making references to a shared physical world existing outside the subjectivity of the speaker. An approach that allows for dialogue or even possibly integration between the two fields of human experience seems much more satisfactory, and is the approach presupposed here.[6]

As Langdon Gilkey has pointed out, dichotomistic "two realms" approaches run the risk of evacuating the biblical language of "God's acts" (including creation) of all real meaning and leaving it empty, abstract and equivocal. To say that God "creates" without any reference to events relating to space and time is to reduce the biblical language to vacuity. "Biblical theology must take cosmology and ontology more seriously," writes Gilkey; ". . . cosmology does make a difference in hermeneutics."[7]

---

[5]Paul Tillich, *Systematic Theology* (London: Nisbet, 1953), 1:280-81. While the neo-orthodox theologies of Karl Barth and Emil Brunner display significant affinities with the "existential" theologies of Bultmann and Tillich, it should be noted that Barth and Brunner do not really exemplify a dichotomous "two realms" approach in matters of science and faith (or an "independence" model: see Ian G. Barbour, *Religion in an Age of Science* [London: SCM Press, 1990)] pp. 10-16, for a helpful typology of various ways of relating science and religion). While Barth shows almost no interest in relating his discussion of Genesis 1 to issues in modern science, he does, significantly, state that Genesis 1:1 does mean that creation took place "in the beginning," that there was a beginning of all things. For Barth, Christian faith "regards the beginning of the world, posited by the will and act of God, not merely as supra-historical, but also as historical": *Church Dogmatics* 3/1, *The Doctrine of Creation.* trans. J. W. Edwards, O. Bussey and H. Knight (Edinburgh: T & T Clark, 1958), pp. 14-15. Similarly, while Brunner understands scientific cosmologies to have only a "remote and indirect relation to the Christian doctrine of creation," he nevertheless affirms the importance of the "event" character of the creation of the universe. "When we say that the world is God's world, we say that it had a beginning. . . . From the standpoint of belief in the Creation, we maintain the finite character both of actual Time and actual Space" (Emil Brunner, *The Christian Doctrine of Creation and Redemption,* vol. 2 of *Dogmatics,* trans. Olive Wyon [London: Lutterworth, 1952], pp. 14-15).

[6]For a discussion of such an approach and related issues, see Barbour, *Religion in an Age of Science,* pp. 16-30.

[7]Langdon Gilkey, "Cosmology, Ontology and the Travail of Biblical Language," *Journal of Religion* 41 (1961): 203. Gilkey's concern was directed at the "Biblical Theology" movement represented, for example, by Bernard Anderson, *Understanding the Old Testament* (Englewood Cliffs, N.J.: Prentice Hall, 1957), and George E. Wright and Reginald Fuller, *The Book of the Acts of God* (Garden City, N.Y.: Doubleday, 1959), in which naturalistic assumptions emptied such terms as "the Exodus event" of concrete empirical reference.

Another source of reluctance to investigate possible areas of convergence between the Genesis creation account and modern science is concern about the tentative nature of scientific theories. As Ian Barbour has correctly noted, "much of contemporary cosmology is tentative and speculative."[8] Similarly, Ernan McMullin is reluctant to see any direct linking of cosmology and theology, due to the "tentative nature of scientific theories" and his view that Scripture does not have a "directly cosmological intent." At most, both theology and cosmology may make their different contributions to a more comprehensive view of the world.[9]

It is, of course, worthwhile to draw attention to the tentative nature of scientific theories. The history of both science and theology attest to the very real danger of a facile reading of current scientific theories into the text of Scripture. Davis Young, for example, has documented a long history of failed attempts since the seventeenth century to read then-current geological theories into the text of Genesis.[10] On the other hand, there is the equally real danger that the tentative nature of science will be overemphasized, such that the genuinely *cumulative* nature of scientific knowledge is overlooked. While it is true that scientific theories change, it is also true that an average scientist today has

---

[8]Barbour, *Religion in an Age of Science,* p. 129.

[9]Ernan McMullin, "How Should Cosmology Relate to Theology?" in *The Sciences and Theology in the Twentieth Century,* ed. A. R. Peacocke (Notre Dame, Ind.: University of Notre Dame Press, 1981), p. 49. McMullin's emphasis on Scripture's primary purpose as theological rather than "scientific" (in the modern sense of this term) is certainly in keeping with a long Christian tradition. Augustine's remarks on the purpose of Scripture are worth noting: "One could ask which shape and form of heaven must be accepted by faith on the authority of Holy Scripture. Many dispute about these things which the sacred writer passed by in silence, because they are without importance for attaining eternal life. . . . In short, the Spirit of God which spoke through them did not wish to teach things which contribute nothing to salvation" (*Genesis ad litteram* 2.9.20). Nevertheless, in the present case it should be noted that the issue of whether the universe had a real beginning in time does have theological significance, as it relates to God's complete sovereignty and transcendence over the created order and his unlimited power to save—a point to be developed later in this discussion. One might wonder if McMullin's reluctance to see anything but the most indirect linking of theology and scientific cosmologies is related to a possible concern, as a scholar in the Roman Catholic tradition, to avoid any repetition of the mistaken assumptions of the Galileo affair, in which the church tied its understanding of Scripture too closely to the Aristotelian and Ptolemaic scientific cosmologies of the time. For recent attempts to develop stronger connections between theology and the natural sciences, see Wolfhart Pannenberg, *Theology and the Philosophy of Science,* trans. Francis McDonagh (London: Darton, Longman & Todd, 1976), and Nancey Murphy, *Theology in the Age of Scientific Reasoning* (Ithaca, N.Y.: Cornell University Press, 1990).

[10]Davis A. Young, "Scripture in the Hands of Geologists," *Westminster Theological Journal* 49 (1987): 1-34, 257-304.

a more extensive and accurate knowledge of the physical universe today than did Galileo or Newton, despite their genius as individuals.

In the present matter of big bang cosmology, while there are various versions of the theory, and all versions have their scientific problems, it is still the case that the model in general has very strong empirical support.[11] As astronomer Joseph Silk has pointed out, if "a better theory of the universe is forthcoming, there seems little doubt that it will incorporate the big bang theory as an appropriate description of the physical universe." Such a revised theory would likely encompass the big bang model in the same way that Einstein's theory of gravitation (General Relativity) encompassed and generalized the concepts of Newtonian gravitation.[12]

In the balance of this discussion, consequently, it will be assumed without further argument that the investigation of possible convergences between the Genesis creation account and modern cosmology is a justifiable enterprise. This assumption is, in fact, quite in keeping with the revival in the last twenty to thirty years in a "new style natural theology" that seeks, in the words of physicist-priest John Polkinghorne, "insight" rather than logical demonstration and that sees theology not as a rival to science but as a discipline that complements the natural sciences in a search for understanding of the physical world.[13] Such an understanding of the nature of the relationship between science and religion is presupposed in the present work.

Genesis 1:1 in Recent Scholarship

Historically, Jewish and Christian scholars have translated the opening words of the Bible as "In the beginning God created the heavens and the earth," understanding the verse as an independent clause in relation to the following verse, "The earth was formless and empty" (NIV). However, since the 1960s a number of translations have taken verse 1 as a dependent clause in relation to what follows, so that the text reads, "When God began to create the heaven and the earth—the earth being unformed and void. God said . . ." (New Jewish Version, 1962). In a similar vein, the New English Bible (1970) renders the verses as "In the beginning of creation, when God made heaven and earth, the

---

[11]The major lines of evidence supporting the big bang model will be discussed below.

[12]Joseph Silk, *The Big Bang,* rev. ed. (New York: W. H. Freeman, 1989), p. 411.

[13]John Polkinghorne, "Contemporary Interactions Between Science and Theology," *Modern Believing* 36, no. 4 (1995): 33-38. Polkinghorne presents a helpful overview of the then-recent work of Ian Barbour, Arthur Peacocke, Paul Davies and others in this field.

earth was without form and void."[14]

To the casual reader the difference in meaning between the traditional and "revisionist" translations may seem slight, but in fact the differences have great theological significance. The newer translations imply that the beginning of God's creative work was not an *ex nihilo* creation but the shaping of a chaotic or formless earth whose prior existence is assumed and left unexplained. In other words, the newer translations take the "beginning" of God's creative work in a relative rather than absolute sense. As a consequence, the absolute transcendence and sovereignty of God over the entire creation is somewhat muted, in comparison to the *ex nihilo* concept presupposed in the traditional rendering.[15]

Interpreters representing a broad variety of theological presuppositions tend to agree that the syntax of Genesis 1:1-3 is difficult, and that syntactically and grammatically both the traditional and revisionist translations can claim justification. Translation decisions tend to be influenced by lexical, theological and especially source-critical considerations. "Source-critical" considerations involve assumptions that the Genesis account of creation is substantially influenced by Babylonian or other ancient Near Eastern myths of creation involving a struggle with primeval chaos or chaos monsters.

In an important article on Genesis 1 that influenced revisionist translations, P. Humbert argued that of the approximately fifty instances of the word *reshit* (beginning) in the Hebrew Bible, only twelve are to be understood in the sense of a true temporal beginning. Humbert argued on the basis of this statistical usage that this was strong warrant for taking verse 1 as a dependent clause, having the meaning "In the beginning, when God began to create . . ."[16] How-

---

[14]These "revisionist" translations of Genesis 1:1 and the assumptions behind them are given extensive discussion in an important article by Gerhard F. Hasel, "Recent Translations of Genesis 1:1: A Critical Look," *The Bible Translator* 22, no. 4 (1971): 154-67. A 1996 Jewish translation by Everett Fox, volume 1 of the Schocken Bible, gives the rendering "At the beginning of God's creating of the heavens and the earth, when the earth was wild and waste . . ." (cited in Edward Hirsch, "In the Beginning: A New Translation of the Hebrew Bible," *Religious Studies News* 11, no. 1 (1996): 1.

[15]The revisionist reading is also adopted by E. A. Speiser, *The Anchor Bible: Genesis* (Garden City, N.Y.: Doubleday, 1964); Sarna, *Understanding Genesis;* Bruce Vawter, *On Genesis: A New Reading* (London: Geoffrey Chapman, 1977); cf. the earlier work by John Skinner, *A Critical and Exegetical Commentary on Genesis,* 2nd ed. (Edinburgh: T & T Clark, 1930), who prefers the rendering "In the beginning of God's creating the heavens and the earth" but admits that "a decision is difficult, and in dealing with v. 1 it is necessary to leave the [traditional] alternative open" (pp. 12-13).

[16]P. Humbert, "Trois notes sur Genese I," in *Interpretationes ad Vetus Testamentum pertinentes Sigmundo Mowinckel missae* (Oslo: Fabritius & Sønner, 1955), pp. 85-96; cited by Walther

ever, as Walther Eichrodt has pointed out, such an argument places too much weight on lexical statistics and not enough on the contexts of the passages in question. Eichrodt further points to Isaiah 40:21 as a clear example of *reshit* used with reference to an absolute beginning in time: "Do you now know? Have you not heard? Has it not been told you from the beginning? Have you not understood since the earth was founded?" The reference to the foundations of the earth, an obvious allusion to Genesis 1, clearly presupposes a true beginning of the earth's history. This use of *reshit* is also in evidence in Isaiah 46:9-10: "I am God, and there is none like me. I make known the end from the beginning, from ancient times, what is still to come." In this text God's complete transcendence over the created temporal order is the basis for the prophet's assurance to Israel in exile that God is able to redeem. Likewise in Proverbs 8:23 the personified Wisdom says, "I was appointed from eternity, from the beginning, before the world began."[17] These usages show that Humbert's argument is far from compelling.

Revisionist translations of Genesis 1:1 have tended to assume that the biblical account has borrowed from or has been significantly influenced by creation myths of the ancient Near East. In Hermann Gunkel's influential work of 1895, *Creation and Chaos,* he argued that the *tehom* ("the deep") of Genesis 1:2 was derived from Tiamat, the goddess slain in the Babylonian creation epic Enuma Elish. In such ancient Near Eastern mythologies, creation is not *ex nihilo* but often begins with a preexisting watery chaos from which the gods and the earth eventually emerge.[18]

Eichrodt, "In the Beginning: A Contribution to the Interpretation of the First Word of the Bible," in *Creation in the Old Testament,* ed. Bernard W. Anderson (Philadelphia: Fortress, 1984), p. 66.

[17]Eichrodt, "In the Beginning," p. 66. For other writers who argue for the traditional translation, see also Umberto Cassuto, *A Commentary on the Book of Genesis,* pt. 1 (Jerusalem: Magnes, 1961); Walther Eichrodt, *Theology of the Old Testament,* vol. 2 (London: SCM Press, 1967; see pp. 101-6 for penetrating theological insights on the Old Testament theology of creation); Gerhard von Rad, *Genesis: A Commentary,* trans. John H. Marks (London: SCM Press, 1961); Bruce K. Waltke, "The Creation Account in Genesis 1:1-3," *Bibliotheca Sacra* 132 (1975): 216-28; Gordon Wenham, *Genesis 1-15* (Waco, Tex.: Word, 1987); Claus Westermann, *Genesis 1-11: A Commentary,* trans. John J. Scullion (London: SPCK, 1984).

[18]For helpful discussions of the ancient Near Eastern context of Genesis, see Westermann, "Creation in the History of Religions and in the Bible," in *Genesis 1-11,* pp. 19-47; Wenham, "Genesis 1-11 and the Ancient Near East," in *Genesis 1-15,* pp. xlvi-l, with extensive bibliography. See also the article by Gerhard Hasel, "The Polemic Nature of the Genesis Cosmology," *Evangelical Quarterly* 46 (1974): 81-102, who argues that Genesis 1, far from being dependent on Babylonian and other ancient Near Eastern mythologies, is in fact a polemic against such polytheistic conceptions. For translations and commentary on the Enuma Elish, see Alexander Heidel, *The Babylonian Genesis: The Story of Creation* (Chicago: University of Chicago Press,

While many modern Old Testament scholars have followed Gunkel's lead, his assumptions have been heavily criticized in recent scholarship. As David Tsumura has pointed out in an important study, the etymological similarity of *tehom* and Tiamat is not a convincing argument for the dependence of Genesis 1 on the Babylonian creation myth. More than one creation tradition existed in ancient Mesopotamia, and in some of the older narratives the creation of the cosmos is not associated with the conflict theme at all.[19] W. G. Lambert, a specialist in Babylonian cuneiform texts, has pointed out that while there is one close parallel between Genesis and the Enuma Elish (splitting of waters/splitting of Tiamat), there is no evidence of Hebrew borrowing from the Babylonian. The separation of heaven and earth motif does not presuppose a cosmic battle; in three Sumerian creation stories, none has the body of a monster slain in battle being cut apart. Lambert concludes that "the case for a battle [in Genesis 1:2] as a prelude to God's dividing of the cosmic waters is unproven."[20] These considerations show that revisionist translations of Genesis 1:1-2 which assume substantial borrowing from Babylonian or other ancient Near Eastern sources are based on highly questionable assumptions.

The traditional rendering of Genesis 1:1 is also contextually consistent with the theology of the overall creation narrative. Eichrodt is correct in seeing the historic independent-clause rendering of verse 1 not as an arbitrary assumption but as a logical expression of the writer's outlook. Creation *ex nihilo* is clearly implied; the idea of "an absolute beginning of the created world" is an "indispensable link in the working out of salvation on behalf of Israel."[21] The complete sovereignty of God over the creation is the theological basis for God's complete sovereignty in redemption. In a similar vein Gerhard von Rad points out that Genesis 1:1 shows how God, "in the freedom of his will, creatively established for 'heaven and earth,' i.e., for absolutely everything, a beginning of its subsequent existence." The true subjects of verse 1 are not mythically personified powers from which the cosmos arose through primeval battle but rather "the one who is neither warrior nor procreator, who

---

1951), and Stephanie Dalley, *Myths from Mesopotamia: Creation, the Flood, Gilgamesh and Others* (New York: Oxford University Press, 1989). Dalley's translation is more recent, but the older discussion by Heidel is still quite valuable.

[19]David T. Tsumura, *The Earth and the Waters in Genesis 1 and 2: A Linguistic Investigation* (Sheffield, U.K.: Sheffield Academic Press, 1989), pp. 156-57.

[20]W. G. Lambert, "A New Look at the Babylonian Background of Genesis," *Journal of Theological Studies* 16 (1965): 294.

[21]Eichrodt, "In the Beginning," p. 72.

alone is worthy of the predicate, Creator."[22]

Genesis 1:1 in the History of Jewish and Christian Interpretation

The great majority of both Jewish and Christian commentators have understood Genesis 1:1 as an independent clause that speaks of a true beginning and implies creation *ex nihilo*.[23] Very significant is the fact that all the ancient versions—the Septuagint, Vulgate, Aquila, Theodotion, Symmachus and Targum Onkelos—construe verse 1 as an independent clause ("In the beginning God created the heavens and the earth").[24]

In Jewish interpretation the earliest explicit statement of creation *ex nihilo* is found in 2 Maccabees 7:28, a text written in Greek and dating from the second century B.C. A Jewish mother urges her son to face martyrdom bravely: "I implore you, my child, to look at the heavens and the earth; consider all that is in them, and realize that God did not create them from what already existed and that a human being comes into existence in the same way." The same God who called the world into being from "nothing" has the power to raise the martyrs from the "nothingness" of death.

Philo, writing in the first century A.D., believed that the idea of an eternal universe was injurious to genuine piety and the biblical notion of providence: "Those who assert that this world is unoriginate unconsciously eliminate that which of all incentives to piety is most beneficial . . . namely, providence. For it stands to reason that that which has been brought into existence should be cared for by its Father and Maker."[25] Moses taught that since this world is visible and perceived by the senses, and since visible objects are subject to becoming and change, "it follows that it must have had an origin." Genesis 1:1 shows that there was no time before the world was created; "time began either simultaneously with the world or after it."[26] One might note here the similarity

---

[22]Von Rad, *Genesis,* pp. 46-47.

[23]For a careful discussion of the problems with the thesis of Gerhard May, *Creatio ex Nihilo: The Doctrine of 'Creation out of Nothing' in Early Christian Thought* (Edinburgh: T & T Clark, 1994), that creation *ex nihilo* is not demanded by the text of the Bible but is basically a creation of early Christian theology, see Paul Copan, "Is *Creatio ex nihilo* a Post-biblical Invention? An Examination of Gerhard May's Proposal," *Trinity Journal* 17, n.s. (1996): 77-93.

[24]Waltke, "Creation Account," p. 223.

[25]Philo *On the Creation (De Opificio Mundi)* 9.10; in *Philo,* trans. F. H. Colson and G. H. Whitaker, Loeb Classical Library (Cambridge, Mass.: Harvard University Press, 1929), 1:11-12.

[26]Ibid. 12.26. Seymour Feldman notes that "Philo accepted Plato's conception [in the *Timaeus*] of an eternal God who brought the world into existence, but could not accept the Platonic theory that God created the world out of eternal preexistent matter. He solved the difficulty by stat-

of Philo's view and Augustine's notion that God created the world with time rather than in some "preexisting" time.[27]

In his *Jewish Antiquities* the first-century A.D. historian Josephus makes reference to the opening words of the Bible, "In the beginning God created the heavens and the earth."[28] Josephus does not elaborate on the details of the text, but it is significant that, like the later Jewish commentator Aquila (second century), he chose the word *ektisen* (created) rather than *epoiesen* (made, produced) used by the earlier Alexandrian translators of the Septuagint. This suggests that Josephus understood Genesis 1:1 as an independent clause and wished to avoid any suggestion that God merely shaped previously existing matter.

Rabbinic commentaries on Genesis reflect an *ex nihilo* understanding of God's creative work. In Genesis Rabbah 1:9 we find the following account: "A certain philosopher asked Rabbi Gamaliel, . . . 'Your God was indeed a great artist, but surely He found good materials which assisted Him?' 'What are they?' said he to him. '*Tohu, bohu,* darkness, water, wind . . . and the deep [Genesis 1:2],' replied he. 'Woe to that man,' he exclaimed. 'The term "creation" is used by Scripture in connection with all of them.' "[29] This rabbinic discussion is consistent with the Jewish tradition reflected in 2 Maccabees, Philo and Josephus that Genesis teaches that the physical universe had a singular beginning in (or "with") time as

ing that God created both the preexistent matter out of nothing, and the world out of the preexistent matter." Feldman, "Creation in Philosophy," in *Encyclopedia Judaica* (Jerusalem: Keter, 1972), 5:1066.

[27] Augustine *Confessions* 11.14: "In no time therefore, hadst thou 'not made' anything; because very time itself was of thy making *[quia ipsum tempus tu feceras],*" in *St. Augustine's Confessions,* trans. William Watts (Cambridge, Mass.: Harvard University Press, 1946), 2:237. For further discussion of Philo's views of creation, see Harry A. Wolfson, *Philo: Foundations of Religious Philosophy,* vol. 1 (Cambridge, Mass.: Harvard University Press, 1947), especially chap. 5, "Creation and Structure of the World," pp. 295-324. On p. 323 Wolfson notes Philo's rejection of Stoic notions of cyclical universes, and the use of some of Philo's ideas by later Christian writers such as Augustine.

[28] Josephus *Jewish Antiquities* 1.26-27, in *Josephus,* trans. Henry Thackeray. Loeb Classical Library (Cambridge, Mass.: Harvard University Press, 1930), 4:13-15.

[29] In *Midrash Rabbah: Genesis 1,* trans. H. Freedman and Maurice Simon (London: Soncino, 1939), p. 8. Louis Rabinowitz observes that this reply "refutes both the existence of primordial matter and the view that God was not the sole creator" ("Rabbinic View of Creation," in *Encyclopedia Judaica* (Jerusalem: Keter, 1972), 5:1063. For further discussion of rabbinic understandings of creation see Ephraim Urbach, *The Sages: Their Concepts and Beliefs,* trans. Israel Abrahams (Jerusalem: Magnes, 1979), especially chap. 9, "He Who Spoke and the World Came into Being."

the sovereign creation of God.[30]

Early Christian tradition is almost uniform in its affirmation of an *ex nihilo* concept of creation. Such a concept, rooted in Genesis 1, is presupposed in New Testament texts such as John 1:3, Romans 4:17, Colossians 1:16, Hebrews 11:3 and Revelation 4:11.[31] Writing in the second century, Justin Martyr is an exception to the later tradition in allowing that Plato's theory of preexisting matter could be accommodated to Genesis, since Plato in fact borrowed his teaching from Moses: "it was from our teachers . . . that Plato borrowed his statement that God, having altered matter which was shapeless, made the world."[32]

With the exception of Justin Martyr, Christian tradition from the second century onward is essentially unanimous in its understanding that the concept of *ex nihilo* creation is to be found in Genesis 1:1. *The Shepherd of Hermas,* probably written in Rome in the second century, states that God "made all things to be out of that which was not."[33] Theophilus, bishop of Antioch in the second century, explicitly criticizes Plato's theory of creation out of preexisting matter, observing that God is more powerful than a human artisan because "out of things that are not He creates and has created things that

---

[30]The one possible exception in early Jewish tradition to the *ex nihilo* understanding of Genesis is *Wisdom of Solomon* 11:17: "For your almighty hand, which created the world out of formless matter . . ." This text, thought to be written by an Alexandrian Jew in the first century B.C., may reflect the Platonic view of creation as the shaping of preexisting matter. On the other hand, the writer may be thinking of Genesis 1:2: "The earth was without form . . ." It is not easy to decide between the two possible interpretations of this text.

[31]John 1:3, "Through him [the *Logos*] all things were made; without him nothing was made that has been made" (John 1:1, "In the beginning was the Word," is an obvious allusion to Genesis 1:1). Romans 4:17, "the God who gives life to the dead and calls things that are not as though they were." Colossians 1:16, "By [Christ] all things were created: things in heaven and on earth, visible and invisible. . . . All things were created through him and for him." Hebrews 11:3, "By faith we understand that the universe was formed at God's command, so that what is seen was not made out of what was visible." Revelation 4:11, "You are worthy, our Lord and God, to receive glory and honor and power, for you created all things, and by your will they were created and have their being."

[32]Justin Martyr *First Apology* 59, in *The Ante-Nicene Fathers,* ed. Alexander Roberts and James Donaldson (reprint Grand Rapids, Mich.: Eerdmans, 1989), 1:182. Justin, citing Genesis 1:1-3, says that "Plato, and those who agree with him . . . have learned that by the word of God the whole world was made out of the substance spoken of before by Moses." Clement of Alexandria, in *Stromata* 14, may also reflect a willingness to accommodate Genesis to Plato, but this is not entirely clear: the Greek philosophers, "having so heard from Moses, taught that the world was created." He cites Plato and the Timaeus but, unlike Justin, does not seem to directly comment on Genesis 1:2 and the issue of preexistent matter.

[33]*Mandate* 1:1; cf. *Vision* 1:6, in *The Apostolic Fathers,* trans. Kirsopp Lake. Loeb Classical Library (Cambridge, Mass.: Harvard University Press, 1913), 2:71; 9.

are."[34] The second-century apologist Tatian in his *Address to the Greeks* states that matter is not eternal but was "brought into existence by the Framer of all things alone."[35]

Tertullian devotes an entire treatise to the refutation of Greek ideas of the eternity of matter. He states that the creation of all things from nothing at the beginning is consistent with the biblical declarations (citing Mt 24:35, "heaven and earth will pass away") that at the end God will bring all things to nothing. Tertullian relates the sovereignty of God in creation to the sovereignty of God in eschatology and judgment.[36]

Like Theophilus of Antioch, Irenaeus, writing in the second century, argues that *ex nihilo* creation demonstrates that God's power far surpasses that of human beings: "While men . . . cannot make anything out of nothing . . . God is in this point preeminently superior to men, that He himself called into being the substance of his creation, when previously it had no existence."[37]

In his *Confessions* Augustine asks, "How, O God, didst thou make heaven and earth?" His answer is, not out of preexisting materials, but "thou spakest, and they were made, and in thy Word [Christ] thou madest them."[38] Time had no existence before the creation; "time itself was created."[39]

In the medieval period this Christian understanding of *ex nihilo* creation was continued by Thomas Aquinas.[40] The doctrine was formally defined as a

---

[34]Theophilus *Apology to Autolycus* 2.4, in *The Ante-Nicene Fathers,* ed. Alexander Roberts and James Donaldson (reprint Grand Rapids, Mich.: Eerdmans, 1989), 2:95.

[35]Tatian *Address to the Greeks* 5, "The Doctrine of Christians as to the Creation of the World," in *The Ante-Nicene Fathers,* ed. Alexander Roberts and James Donaldson (reprint Grand Rapids, Mich.: Eerdmans, 1989), 2:67.

[36]Tertullian *Against Hermogenes* 34 ("Containing an Argument Against His Opinion That Matter Is Eternal"); cf. 4, "Matter will be equal with God when it is held to be eternal." In chapters 19-22 Tertullian refutes Hermogenes's misuse of Genesis 1:1-2. In *The Ante-Nicene Fathers,* ed. Alexander Roberts and James Donaldson (reprint Grand Rapids, Mich.: Eerdmans, 1989), 3:477-502.

[37]Irenaeus *Against Heresies* 2.10.4, in *The Ante-Nicene Fathers,* ed. Alexander Roberts and James Donaldson (reprint Grand Rapids, Mich.: Eerdmans, 1989), 1:370.

[38]Augustine *Confessions* 21.6 (*St. Augustine's Confessions,* 2:221).

[39]Augustine *City of God* 12.15, trans. Marcus Dods, in *Nicene and Post-Nicene Fathers* (reprint Edinburgh: T & T Clark, 1988), p. 236.

[40]In the *Summa Theologica* 1.q45, "Whether to Create Is to Make Something from Nothing," Aquinas answers in the affirmative and explains that "when anything is said to be made from nothing, this preposition from *[ex]* does not signify the material cause, but only the order; as when we say, from morning comes midday—i.e., after morning is midday." In *The Summa Theologica of St. Thomas Aquinas: Part I,* trans. Fathers of the English Dominican Province (London: R. & G. Washbourne, 1912), pp. 220-22. In the *Summa contra Gentiles* 2.38

dogma of faith in 1215 by the Fourth Lateran Council[41] and reaffirmed at the First Vatican Council in 1870.[42]

This long and extensive agreement of both Jewish and Christian tradition represents weighty support for the conclusion, also arguable on lexical, grammatical and theological grounds, that Genesis 1:1 indeed does teach a true, singular origin of the universe, a creation *ex nihilo.*

Genesis 1 and Other Ancient Cosmologies

Before turning to consider recent scientific cosmologies, it will be worthwhile to briefly comment on some features of three ancient cosmological theories—those of Plato, Aristotle and the Stoics. These are selected both because they form notable contrasts to the biblical concept of a singular beginning of the universe in time and because they also find parallels in certain modern theories.

Plato's most extensive discussion of cosmology is found in the *Timaeus.* Here he states that when God "took over all that was visible, seeing that it was not in a state of rest but in a state of . . . disorderly motion . . . brought it into order out of disorder."[43] Creation is not *ex nihilo* but involves the ordering of preexisting matter. As we have seen, many of the church fathers drew contrasts between this concept and the biblical view in Genesis.

For Plato the cosmos has "come into existence as a Living Creature endowed with soul and reason owing to the providence of God."[44] His concep-

---

Aquinas concludes that rational arguments for the noneternity (creation in/with time) of the world may have some probability but lack "absolute and necessary conclusiveness." The implication is that for Aquinas *ex nihilo* creation is accepted on the basis of biblical revelation, not on the basis of rational arguments alone (*Summa contra Gentiles,* book 2, *Creation,* trans. James F. Anderson (Notre Dame, Ind.: University of Notre Dame Press, 1975), pp. 112-15. Cf. Immanuel Kant's conclusion that neither the eternity of the world nor the beginning of the world in time is capable of rational proof, since both transcend possible empirical employments of the understanding (*Critique of Pure Reason,* trans. Norman Kemp Smith [London: Macmillan, 1963], p. 455, on the antinomies of reason).

[41]Constitutions 1, "On the Catholic Faith": The one triune God, "by his almighty power at the beginning of time *[ab initio temporis]* created from nothing *[de nihilo]* all things invisible and visible, spiritual and corporeal." In *Decrees of the Ecumenical Councils,* vol. 1, *Nicaea I to Lateran V,* ed. Norman P. Tanner (London: Sheed & Ward, 1990), p. 230.

[42]Canon 1, "On God the Creator of All Things," 5: "If anyone does not confess that the world and all things which are contained in it, both spiritual and material, were produced, according to their whole substance out of nothing *[ex nihilo]* by God . . . let him be anathema." In *Decrees of the Ecumenical Councils,* vol. 1, *Nicaea I to Lateran V,* ed. Norman P. Tanner (London: Sheed & Ward, 1990), 2:810.

[43]Plato *Timaeus* 30A, in *Plato,* trans. R. G. Bury (Cambridge, Mass.: Harvard University Press, 1929), 9:55.

[44]Ibid.

tion of the world as an animated being endowed with reason introduced teleology and purpose into the natural order, elements that had been denied by the Sophists and the earlier Greek atomistic philosophers.

During the medieval and early modern periods, however, it was the cosmology not of Plato but of Aristotle (together with Ptolemy's astronomy) that became "canonical" for the Christian church. For Aristotle the universe as a whole is eternal. After extensive discussion of the views of earlier thinkers, Aristotle concludes, "We may take it that the world as a whole was not generated and cannot be destroyed, but is unique and eternal, having no beginning or end of its whole life, containing infinite time."[45] It should be noted that it is the universe *as a whole* that is eternal for Aristotle. The upper heavenly spheres, composed of "aither" are ungenerated, indestructible and eternal. Below the eternal, heavenly spheres of aither come the sublunary regions, composed of the elements of earth, air, fire and water, each having its "natural" motion. None of these sublunary elements are eternal per se; they are generated from each other and pass into one another again.[46] The transformations of the four sublunary elements in Aristotle's cosmology would seem to bear some resemblance to the notion of the transformation and conservation of mass-energy in modern physics. The universe as a whole could be said to be in a "steady state,"[47] with eternal, unchanging circular motions above and ceaseless transformations (with aggregate "conservation") below.

For approximately five hundred years—from the second century B.C. to the third century of the Christian era—one of the most influential cosmologies among the educated was that of the Stoics, with its vision of a cyclical universe. [48] For the Stoics the present cosmic order, which originated in the dis-

---

[45]Aristotle *On the Heavens (De caelo)* 2.1, trans. W. K. C. Guthrie (Cambridge, Mass.: Harvard University Press, 1939), 6:131, 133.

[46]For a brief, clear explanation of Aristotle's cosmological system, see Guthrie's introduction to ibid., pp. xii-xv. Related discussion may be found in Arnold Ehrhardt, *The Beginning: A Study in the Greek Philosophical Approach to the Concept of Creation from Anaximander to St. John* (Manchester, U.K.: Manchester University Press, 1968), especially chap. 7, "Aristotle"; and G. E. R. Lloyd, "Greek Cosmologies," chap. 8 in *Ancient Cosmologies,* ed. Carmen Blacker and Michael Loewe (London: George Allen & Unwin, 1975).

[47]The modern "steady state" cosmology proposed by Hermann Bondi, Thomas Gold and Fred Hoyle in 1948 will be discussed below.

[48]The primary sources for early Stoicism are fragmentary. Not a single treatise from third-century Stoicism has survived intact. Scholarly reconstructions must unfortunately rely on second- or third-hand sources or later Stoic writers.

tant past, is not eternal but will eventually perish. An enormous conflagration *(ekpyrosis)* will dissolve all the elements into fire. After a time the world order will come into existence again, this future cosmos being identical to the present one in every respect—even the people being the same. The unending history of the cosmos will be an ongoing cycle of destruction and restoration.[49] The Stoic view of the universe, which has some antecedents in Heraclitus, the Pythagoreans and Plato, reflected a notion of the "cosmic year" that was deeply ingrained in the Greek mind. The annual cycle of the seasons sug-gested that cosmic history itself was cyclical in nature.[50] This cyclical notion of the cosmos invites comparison with modern scientific proposals for "oscil-lating universes," to be discussed below.[51]

Modern Scientific Cosmologies

From the time of Ptolemy (second century) until the third decade of the twen-tieth century it was generally believed that the universe is static. The expan-sion of the universe was discovered in 1929 by American astronomer Edwin Hubble, who measured the red shifts in starlight from distant galaxies. The reality of an expanding universe was "one of the greatest missed opportunities of theoretical physics," according to Stephen Hawking. "It should have been predicted even by Newtonian gravity."[52] Given the universal reach of gravita-tional force, the universe cannot be static but has to be either expanding or contracting.

In the first section of this chapter I have argued that Genesis 1:1 teaches that the universe had a singular beginning in time and that later Jewish and Christian traditions were justified in seeing creation *ex nihilo* as a further

---

[49]This synopsis of the Stoic view is found in the excellent treatment of David E. Hahm, *The Ori-gins of Stoic Cosmology* (Columbus: Ohio State University Press, 1977), p. 185. Additional dis-cussion may be found in David C. Lindberg, "Epicureans and Stoics," in *The Beginnings of Western Science* (Chicago: University of Chicago Press, 1992), pp. 76-83; and in Samuel Sam-bursky, *Physics of the Stoics* (New York: Macmillan, 1959).

[50]Hahm, *Origins of Stoic Cosmology,* pp. 185, 194.

[51]It may also be noted that the notion of a cyclical universe is also found in Hindu mythology. In certain of these traditions, at the end of each cosmic cycle *(kalpa)* the universe is destroyed by fire and remains submerged in the cosmic waters for a period while Brahma sleeps. Brahma then awakes from sleep, and the cycle of cosmic expansion and subsequent collapse begins anew. See Wendy Doniger O'Flaherty, *Hindu Myths: A Sourcebook Translated from the Sanskrit* (New York: Penguin, 1975), pp. 43-55.

[52]Stephen W. Hawking, "The Quantum Theory of the Universe," in *Intersections Between Elemen-tary Particle Physics and Cosmology,* ed. Tsvi Piran and Steven Weinberg (Philadelphia: World Scientific, 1986), p. 73.

implication of the text. Genesis stands essentially alone among the world's ancient cosmologies in advancing such a concept of creation. In this section the primary question to be considered is, do modern scientific cosmologies teach a singular origin of the universe in time? If this is indeed the case, the theological implications of the apparent convergence between Genesis and big bang cosmology will be considered.

The "standard" big bang model. In 1965 two Bell Laboratory radio astronomers, Robert Wilson and Arno Penzias, discovered cosmic microwave background radiation, the cooled remnant of the primeval fireball that exploded to constitute the early universe.[53] This faint "echo" of the big bang, observed to be uniform from every direction of space, was decisive in convincing most scientists that some form of the big bang model of the origin of the universe was likely to be true.

Cosmic background radiation, red-shifted light from distant galaxies, and the observed abundance of hydrogen and helium in the universe constitute the three major lines of evidence that support the big bang model—a model in which the universe "explodes" from an unimaginably tiny, hot and dense point to form the universe as we now observe it.[54] During the 1920s Edwin Hubble discovered evidence not only for red-shifted starlight but also that the rate at which the galaxies were receding was directly proportional to the distance of the galaxies: the farthest galaxies were receding fastest.[55] The observed galaxies were speeding away from one another like spots on a balloon being blown up. The clear implication of this evidence for receding galaxies, when extrapolated backward, was that the universe's expansion must have had a beginning, at t=0 when the big bang first occurred.

During the 1960s various scientists made theoretical calculations of the rel-

---

[53]The original report of their discovery is A. A. Penzias and R. W. Wilson, "A Measurement of Excess Antenna Temperature at 4080 Mc/s," *Astrophysical Journal* 142 (1965): 419-21. Penzias and Wilson were later awarded the Nobel Prize for their discovery.

[54]Among the many accessible discussions of the standard big bang model and the evidence for it are James S. Trefil, *The Moment of Creation* (New York: Macmillan, 1984); Stephen W. Hawking, *A Brief History of Time: From the Big Bang to Black Holes* (London: Bantam, 1988); Joseph Silk, *The Big Bang,* rev. ed. (New York: W. H. Freeman, 1989); Alan Lightman, *Ancient Light: Our Changing View of the Universe* (Cambridge, Mass.: Harvard University Press, 1991); Malcolm S. Longair, *Our Evolving Universe* (Cambridge: Cambridge University Press, 1996). Somewhat more technical discussions are found in Jayant V. Narlikar, *Introduction to Cosmology,* 2nd ed. (Cambridge: Cambridge University Press, 1993), and Matt Roos, *Introduction to Cosmology* (New York: John Wiley & Sons, 1994). These authors also address "inflationary universe" variants of the standard model, which will not be examined here.

[55]Silk, *Big Bang,* p. 54.

ative abundance in the universe of hydrogen and helium that would have been expected to have been produced in the first few minutes after the big bang. The fact that observations of the actual abundance—on the order of 75 percent hydrogen and 24 percent helium—match well with the theoretical calculations is seen by most scientists as strong evidence for the big bang.[56] Problems do exist with the "standard" model, but most scientists believe that future cosmological theory will incorporate the major features of the big bang model rather than completely replace it.

Alternatives to the big bang? In 1948 astronomers Hermann Bondi, Thomas Gold and Fred Hoyle proposed a "steady state" theory of the universe as an alternative to the big bang.[57] In this theory the observed expansion of the universe would be "balanced" by the continuous creation of matter, such that the average density of matter per volume of space in the universe would remain constant over time. The model would avoid the problem of an apparent breakdown of the known laws of physics at t=0, since the process of continuous creation would have no beginning in time.

It is said that this theory originated one evening in 1946 after Bondi, Gold and Hoyle had seen a movie of a ghost story with a circular plot in which the end was identical to the beginning. "What if the universe is constructed like that?" asked Gold, as the three men chatted over brandy in Bondi's rooms at Trinity College in Cambridge. "From that curious beginning," according to John D. Barrow and Joseph Silk, "the steady-state theory of the universe was born."[58]

Hoyle stated that his proposal was substantially motivated by "aesthetic objections" to the idea of a singular creation event in the remote past. Such a singular event would imply effects arising from "causes unknown to science," and his theory would avoid the awkward situation of a breakdown in the applicability of the known laws of physics.[59]

The steady state theory never won a substantial following among practicing

---

[56]Lightman, *Ancient Light,* p. 130, and Silk, *Big Bang,* p. 83.

[57]Hermann Bondi and Thomas Gold, "The Steady-State Theory of the Expanding Universe," *Monthly Notices of the Royal Astronomical Society* 108 (1948): 252-70; Fred Hoyle, "A New Model for the Expanding Universe," *Monthly Notices of the Royal Astronomical Society* 108 (1948): 372-82.

[58]The account is related in John D. Barrow and Joseph Silk, *The Left Hand of Creation: The Origin and Evolution of the Expanding Universe* (London: Heinemann, 1983), p. 13.

[59]Hoyle, "New Model," p. 372. For a fascinating discussion, based on extensive interviews with leading cosmologists, of how metaphysical questions and presuppositions have influenced scientific research in this area, see Alan Lightman and Roberta Brewer, *Origins: The Lives and Worlds of Modern Cosmologists* (Cambridge, Mass.: Harvard University Press, 1990).

scientists. The postulated continuous creation of matter—which Bondi and Gold admitted in their theory was at a rate "far too low for direct observation"[60]—violated the most fundamental conservation laws of physics. The 1965 discovery of microwave background radiation provided irrefutable evidence for an early hot and dense state of the universe that was radically different from the present. The steady state theory had no plausible explanation for this background radiation. The scientific community was convinced that the observational evidence drove a massive nail into the coffin of the steady state proposal. This theory, according to Silk, "is now little more than a footnote of considerable historical interest in the development of modern cosmology."[61]

During the 1950s and 1960s the so-called oscillating-universe model had some support among astronomers.[62] In this model the universe, after collapsing in a "big crunch," would "bounce" back in a new expansion, beginning a new cycle of expansion and contraction that would conceivably continue forever. For astronomers such as Robert Dicke and his associates such a model had a great philosophical advantage, for it "relieves us of the necessity of understanding the origin of matter at any finite time in the past."[63] And as Paul Davies has noted, such oscillating-universe theories also seem to appeal to those influenced by "Hindu and Buddhist mythology, in which cycles of . . . creation and destruction figure prominently."[64]

The oscillating-universe proposal was dealt a heavy blow during the late 1960s and early 1970s by the theoretical work of Stephen Hawking and Roger Penrose, who demonstrated that there were no plausible physical mechanisms for endless cycles of "bangs" and "bounces." Such oscillations, concluded Hawking and Penrose, do not seem "realizable within the framework of general relativity,"[65] the fundamental mathematical framework developed by Albert Einstein to describe the large-scale structures of the universe. For such bounces to occur after the "big crunch," there would have to be some sort of antigravitational force to reverse the momentum of the collapsing universe,

---

[60]Bondi and Gold, "Steady-State Theory," p. 252.

[61]Silk, *Big Bang,* p. 6.

[62]Lightman, *Ancient Light,* p. 51.

[63]R. H. Dicke et. al., "Cosmic Black-Body Radiation," *Astrophysical Journal* 142 (1965): 415.

[64]Paul Davies, *The Last Three Minutes: Conjectures About the Ultimate Fate of the Universe* (London: Weidenfeld & Nicolson, 1994), p. 141. See note 50 above; cf. also the discussion of the Stoics' cyclical cosmology.

[65]Stephen W. Hawking and Robert Penrose, "The Singularities of Gravitational Collapse and Cosmology," *Proceedings of the Royal Society of London* A314 (1970): 530.

and no such force is known.[66]

The oscillating-universe model is also inconsistent with established observations of cosmic background microwave radiation. From the fact that there is a specific, finite amount of background radiation it can be inferred that the universe could have undergone at best only a finite number of repeated "bounces." Otherwise too much radiation would have been pumped into the observed universe during earlier cycles of expansion.[67]

Furthermore, various scientists have pointed out that the oscillating-universe model is inconsistent with the second law of thermodynamics, which requires that in a closed system the amount of entropy or disorder can only increase over time. Various nonsymmetric processes that would be occurring during each cycle—starlight being pumped into space, matter being swept into black holes—would mean that the universe would eventually run down, less energy being available for useful work in the succeeding cycles.[68]

Given the observational data and the grave theoretical problems with the cyclical theory, astronomer Silk has concluded that "the beginning of time is unavoidable."[69] The oscillating-universe model has been largely abandoned and has little or no support among the working scientific community today.[70]

Recent speculative proposals: Quantum cosmology. With the demise of steady state and oscillating-universe models, serious scientific cosmologies have proceeded on the premise that the universe did have a singular beginning. What was the nature of this singular "creation event," and what are the limits, if any, of scientific theory to explain it? Since the 1970s physicists have been attempting to combine the theoretical tools of elementary particle physics, general relativity and quantum mechanics to explain the origin and development of the very early universe. Let's explore some of the features and impli-

---

[66]Davies, *Last Three Minutes,* p. 142.

[67]Silk, *Big Bang,* p. 390.

[68]Ya B. Zel'dovich and I. D. Novikov, in *The Structure and Evolution of the Universe,* trans. Leslie Fishbone (Chicago: University of Chicago Press, 1983), pp. 659-60, conclude that "the second law of thermodynamics forbids an oscillating model. This is because the entropy of the universe only grows . . . in the course of both expansion and contraction [e.g., because of starlight and the formation of black holes]." Physicist Davies agrees: "The conclusion seems inescapable. . . . Any cyclic universe . . . will not evade the degenerative influences of the second law of thermodynamics" (*Last Three Minutes,* p. 46).

[69]Silk, *Big Bang,* p. 391.

[70]For a worthwhile review of the idea of an oscillating universe in the history of science, see Stanley L. Jaki, "The History of Science and the Idea of an Oscillating Universe," in *Cosmology, History and Theology,* ed. Wolfgang Yourgrau and Allen D. Beck (New York: Plenum, 1977), pp. 233-51.

cations of these rather speculative "quantum cosmologies."[71]

In 1973 Edward Tryon, a physicist at Hunter College of the City University of New York, published an article with the provocative title "Is the Universe a Vacuum Fluctuation?" Taking it as well established that some version of the big bang theory is correct, Tryon proposed that the universe emerged as a quantum fluctuation of the vacuum, where "vacuum" is understood as an energy field, as described in quantum-mechanical theory.[72] Tryon's article inspired a number of subsequent speculative papers that envisaged the universe spontaneously emerging from (almost) "nothing" as some form of quantum-mechanical fluctuation.[73]

Tryon observed that the spontaneous appearance of particle/antiparticle pairs (e.g., electrons and positrons) is a well-known phenomenon in elementary particle physics. Could this phenomenon be generalized to the universe as a whole, so long as such a model had a net zero value for all conserved quantities such as energy and charge? Tryon hypothesized that the net positive energy of the universe's mass ($E=mc^2$) might be balanced by the net gravitational energy of the universe, defined in physics as a negative quantity. If the universe has zero net values for all conserved quantities, suggested Tryon, "our universe could have appeared from nowhere without violating any conservation laws." As to the question of *why* it happened, wrote Tryon, "I offer the modest proposal that our Universe is simply one of those things which happen from time to time."[74]

Tryon's ideas were given further development in the 1970s and 1980s by

---

[71]These proposals are speculative on both theoretical and experimental grounds. Quantum cosmologies attempt to apply both general relativity and quantum mechanics to the very early universe (e.g., prior to 10^{-35} seconds after the big bang), when quantum-mechanical effects become very important, but at this time no satisfactory way of unifying these two very different mathematical formalisms has been achieved. Experimentally, the energies needed to test such theories are far beyond those available on any existing particle accelerators, indeed, of any particle accelerators that are likely to be built in the foreseeable future. See Horgan, "Particle Metaphysics," note 2 above.

[72]Edward P. Tryon, "Is the Universe a Vacuum Fluctuation?" *Nature* 264 (December 14, 1973): 396-97.

[73]Tryon's proposal was not, strictly speaking, one of a creation *ex nihilo,* since the energy field from which the universe presumably arose was "something" rather than "nothing." As noted by A. D. Linde, *Inflation and Quantum Cosmology* (New York: Academic Press, 1990), p. 16, "according to quantum field theory, empty space is not entirely empty. It is filled with quantum fluctuations of all types of physical fields. These fluctuations can be regarded as waves of physical fields with all possible wavelengths, moving in all possible directions."

[74]Tryon, "Is the Universe a Vacuum Fluctuation?" p. 397.

other physicists. Assuming the prior existence of a flat space, R. Brout and his associates at the University of Brussels argued that the laws of quantum mechanics are "perfectly consistent with the spontaneous creation of all the matter and radiation in the universe," and proposed their own mathematical model.[75] In 1982 David Atkatz and Heinz Pagels of Rockefeller University in New York published a paper in which they proposed that the universe emerged as a "quantum tunneling event" from a "stable space-time configuration." The big bang would be analogous to a single radioactive decay event, on a huge scale.[76]

As already noted, these are not true *ex nihilo* scenarios; "something," the energy field or the space-time manifold, does exist before the emergence of the universe. As Brout admitted in his 1978 paper, one fundamental problem for such scenarios is to explain the actual observed preponderance of matter over antimatter.[77] The conservation laws of physics imply the creation of equal amounts of matter and antimatter in the vacuum fluctuation hypotheses, but the universe as we actually observe it is almost exclusively composed of normal matter. If the quantum fluctuation hypothesis is true, where is all the missing antimatter? And if it exists, what is to prevent the universe from annihilating itself in an enormous flash of light as particles and antiparticles collide?

There is also the troubling question of the prior existence of the space-time manifold. Where did it come from? "This is a question," Atkatz and Pagels admit, that "we cannot answer."[78]

In 1982 Alexander Vilenkin, a physicist at Tufts University in Massachusetts, pushed these speculative models even further, proposing a cosmological scenario "in which the universe is spontaneously created from literally *nothing.*" In quantum mechanics particles can tunnel through potential barriers; this suggests, according to Vilenkin, that "the birth of the universe might be a quantum tunneling effect."[79]

Vilenkin realizes that the notion of a universe emerging spontaneously from nothing is a "crazy one." The advantage of the speculative model that he proposed is primarily "aesthetic," since it avoids the problem of the singularity at t=0 in the usual big bang models. He also admits that the only verifiable

[75]R. Brout et al., "The Creation of the Universe as a Quantum Phenomenon," *Annals of Physics* 115 (1978): 78.

[76]David Atkatz and Heinz Pagels, "Origin of the Universe as a Quantum Tunneling Event," *Physical Review* D25, no. 8 (1982): 2065-73.

[77]Brout et al., "Creation of the Universe," p. 98.

[78]Atkatz and Pagels, "Origin of the Universe," p. 2072.

[79]Alexander Vilenkin, "Creation of Universes from Nothing," *Physics Letters* B117 (1982): 26.

prediction his model can make is that the universe must be closed (i.e., not expanding forever); however, a problem even here is that "we shall have to wait a long time until . . . [this] can be determined experimentally."[80]

Vilenkin's proposal is a good example of a speculative theory "underdetermined by the data." The one prediction made by the theory—that the universe must be closed—not only is, as he admits, unlikely to be experimentally verified in the foreseeable future, but is also consistent with any number of alternative cosmological models. A mathematical model such as Vilenkin's which is not readily either verifiable or falsifiable by experiment does not have impressive credentials as a good scientific theory.

Another speculative cosmological model that, because of the high public visibility of one of its authors, has received considerable attention in recent years, is the so-called Hawking-Hartle proposal. In 1983 Stephen W. Hawking, known to the general public as the author of the bestselling *A Brief History of Time,* and his associate J. B. Hartle published an article with the modest title "Wave Function of the Universe."[81] In this mathematical model of the origin of the universe, space-time forms a surface that is finite in size but with no boundary or edge (like a globe or a torus—doughnut shape). There is no "singularity" at t=0, where the laws of physics break down. In the Hawking-Hartle proposal time emerges gradually from space in a "fuzzy," quantum-mechanical fashion; strictly speaking, there is no single point for the "origin" of time.[82]

In this model of the universe, where the universe is completely self-contained and not affected by anything outside of itself, the universe is neither created or destroyed; it merely "is." Hawking poses the question, "What place, then, for a creator?"[83]

Some science writers have concluded that the Hawking-Hartle model has eliminated the need to appeal to God or to metaphysics for an ultimate explanation of the universe. According to John Gribbin, thanks to Hawking and Hartle it is now possible to give a good scientific answer to the question "Where do we come from?" without "invoking either God or special boundary conditions . . . at the moment of creation. . . . It is the metaphysi-

---

[80]Ibid., p. 27.
[81]J. B. Hartle and Stephen W. Hawking, "Wave Function of the Universe," *Physical Review* D (1983): 2960-75. The model is described in popular language in Hawking, *Brief History of Time,* p. 136.
[82]Roos, *Introduction to Cosmology,* p. 191.
[83]Hawking, *Brief History of Time,* p. 136.

cians who are out of a job."[84]

Significantly, Hawking himself does not agree with the sweeping conclusions that Gribbin and others draw from his model. Hawking notes that his theory is just a set of mathematical rules and equations; such a mathematical model cannot answer the question of "why there should be a universe for the model to describe." Why should the theory be instantiated in an actually existing universe? "What is it," Hawking wonders, "that breathes fire into the equations and makes a universe for them to describe?" [85] Hawking does not answer the fundamental question that he poses.

Various commentators have pointed to substantial problems that are inherent in the Hawking-Hartle proposal. Because no one has yet succeeded in unifying quantum mechanics and general relativity, there is no good theory of quantum gravity—that is, a theory that can describe gravity in the very earliest universe, prior to the "Planck time" 10^{-43} seconds after the big bang. Lacking such a theory, Hawking and Hartle cannot produce detailed calculations concerning the very early state of the universe; even with such a theory the calculations might be too complex to carry out in practice.[86]

J. V. Narliker has expressed uneasiness about speculative theories such as Hawking's about the very early universe that are based on "no direct observational evidence."[87] Such speculative scenarios purport to deal with conditions prior to ten seconds after the big bang that happened only once and will never happen again; they lack the *experimental repeatability* that characterizes standard physical theories. By way of contrast, astrophysical theories concerning the synthesis of elements in stars refer to ongoing processes with "each star as an independent experiment."[88]

As Heinz Pagels has observed, these theories in quantum cosmology involve extrapolating current theories and concepts far beyond where they have been tested; they are no more than "imaginative guesses." Theory build-

[84]John Gribbin, *In Search of the Big Bang: Quantum Physics and Cosmology* (London: Heinemann, 1986), p. 392. Gribbin no doubt would add theologians to his list of the potentially unemployed!

[85]Hawking, *Brief History of Time,* p. 174.

[86]Lightman and Brewer, *Origins,* p. 39.

[87]Narliker, *Introduction to Cosmology,* pp. 378-79. For additional criticism and analysis of the Hawking-Hartle proposal, see an article by physicist C. J. Isham, "Creation of the Universe as a Quantum Process," in *Physics, Philosophy and Theology: A Common Quest for Understanding,* ed. Robert J. Russell, William R. Stoeger and George V. Coyne, (Vatican City: Vatican Observatory, 1988), pp. 375-405, especially "Assumptions" and "Problems."

[88]Ibid., p. 379.

ing, he notes, "is never a substitute for experiment and observation."[89] No existing particle accelerator—or any likely to be built in the foreseeable future—can deliver the extremely high energies needed to test such theories. A collider capable of probing the quantum gravity realm would need to be as much as one thousand light-years in circumference; the entire solar system is only one light-day around.[90]

Superstrings and theories of everything. In recent years quantum cosmologies of the very early universe have become part of a larger quest in the physics community for what has been termed a "Theory of Everything." Such a "final theory" would unify quantum mechanics with general relativity and provide a unified understanding of the four fundamental forces of nature (gravity, electromagnetism, and the strong and weak nuclear forces). Such a theory would, in principle, allow physicists to explain the origin of the universe and calculate its successive states from the time of the big bang until the present. Many physicists believe that exotic "superstring" theories, which postulate the existence of unimaginably small, vibrating "strings" as the ultimate constituents of the elementary particles, may provide the mathematical basis for such a grand unification of the known laws of physics.[91] The question naturally arises, what would be the theological implication of the successful development of such a theory of everything? Would the "God hypothesis" then no longer be necessary as the final explanation of the universe's existence?

Some physicists, such as Paul Davies, seem to suggest that a final theory

---

[89]Heinz R. Pagels, *Perfect Symmetry: The Search for the Beginning of Time* (London: Michael Joseph, 1985), p. 348.

[90]Horgan, "Particle Metaphysics," p. 72. For further discussion of the philosophical and theological implication of the Hawking-Hartle proposal, see the important book by William Lane Craig and Quentin Smith, *Theism, Atheism and Big Bang Cosmology* (Oxford: Clarendon, 1993), especially chaps. 11 and 12, "Theism, Atheism and Hawking's Quantum Cosmology." Craig argues for a theistic position and Smith for an atheistic one. The book is given an insightful review, from a perspective sympathetic to Craig's classical theism, by John Leslie in *Zygon* 30, no. 4 (December 1995): 652-56. Leslie believes that Smith's arguments are unconvincing and that at the end of the day "there is no physical basis in ordinary quantum theory for the claim that the universe itself is uncaused, much less for the claim that it sprang into being uncaused from literally nothing" (p. 656.)

[91]For very preliminary discussion of superstring theories, see Horgan, "Particle Metaphysics," pp. 74-75; for technical treatments see the articles in H. J. de Vega and N. Sanchez, *String Theory, Quantum Cosmology and Quantum Gravity* (Singapore: World Scientific, 1987). For an overview of current attempts to develop a theory of everything, see Madhusree Mukerjee, "Explaining Everything," *Scientific American* 274, no. 1 (January 1996): 72-78, and John D. Barrow, *Theories of Everything: The Quest for Ultimate Explanation* (Oxford: Clarendon, 1991).

would be a final and sufficient explanation for the universe. Perhaps the ultimate "superlaw," when and if it is discovered, "will emerge to be the only logically possible physical priniciple."[92] Stanley Jaki, however, has argued that such claims for a "logically necessary" and complete physical theory are impossible to demonstrate, given the limitations placed on logical proof by Gödel's theorem. Gödel demonstrated that no nontrivial set of mathematical propositions (which would include the formalism of a final theory) can contain the proof of its own consistency and completeness. We could never be sure of the final consistency and completeness of such a theory of everything.[93]

Most physicists, however, seem to take the view that any final theory, should it be discovered, will not be a logically necessary one. Nobel laureate Steven Weinberg, for example, has concluded that "whatever the final theory may be, it will certainly not be *logically* inevitable. . . . We still have to ask why . . . nature should obey the rules of quantum mechanics."[94] Why should a final theory have one form rather than some other? And even more fundamentally, as Weinberg observes, there is still the question "Why is there anything at all?"[95]

Physicist James Trefil notes that even if the laws of some final theory appeared to be the only ones that were logically consistent with one another, the question could still be asked, "Who made the laws of logic?" He concludes that no matter "how far back the boundaries are pushed . . . there will always be room for religious faith and a religious interpretation of the physical world."[96]

Weinberg, Trefil and Hawking seem to realize that any "final theory" is still just a set of mathematical equations that call for a greater, more final causal reality to give them life. Thus it seems clear that a final theory, should it ever

---

[92]Paul Davies, *God and the New Physics* (London: J. M. Dent & Sons, 1983), p. 217. David Lindley has pointed out, however, that such speculative theories are becoming increasingly removed from what can be measured or experimentally detected, leading to the danger that cosmology could come to be ruled more by aesthetic preferences or prejudice than by the traditional criteria of science (David Lindley, *The End of Physics: The Myth of a Unified Theory* [New York: Basic-Books, 1993], p. 131).

[93]Stanley L. Jaki, *God and the Cosmologists* (Edinburgh: Scottish Academic Press, 1989), as cited in the review by Peter Hodgson in *Zygon* 27, no. 4 (1992): 476.

[94]Steven Weinberg, *Dreams of a Final Theory* (London: Hutchinson Radius, 1993), p. 188.

[95]Ibid. In a similar vein, Heinz Pagels raises the question "What 'tells' the void that it is pregnant with a possible universe? It would seem that even the void is subject to law, a logic that exists prior to space and time" (*Perfect Symmetry,* p. 347). From the perspective of biblical theism it is, of course, God who is the ultimate source of the laws of logic and quantum mechanics and the ultimate reference point for explaining the universe's existence.

[96]James S. Trefil, *The Moment of Creation: Big Bang Physics from Before the First Millisecond to the Present Universe* (New York: Charles Scribner's Sons, 1983), pp. 222-23.

be developed, would be no threat to biblical faith. From the perspective of faith, it is the God of biblical revelation who "breathes fire into the equations" and brings a *possible* universe into *actual existence* through mathematical equations and quantum-mechanical laws that he himself has designed.

Some Concluding Reflections

We have seen that Genesis 1:1 does indeed teach that the universe had a singular beginning, and that the mainstream Jewish and Christian traditions were justified in drawing the further inference that this was a creation *ex nihilo*. The concept of *ex nihilo* creation is consistent with the pervasive biblical witness to God's complete transcendence over the entire created order, and God's unlimited power to redeem his people.

Genesis' concept of a singular, *ex nihilo* beginning of the universe essentially stands alone among the cosmologies of the ancient world and exhibits, at this point, convergence with recent big bang cosmological models. Given the long history of an often conflict-ridden relationship between Christian theology and the natural sciences,[97] this aspect of convergence is to be welcomed as having potential for fostering fruitful dialogue among astronomers, physicists, philosophers and theologians.

If at some point in the future one or more of the speculative quantum cosmologies discussed here, or even a grand theory of everything, comes to be established as a firm scientific theory, this should not be seen as a threat to Christian faith. From the perspective of Christian theology, it is the God of Genesis 1:1 who, working through the mathematical and physical laws uncovered by the sciences, "breathed fire into the equations" and who called a *possible* universe into *actual existence* by the power of his almighty word. Genesis 1:1 and modern cosmologies can be understood as complementary rather than competing accounts of the origin of the universe. The equations of any "final theory" would describe *how* the universe was created "in the beginning"; Genesis 1:1 tells us *who* created the universe and allows us to relate scientific knowledge to the broader moral, aesthetic and religious dimensions of human experience.

---

[97]For a fine bibliographic essay on the history of scholarship, including recent revisionist historiography, on the "warfare" thesis of Andrew Dickson White (1832-1918) and John W. Draper (1811-1882), see David C. Lindberg and Ronald L. Numbers, introduction to *God and Nature: Historical Essays on the Encounter Between Christianity and Science* (Berkeley: University of California Press, 1986), pp. 1-18. Recent historiography on the relationship of science and religion has demonstrated that Draper and White had very selective readings of this relationship and overemphasized conflict to the detriment of the more positive aspects.

2

Quantum Indeterminacy
& the Omniscience of God

*D*oes the reality of quantum indeterminacy in nature require a revision of classical theism's understanding of the omniscience of God? At least one prominent scientist-theologian believes that it does. According to Oxford's Arthur Peacocke, a leading contributor to the growing body of literature relating theology to the natural sciences, "God has so made the natural order that it is, in principle, impossible even for God, as it is for us, to predict the precise, future values of certain variables."[1] To illustrate his point, Peacocke argues that in this "self-limited omniscience" God "does not know *which* of a million radium atoms will be the next to disintegrate in, say, the next 10 seconds, but

---

[1]Arthur Peacocke, "God's Interaction with the World," in *Chaos and Complexity*, ed. Robert John Russell, Nancey Murphy and Arthur Peacocke (Vatican City: Vatican Observatory, 1995), p. 280 (hereafter cited as *GIW*).

only . . . what the average number will be that will break up in that period of time."[2]

In an earlier generation the theologian was occasionally faced with a question such as, could God make a stone so heavy that he could not lift it? Peacocke appears to be arguing that turn-of-the-millennium physics confronts the theologian with new questions: Given the laws of quantum mechanics, has God made radium atoms that not even he knows when they will split?

Here we will consider only the specific question of the possible impact of quantum physics on the traditional Christian understanding of the omniscience of God. A general acquaintance with selected features of quantum mechanics such as Heisenberg's uncertainty principle and Bohr's principle of complementarity is assumed.[3] I will make no attempt to adjudicate between the various competing interpretations of quantum theory that are held in the scientific community.[4] The broader issues of "divine action," providence and the question of how God interacts causally with the physical world, while obviously related to the matter at hand, are also beyond

---

[2]Peacocke also argues for this concept of "self-limited omniscience" in Arthur Peacocke, *Theology for a Scientific Age*, 2nd ed. (London: SCM Press, 1993), pp. 121-24 (hereafter cited as *TSA*).

[3]Nontechnical introductions to quantum mechanics may be found in J. C. Polkinghorne, *The Quantum World* (London: Longman, 1984); Nick Herbert, *Quantum Reality: Beyond the New Physics* (London: Rider, 1985); P. C. W. Davies, *The Ghost in the Atom* (Cambridge: Cambridge University Press, 1986), especially chap. 1, "The Strange World of the Quantum"; and Nancy R. Pearcey and Charles B. Thaxton, *The Soul of Science: Christian Faith and Natural Philosophy* (Wheaton, Ill.: Crossway, 1994), chap. 9, "Quantum Mysteries: Making Sense of the New Physics." Polkinghorne also deals with issues raised by quantum mechanics in *Reason and Reality: The Relationship Between Science and Theology* (Philadelphia: Trinity Press International, 1991), and in *Science and Providence: God's Interaction with the World* (Boston: Shambala, 1989), but in neither of these is the issue of divine omniscience given extensive analysis.

[4]The various schools of interpretation are presented in the works by Davies and Herbert cited in note 3 above. More technical discussions of the historical development of quantum mechanics and the philosophical issues raised by it may be found in Max Jammer, *The Philosophy of Quantum Mechanics* (New York: John Wiley & Sons, 1974); Bernard D'Espagnat, *Conceptual Foundations of Quantum Mechanics* (Menlo Park, Calif.: W. A. Benjamin, 1971), and *Reality and the Physicist: Knowledge, Duration and the Quantum World* (Cambridge: Cambridge University Press, 1989); John Archibald Wheeler and Wojciech H. Zurek, eds., *Quantum Theory and Measurement* (Princeton, N.J.: Princeton University Press, 1983); Roland Omnes, *The Interpretation of Quantum Mechanics* (Princeton, N.J.: Princeton University Press, 19944); Asher Peres, *Quantum Theory: Concepts and Methods* (Dordrecht, Netherlands: Kluwer Academic, 1993). Jammer writes that never "in the history of science has there been a theory . . . which scored such spectacular successes in the prediction of such an enormous variety of phenomena. . . . [Yet] the interpretation of this formalism . . . is . . . still an issue of unprecedented dissension" (*Philosophy of Quantum Mechanics,* p. v).

the scope of this chapter.[5]

During the twentieth century it became increasingly clear that modern physics has dramatically altered our understandings of the nature of space, time, matter and energy. Modern understandings of nature have been as deeply affected by the discoveries of quantum physics as the medieval view of the solar system was by the discoveries of Galileo. It is not clear, however, what implications the new view of nature holds for traditional Christian understandings of God. Here I will examine Peacocke's proposal and relate it to historical and contemporary theological discussions of divine omniscience. A "revisionist" model of classical theism which affirms both contingency in nature and unlimited knowledge in God will then be presented as an alternative to the Peacocke proposal.

The Peacocke Proposal: "Self-Limited Omniscience"

It is to Peacocke's credit that he is one of the few contemporary theologians who have wrestled extensively with the specifically *theological* implications of quantum mechanics.[6] Peacocke would seem to be correct in discerning that revolutions in human understanding of nature inevitably affect understandings not only of God's relationship to nature but, even more fundamental, understandings of the divine nature itself.

Peacocke believes that quantum theory and the countless experiments that have verified its predictions imply *a real indeterminacy in nature*, not merely a "fuzziness" or imprecision in human knowledge of nature. He shares the current majority view in the physics community that there are not in fact "hidden variables" that, if known, would allow an exact and deterministic picture of subatomic realities in the fashion of classical physics. Contingency and unpredictability on this view represent *ontological* features of nature itself, not merely *epistemological* limitations on human knowledge of nature. As a fur-

---

[5]Helpful discussions of these matters are found in Owen C. Thomas, ed., *God's Activity in the World: The Contemporary Problem* (Chico, Calif.: Scholars Press, 1983), and Ian G. Barbour, *Religion in an Age of Science* (London: SCM Press, 1990), chap. 9, "God and Nature," surveying classical theism, neo-Thomism, process theology and other alternatives.

[6]In this regard the earlier work of William Pollard, *Chance and Providence: God's Action in a World Governed by Scientific Law* (New York: Charles Scribner's Sons, 1958), should be acknowledged, as well as the section "Quantum Theory" in Barbour, *Religion in an Age of Science.* At this point the term *theological* is used in the narrow sense of the doctrine of God and the divine attributes per se, in distinction from the broader issues of the nature of God's relationship to nature.

ther consequence, Peacocke believes, this "inherent unpredictability also represents a limitation of the knowledge even an omniscient God could have" of events at the quantum level.[7]

According to Peacocke, God has voluntarily limited his omniscience in order to make a world of a particular sort: one characterized by freedom and contingency. In this conception, God "has allowed his inherent . . . omniscience to be . . . restricted and curtailed by the very open-endedness that he has bestowed upon creation."[8] God has chosen to make a world in which some future states, such as the precise time when a radium nucleus will decay, are unknowable even by an "omniscient" being. Omniscience is redefined to mean "knowledge of all things that are *possible* to know" rather than "knowledge of all things that could *conceivably* be known."

This voluntary self-limitation of God's knowledge is not a strictly logical one, in the way, for example, that it is logically impossible to know a proposition such as "2 + 3 = 6." This latter proposition cannot be "known" in any possible state of affairs or any possible universe, because it is inherently false and contradictory. In the Peacocke proposal, on the other hand, though God could have chosen to create a (deterministic) universe in which his knowledge would have been unlimited in the traditional sense, he has in fact decided to actualize a universe with an unpredictable character, and so chosen to limit his knowledge of its future states.[9]

In Peacocke's view the future has "no ontological status"—that is, it "does not exist in any sense"—and consequently there is no content of "future events" for even God to know.[10] He appears to qualify this statement, however,

---

[7]Peacocke, *GIW*, p. 279. I am in agreement with Peacocke on this point: true contingency and indeterminacy are features of the quantum world itself. Since 1965 an important theorem established by the physicist John Bell ("Bell's Theorem") and experiments based on it have led most physicists to conclude that "hidden variables" versions of quantum mechanics, which have attempted to preserve a "classical" view of subatomic reality, are no longer viable. See Fritz Rohrlich, "Facing Quantum Mechanical Reality," *Science* 221 (1983): 1251-55; Bernard D'Espagnat, "The Quantum Theory and Reality," *Scientific American* 241 (1979): 128-40; and on recent experimental tests, James Glanz, "Measurements Are the Only Reality, Say Quantum Tests," *Science* 270 (1995): 1439-40. (The title of this latter article is somewhat misleading. Glanz's main point is that recent experiments give further evidence that "commonsense" notions are inadequate to describe quantum realities.) On Bell's Theorem and its implications, see James T. Cushing and Ernan McMullin, eds., *Philosophical Consequences of Quantum Theory: Reflections on Bell's Theorem* (Notre Dame, Ind.: University of Notre Dame Press, 1989).
[8]Peacocke, *TSA*, p. 121.
[9]Ibid., p. 122.
[10]Peacocke, *GIW*, p. 280.

in cases where deterministic laws apply and where God could have an infinitely precise knowledge of all the relevant initial conditions.[11] Presumably God *could* know future events such as eclipses of the sun or moon that are calculable by the laws of classical physics. In the quantum realm, however, Peacocke believes that God can know the future only in terms of *probabilities* and the various *possible trajectories* of such systems; there is nothing else that even God can know.[12] God could know the probability of finding an electron at a given distance from the nucleus of a helium atom, but neither we nor God could know simultaneously, with unlimited precision, both the position and the momentum of that electron. Peacocke believes that God has chosen to create a universe in which God's own knowledge is limited by the Heisenberg Uncertainty Principle.[13]

In the Peacocke proposal, then, God has bestowed a substantial degree of autonomy not only on human beings but also on the natural order itself. The natural order is allowed to develop "in ways that God chooses not to control in detail," such that there is an inherent "open-endedness and flexibility" in nature.[14] Peacocke believes that this view of the created order has the advantage of making it easier to understand the emergence of the "flexibility of conscious organisms" and, perhaps, the emergence of human freedom itself.[15]

There is no doubt that Peacocke's vision of an open-ended and contingent creation has both considerable empirical plausibility and intellectual and aesthetic appeal. It remains, however, to examine this proposal more closely in the light of classical theism's understanding of divine omniscience and God's relationship to time.

God's Knowledge of Contingent Future Events in Classical Theism

The Peacocke proposal addresses, in the light of modern physics' understanding of nature, issues that have been discussed for centuries by philosophers and theologians: Can God know with certainty the choices that a free moral agent will make at some time in the future? If God can know with certainty such choices, how can divine foreknowledge be reconciled with genuine

---

[11]Ibid.

[12]Ibid., p. 281.

[13]Peacocke, *TSA*, p. 122: The Heisenberg Uncertainty Principle "is, then, a limitation on God's omniscience. . . . It is a *self*-limitation, because God as Creator 'chose' . . . to create a world in which these subatomic constituents . . . had such an unpredictable character."

[14]Peacocke, *GIW*, p. 281.

[15]Ibid.

human freedom? Does divine foreknowledge inevitably lead to fatalism? If God knows with infallible certitude what I will choose to eat for breakfast tomorrow morning, am I free to choose otherwise? Is my "free" choice really an illusion?

It is readily apparent that the issues raised by the contingency of the human will are conceptually parallel to those raised by the contingency of quantum phenomena. While it is true that the two cases are metaphysically dissimilar in that one deals with the personal order and the other with the impersonal, the cases are in some respects metaphysically *similar* in that the issue involves the possibility of a divine being's knowing the possible future states (or choices) of finite, contingent entities (the human will, a radioactive nucleus) that are embedded in the temporal order. To that extent, it is relevant to examine the long tradition of philosophical and theological discussion regarding divine foreknowledge of future contingent events in order to see what light might be shed on Peacocke's proposal.

A paradigmatic expression of the standpoint of the theological tradition of "classical theism" may be found in Thomas Aquinas's discussion "Has God Knowledge of Contingent Future Events?" in the *Summa Theologiae* 1a.14.13.[16] According to Aquinas, God knows not only those things that exist in actuality but also those things that "are in the potency of himself or of a creature" *(quae sunt in potentia sua vel creaturae).* That is, God fully knows all things that he could, by an act of his will, choose to create at some time in the future—say a new star or species of plant. Further, he knows fully the potentialities inherent in all creatures, such as the potentiality for an acorn to become an oak tree; for a human embryo to become an adult. While Aquinas did not, of course, have in view the quantum realities discovered only in the twentieth century, it would seem the implication of his view would be that God has a comprehensive knowledge of all the potentialities inherent in a radioactive nucleus. In this case "potentiality" could correspond to the quantum-mechanical *probability* that the nucleus would decay at a given time t. For

---

[16]Thomas Aquinas, *Summa Theologiae,* vol. 4, *Knowledge in God* (1a.14-18), Blackfriars edition, trans. Thomas Gornall (New York: McGraw-Hill, 1964), pp. 45-52. The discussion of Aquinas is significantly influenced by the earlier work of the neo-Platonist philosopher Boethius (A.D. 480-524), especially in the matter of the "timelessness" of God. For a penetrating exposition and analysis of the history of the discussion of this issue prior to the eighteenth century, see William Lane Craig, *The Problem of Divine Foreknowledge of Future Contingents: From Aristotle to Suárez* (Leiden, Netherlands: E. J. Brill, 1988), examining the views of Aristotle, Augustine, Boethius, Aquinas, Molina and others.

Aquinas, for whom there are no uncaused events (every effect having a sufficient cause), there would be the further implication that there is a causal nexus that accounts for the actual decay of a given radioactive nucleus at time *t1* rather than *t2*. Given that God has comprehensive knowledge both of the internal structure of the radioactive nucleus and the causal nexus in which it is embedded, God can know when a certain potentiality of the creature—in this case the decay of a nucleus—will be actualized.

How can God have such knowledge of the potentialities of a creature? For Aquinas a crucial element in the answer to this question is found in God's relationship to time. God does not know contingent future events successively, as we do. Rather, God's knowledge is "measured by eternity, as is also his existence." That is, everything that takes place in time "is eternally present to God," not merely in the sense that their intelligible essences or forms are present in the divine mind, but because "he eternally surveys all things *[quia ejus intuitus fertur super omnia ab aeterno]* as they are in their presence to him." In this "intuitionist" or "perceptual" model of the divine knowledge, God "sees" all creatures and events in one "eternal present."[17]

It is obvious that the notion of *eternity* presupposed in this model of the divine knowledge is critical. Aquinas explains his understanding of eternity in the *Summa Theologiae* 1a.10.1-2, "The Eternity of God."[18] Eternity, he says, has two characteristics: *unending duration,* or lack of a beginning or ending, and *lack of succession*, or eternity existing as an "instantaneous whole."[19] It is this latter "timeless" aspect of eternity that Aquinas stresses in relation to God. He explains that when it is said that God is "eternal," this means that God is "utterly unchangeable," beyond time, the notion of time itself deriving from change. When Scripture describes God using different verb tenses (such as God's being wrathful in the past but not in the present or future), this does not

---

[17]In the theological tradition this type of divine knowledge is known as "knowledge of vision." A traditional illustration of this notion of simultaneous knowledge in an "eternal present" is that of an observer at the top of a tower looking down on a road. A person on the road can see travelers on the road only successively, as they come around the bend, while the observer at the top of the tower can see them simultaneously.

[18]Thomas Aquinas, *Summa Theologiae,* vol. 2, *Existence and Nature of God* (1a.2-11), Blackfriars edition, ed. Timothy McDermott (New York: McGraw-Hill, 1964), pp. 137-55.

[19]To illustrate the notion of eternity as "timelessness," one could think of pure numbers existing in a transcendent Platonic realm of the Forms. Numbers exist in an ideal realm apart from space, time and succession. On the other hand, the "eternal life" offered to believers in Scripture implies not complete transcendence of space and time but "unending life/duration," though, to be sure, in a qualitatively new dimension of existence.

mean, according to Aquinas, that God actually varies from the past to the future but that "his eternity comprehends all phases of time." Just as Scripture can describe God metaphorically in bodily terms (face, arm and the like), so it can describe God's timeless eternity in temporal and successive terms.[20]

It is apparent that this notion of divine "timelessness," in which Aquinas has followed Boethius, pays a high price theologically in order to explain how God can know future contingent events. If God's eternity *must* entail the exclusion of any sort of succession in the divine nature, then it is difficult to see how there could be any change in the emotional states of an "eternal" God. As it has been said, such a God is "religiously unavailable." A God whose emotional states never change is not the God of the Bible; the personal and living God of biblical theism is a God who changes not in his essential nature, character or purposes but does change in the way he responds to his covenant people. It remains to be seen whether one is in fact forced, logically and theologically, to choose between a "timeless" God who is omniscient (but impersonal and unresponsive) and a "temporal" God who is personal but limited in the scope of his knowledge.

In recent decades the issues of divine foreknowledge, omniscience and the "timelessness" of God have been major objects of attention among philosophers and theologians. The 1970 book by the philosopher Nelson Pike, *God and Timelessness,* is a major contribution to this discussion and has generated a considerable number of responses. Pike expressed a quite negative view of the notion of God's timelessness, noting the criticism of contemporary theologians, influenced by Alfred North Whitehead, that such an utterly transcendent and timeless God is not "religiously available" to respond to human actions and petitionary prayer.[21] In the conclusion of his book Pike expresses the suspicion that the doctrine of God's timelessness was introduced into Christian theology because Platonic thought was fashionable at the time and that "once introduced, it took on a life of its own."[22] Pike believes that the notion of time-

---

[20]For a modern example of this concept of God's "timelessness" see the neo-Thomist theologian Reginald Garrigou-Lagrange: God's eternity implies that the divine essence is beyond time and space; in God there is not beginning or end nor "change of any kind." He believes that the exclusion of any idea of succession in the concept of God's eternity "though apparently not as yet a dogma of the Catholic faith, nevertheless is a certain truth, proximate to the faith" (Reginald Garrigou-Lagrange, *God: His Existence and Nature,* trans. Dom Bede Rose [St. Louis: B. Herder, 1934], 1:3-4).
[21]Nelson Pike, *God and Timelessness* (London: Routledge & Kegan Paul, 1970), p. xi.
[22]Ibid., p. 189.

lessness is not required by either the biblical or the confessional traditions, nor is it logically entailed by an Anselmian concept of God as a being greater than which none can be conceived.[23] Pike sees little advantage in the doctrine of God's timelessness and wonders why it continues to be defended by Christian theologians.

One of the most significant recent contributions to this debate is by the evangelical philosopher of religion William Lane Craig, *Divine Foreknowledge and Human Freedom* (1991).[24] Craig recognizes that the two fundamental questions in the debate are "How is genuine contingency preserved in the face of infallible divine foreknowledge?" and "*How* can God know future contingent propositions?" He rejects as inadequate solutions limitations on the divine omniscience and denials that future contingent propositions can have truth value, and argues that divine omniscience can be affirmed without endorsing fatalism.[25] Craig and others in this conversation are concerned with *human* contingency, but as I have previously noted, the issues raised by *quantum* contingency in relation to divine omniscience and timelessness are conceptually parallel.

Craig notes at the outset of his discussion that God's foreknowledge of contingent future events is assumed in biblical theism. This unlimited divine foreknowledge is not a tangential teaching but is fundamental to the biblical view of history and serves to distinguish the God of Israel from the false gods of the surrounding nations (Is 41:21-42; 44:6-8; 46:9-10).[26] This teaching is affirmed in both Testaments; the same sort of foreknowledge ascribed to Yahweh in the Old Testament is ascribed to Jesus in the New (Mk 8:31; 9:31; 10:32-34; 14:13-15,

---

[23]Ibid., pp. 165, 190.

[24]William Lane Craig, *Divine Foreknowledge and Human Freedom: The Coherence of Theism— Omniscience* (Leiden, Netherlands: E. J. Brill, 1991), hereafter cited as *DFHF.*

[25]Other important recent contributions to this discussion include William Hasker, *God, Time and Knowledge* (Ithaca, N.Y.: Cornell University Press, 1989; limits foreknowledge to avoid fatalism); Richard M. Gale, *On the Nature and Existence of God* (Cambridge: Cambridge University Press, 1991), chap. 3, "The Omniscience-Immutability Argument" (argues forcefully against "timelessness" in the interests of a "religiously available" God); in Thomas V. Morris, ed., *The Concept of God* (Oxford: Oxford University Press, 1987), the essays by Alvin Plantinga, "On Ockham's Way Out," pp. 171-200 (attempts to reconcile unlimited divine knowledge with human freedom), and Eleonore Stump and Norman Kretzmann, "Eternity," pp. 219-52 (defends a Boethian concept of a timeless, eternal God); H. P. Owen, *Christian Theism: A Study in Its Basic Principles* (Edinburgh: T & T Clark, 1984; accepts limits on divine foreknowledge); and Jonathan L. Kvanvig, *The Possibility of an All-Knowing God* (London: Macmillan, 1986; argues for the adequacy of a Molinistic account of maximal divine omniscience).

[26]Craig, *DFHF,* p. 12.

18-20, 27-30, and parallels). God's foreknowledge encompasses the most contingent events, even the thoughts that a person will think (Ps 139:1-6).[27] The
plausible implication of the biblical outlook is that God would also know (in a
more than probabilistic sense) when a given radioactive nucleus would split.

Craig argues for the compatibility of unlimited divine knowledge and genuine finite contingency by appealing to the doctrine of "middle knowledge"
developed by the Counter Reformation Jesuit theologian Luis Molina (1553-
1600).[28] In his own attempt to reconcile the sovereignty of God and divine
omniscience with human freedom Molina postulated the existence of a third
type of divine knowledge—"middle knowledge"—that is intermediate
between the two types of divine knowledge then recognized in traditional
Thomism: the "natural" and "free" knowledge of God. "Natural" knowledge
is God's knowledge of everything that is possible (or necessary) in any universe, given the nature of logic and God's own nature. For example, God's
natural knowledge would include his knowledge of his own necessary existence, or, in the more trivial case of the toss of a coin, his knowledge of the
three possible outcomes: heads, tails or (very improbably) landing on the
edge. Such "natural" knowledge is not dependent on an act of the divine will
but is "necessary" in the sense of being entailed by God's nature and the laws
of logic. The "free" knowledge of God, on the other hand, is dependent on the
divine will, on God's choice to actualize one state of affairs rather than
another. God foresaw that human beings would disobey but willed to permit
the Fall, though God could have chosen to prevent it. Such "free" knowledge
is necessitated neither by the laws of logic nor by the divine nature as such.

According to Molina, there is in the mind of God a "middle" knowledge,
such that God knows that "if an agent X is placed in circumstance Y, then X
will freely choose to do Z." There is, according to Molina, a "supercomprehension" in the infinite divine intellect that discerns every individual essence,
these essences existing conceptually in the divine mind. Thus in the question
of divine grace and predestination, God infallibly foresees that if X is offered
the grace of salvation in circumstance Y, then X will choose to respond posi-

[27]Ibid.
[28]The parts of Molina's work most immediately relevant to the present discussion are now available in translation: Luis Molina, *On Foreknowledge,* part 4 of the *Concordia,* trans. Alfred J.
Freddoso (Ithaca, N.Y.: Cornell University Press, 1988); for an exposition of Molina, see Craig,
Problem of Divine Foreknowledge, chap. 7. Without apparently being aware of Molina, Alvin
Plantinga, in *The Nature of Necessity* (Oxford: Clarendon, 1974), pp. 174-80, developed a view
quite similar to that of the sixteenth-century Jesuit.

tively to the offer; God chooses to actualize circumstance Y and so "predestines" agent X in this sense. Thus, according to Molina, can God's foreknowledge and sovereignty be reconciled with genuine human freedom.

After extensive and intricate analysis, Craig concludes that the arguments against middle knowledge[29] are not convincing, and that middle knowledge is at least *possible.* Craig argues that this possibility of middle knowledge "is all that needs to be proved in order to show that God's knowledge of future contingent propositions is not impossible."[30] Extending Craig's conclusion to the case at hand, one could say that by virtue of his middle knowledge, God knows that a given radium atom, placed in a given causal nexus, would or would not split at a given time $t;$ and given this middle knowledge, God could choose to actualize or not actualize such a set of circumstances. In the subsequent discussion a revised version[31] of Molina's middle knowledge will be incorporated into my own proposal for unlimited divine knowledge of quantum realities.

Divine Omniscience and Quantum Indeterminacy: A Revisionist Proposal

Now for an alternative to Peacocke's proposal. This model of "neoclassical theism" will attempt to incorporate revised forms of both divine "timelessness" and Molina's middle knowledge. I will argue that such a model is capable of recognizing true indeterminacy in nature at the quantum level and at the same time can give an account of how God can have comprehensive knowledge of such quantum events—omniscience in the traditional sense.

The neoclassical model presented here assumes concepts of space and time

---

[29]Traditional Thomists reject middle knowledge because they believe that it has no real object (in the case of true contingency there is "nothing there" for God to know) and because it posits a passivity or dependency of God's knowledge upon the creature, inconsistent with the divine independence or aseity; see Craig, *DFHF,* pp. 242-46.

[30]Craig, *DFHF,* p. 278.

[31]I differ from Craig in two respects. Rather than favoring an "innatist" explanation of middle knowledge—that God has a "supercomprehension" of every individual essence based on the conceptual existence of such essences in the divine mind—I favor a "perceptual" model in which God immediately "sees" every existing entity in the created order from the divine perspective, unlimited by space or time. The innatist perspective seems to be in danger of undermining the dynamic aspect of events in space and time by associating them too closely with the divine mind and essence. In the second place, Craig appears to follow Molina (*DFHF,* p. 241) in holding that "it is not within the scope of God's power to control what free creatures would do if placed in any set of circumstances." I hold that in biblical theism, God not only foreknows the potentialities and inclinations of contingent entities in all circumstances but is also free—through divine sovereignty and immanence within the created order—to alter or redirect those inclinations should he so desire.

as generally understood in Einstein's special and general theories of relativity. Space and time are assumed to be relational concepts, the forms and structures of orderly events in the universe, not absolute "receptacles" or "containers" that exist apart from the universe's mass and energy.[32] Space and time are not separate entities but part of a four-dimensional space-time continuum. Following Augustine, one could understand God's *ex nihilo* creation to involve the creation of the universe not "in" (preexisting) time but "with" time: God creates mass-energy *together with* the space-time manifold, this manifold being a creaturely reality ontologically distinct from the divine essence.[33]

In modern physics and cosmology the dynamic development of the physical universe from the moment of the initial big-bang singularity to the present is often visually modeled in terms of a "light cone" (see figure 1).

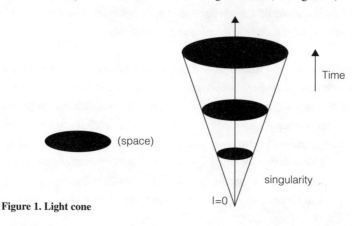

Figure 1. Light cone

---

[32] For philosophical treatments of space and time, incorporating modern physical theory, see Hans Reichenbach, *The Philosophy of Space and Time,* trans. Maria Reichenbach and John Freund (New York: Dover, 1958; argues against idealist and subjectivist views of space-time from a realist standpoint); G. J. Whitrow, *The Natural Philosophy of Time* (London: Thomas Nelson & Sons, 1961; argues against the "block universe" concept of time, in which time and becoming are only apparent to the observer); Adolf Grunbaum, *Philosophical Problems of Space and Time* (Dordrecht, Netherlands: D. Reidel, 1973; very technical discussion of issues raised by Einstein's special and general theories of relativity); Lawrence Sklar, *Space, Time and Spacetime* (Berkeley: University of California Press, 1974; suspicious of attempts to reduce spatiotemporal categories to something else). For recent attempts to incorporate twentieth-century concepts of space-time in theological analysis, see the important works of Thomas F. Torrance, *Space, Time and Incarnation* (Oxford: Oxford University Press, 1969), and *Space, Time and Resurrection* (Edinburgh: Handsell, 1976).

[33] Cf. Augustine *Confessions* 11.14: "In no time, therefore, hadst thou 'not made' anything; because time itself was of thy making *[quia ipsum tempus tu feceras]"* (*St. Augustine's Confessions,* trans. William Watts [Cambridge, Mass.: Harvard University Press, 1946], 2:237); see also *City of God* 12.15.

The horizontal surfaces of figure 1's cone represent the three dimensions of space, while the vertical axis represents the dimension of time. It should be emphasized that such diagrams are only conceptual models; it is obviously impossible to represent with full adequacy the reality of a changing four-dimensional universe with a static diagram drawn on a two-dimensional surface. Taking such diagrams "literally" gives rise to unnecessary objections concerning a "block universe" in which time is robbed of reality and movement. The diagram is presented here not to endorse some static model of a universe like Parmenides's in which there is only "Being" and no "becoming," but merely as a conceptual tool to aid in the discussion of God's relationship to the spatiotemporal order.

As an alternative to the doctrine of divine "timelessness" found in Boethius and Aquinas, God's relationship to space-time is here understood in terms of a concept of transcendence-immanence complementarity (TIC). In this TIC principle, God is understood to be both immanent within the space-time order and transcendent of it. The language of biblical theism speaks of God's "eternity" both as an unending life within a temporal order, a life without beginning or end, and in the more absolute sense of a life that transcends time altogether.[34] These different ways of speaking of God's relationship to time in the biblical texts are understood to be complementary rather than contradictory, reflecting the different purposes of the biblical authors in a given text.

The language of "complementarity" is borrowed from Niels Bohr's philosophical reflections on quantum theory.[35] Rather than asking whether an electron is "really" more like a particle or a wave, in this view we can understand that "wave" and "particle" are two complementary ways of describing the electron, whose appropriateness depends on the particular experiments and measurements that are being performed. In certain experimental contexts the wavelike characteristics of the electron are manifest, while its particlelike characteristics are manifest in others. The two models are not visually commensurable, but each is valid in its own context.

---

[34]On the concept of the divine eternity and God's relationship to time in the biblical writings, see Hermann Sasse, "*aion, aionios,*" in *Theological Dictionary of the New Testament,* ed. Gerhard Kittel, trans. Geoffrey W. Bromiley (Grand Rapids, Mich.: Eerdmans, 1964-1976), 1:197-209.

[35]For discussion of Niels Bohr's principle of complementarity and other aspects of quantum theory, see John Honner, *The Description of Nature: Niels Bohr and the Philosophy of Quantum Physics* (Oxford: Clarendon, 1987). Honner is quite sympathetic to Bohr's standpoint and argues that Bohr was more of a philosophical realist and less an "instrumentalist" than usually thought.

If we apply such a model to the present discussion, we can recognize that in some contexts the biblical writers are concerned with God's presence and relationship to his creatures within space and time, while in others the focus is on God's transcendence over the created order. In terms of the light-cone diagram of figure 1, the God of biblical theism is free to be present within the space-time manifold (immanence) but at the same time is not contained or limited by it (transcendence). In his transcendent aspect God stands "outside" the light-cone and immediately "sees" every point along the temporal axis—including the decay of radioactive nuclei. But in his *immanent* relationship to the created order, God enters into real relationships to his creatures, responding to them as the personal, living God, changing not in character, essence or ultimate purpose but in the way in which he may relate to them at a given moment.[36]

In principle, of course, classical theism has always recognized both the transcendence and immanence of God. In discussions of divine "timelessness," however, it seems that Aquinas and others have taken an unbalanced approach, overemphasizing transcendence at the expense of immanence, in an attempt to safeguard divine omniscience. The present proposal, with its appeal to transcendence-immanence complementarity, is an attempt to correct that imbalance.

A second element in the model being advanced here as an alternative to Peacocke involves a modified form of Molina's middle knowledge and of classical Thomism's understanding of divine causality in relation to contingent events. According to the doctrine of middle knowledge, it will be recalled, God knows immediately, through "supercomprehension" or "knowledge of vision," how a contingent being X will act in circumstance Y. God "sees" both the essential nature of the creature and the laws and structures constituting the causal nexus in which the creature is embedded. In the case of the radioactive

---

[36]Torrance expresses a similar understanding in *Space, Time and Incarnation*, p. 67: "While the Incarnation does not mean that God is limited by space and time, it asserts the reality of space and time for God in the actuality of His relations with us." See also Alan G. Padgett, "God and Time: Toward a New Doctrine of Divine Timeless Eternity," *Religious Studies* 25 (1989): 213: "God, then, can enter into our space-time at will, but is not contained within it of necessity. And this is as one might expect, since God is the Creator of space and time. It is he that calls the universe into existence, and he cannot be limited by anything that is wholly dependent upon him." In Padgett's view, God is "relatively timeless"; that is, God's life is not limited to the time of our space-time universe, rather than being "absolutely timeless" in the sense of Plato, Boethius and Aquinas.

nucleus, the causal nexus is constituted by the space-time manifold, the energy fields and the laws of quantum mechanics.

Now it is well known that one of the major objections raised by classical Thomists to Molinistic middle knowledge concerns the alleged "passivity" in God that is entailed by this concept. According to classical Thomists, middle knowledge would involve a dependency of God's knowledge on the contingent acts of the creature, and as such it would be inconsistent with God's "pure actuality." From the perspective of classical Thomism, God knows with certitude a future contingent state of affairs Z precisely because he knows the act of his own will that has determined that Z shall obtain. Reginald Garrigou-Lagrange states the Thomistic objection concerning "passivity" this way: "Either God is the first determining Being, or else He is determined by another; there is no other alternative. . . . *Scientia media* involves an imperfection, which cannot exist in God."[37] Garrigou-Lagrange believes that a maximally perfect Being can in no way be dependent on the creature, and middle knowledge, he argues, implies such a passive dependence of God's knowledge on the actions of the creature. God, as it were, "must look at the weathervane in order to learn which way the wind is blowing"—rather than knowing the direction of the wind and the weathervane by a prior determining act of his will.

The modification here proposed to the standard Thomistic understanding argues that, contrary to Garrigou-Lagrange, there is in fact a third alternative to God's either being the "first determining Being" or being determined by another. This revision of classical Thomism posits a concept of bilateral, a posteriori determination of contingent events by acts of the divine will. The term *bilateral* calls attention to the fact that the futurition of many events is the product of a joint causality involving both the creature and the Creator. At the level of secondary causes, it is true to say that "sunlight and the process of photosynthesis cause the grass to grow," while at the level of primary causation, it is true to say that "God causes the grass to grow." Both statements are true; they address different levels of reality. On the other hand one could speak of "unilateral" causation, in which the actualization of some state of affairs is caused by an act the divine will alone. The creation of a physical universe *ex*

---

[37]Cited in Freddoso's introduction to Molina, *On Foreknowledge,* p. 66. In pp. 1-81 of this work Freddoso provides an extensive introduction to, and philosophical defense of, the Molinist perspective.

nihilo would be an example of such "unilateral" divine causality; there would be no finite, contingent beings yet in existence that could contribute to the causal efficacy of such a divine creative act.

The concept here termed "bilateral causation" is, of course, recognized in classical Thomism's distinction of primary and secondary causes. It seems worthwhile, however, to call attention again to the reality of bilateral causation, in that there seems to be a tendency in classical Thomism to deemphasize—in the interests of guarding God's "pure actuality"—the creature's causal contributions, especially those contributions that might be thought to initiate or determine future states of affairs.

The term *a posteriori* in the phrase "bilateral, a posteriori determination of contingent events" (by the divine will) is intended to recognize creaturely initiative in the futurition of certain contingent events. In this model of God's action in the world, God, at any given time *t1,* "sees" the tendencies and potentials in a creature *X*—say, a radium nucleus—and because of this comprehensive knowledge of both the essential nature and potentials of the creature, and of the causal nexus in which it is embedded, knows that nucleus *X* is about to disintegrate at some time *t2*. By an a posteriori determination of his will, based on the immediate and comprehensive knowledge of vision, God then chooses to concur in the creaturely tendency and render certain the decay of the nucleus at time *t2*. The determination by the divine will is a posteriori in the sense that it is a "foreseen" response to a set of tendencies *initiated within* the creature.[38] This would be contrasted with a purely a priori determination of a future event that in no way responded to or took into account the existing tendencies of the creature.

In this proposal it could be said that—in some cases—"the creature proposes but God disposes." That is, so to speak, the radium nucleus "proposes" to decay at time *t2,* but unless God chooses to concur in or "ratify" the creaturely tendency, the possible future contingent event does not actually transpire. This model attributes real causal initiative to the creature in a way that traditional Thomism seems to deny. That is to say, in certain cases the initiative for a given chain of events is understood to come from the creature; the creature is seen as a real source of metaphysical *novelty,* insofar as God has delegated to the creature some of his own creative power.

---

[38]Strictly speaking, of course, the tendencies of the radium atom are not "foreseen" but simply "seen" by God, standing outside of and transcending the space-time continuum.

Admittedly, this revision of classical Thomism does attribute a measure of "passivity" to God, if divine passivity is defined as including any element of responsiveness to the creature. In traditional Thomism this seems to be seen as an "imperfection"; but this revisionist proposal questions such a notion of "perfection." In biblical theism, God's responsiveness to the creature is not a weakness but a strength, not an "imperfection" but indeed a perfection, an expression of his unsurpassable, unchanging nature as a living and personal God.

This concept of bilateral, a posteriori determination of future contingent events allows a measure of divine responsiveness to creatures that makes God "religiously available" to the believer, thus avoiding some of the problems associated with the timeless, impassible God of classical theism. At the same time, the proposal involves a revision of the Molinist concept. According to Molina, it is not in the scope of God's power to *control* what free creatures will do in a given circumstance, though God can *know* their inclinations and choices and choose to actualize the circumstances accordingly.[39] In the model of divine action being argued here, God reserves the right to intervene in creaturely reality—not merely in circumstances external to a creature—and to redirect, change or override a creature's preexisting tendency. In this proposal the creature is given a genuine "voice and vote," but God retains the right to veto the creaturely inclination. This positing of the possibility of divine revisionary action within the creature as well as external to it seems more in keeping with the "interventionist" element of biblical theism, which asserts that, in a redemptive context, "God has mercy on [softens] whom he wants to have mercy, and he hardens whom he wants to harden" (Rom 9:18).

This proposal, then, attributes less control to God than does traditional Thomism, in that it recognizes the possibility of genuine causal initiatives on the part of the creature; at the same time it recognizes more control than does Molinism, for it views God as remaining free to change or redirect inclinations and tendencies internal to the creature. Such revisions of both traditional Thomism and Molinism produce a model of divine causation that can account for maximal divine knowledge of future events while at the same time recognizing genuine contingency in nature and causal ini-

---

[39]At the personal level of grace and conversion, for Molina grace is not *intrinsically* efficacious (as in the Augustinian and Calvinistic concept of "irresistible" grace) but *extrinsically* efficacious for those who choose to cooperate with it (as in the Arminian view); see Craig, *DFHF,* p. 241.

tiatives by the creature.[40]

In conclusion, then, I have argued, as an alternative to Peacocke's model of "self-limited omniscience," that it is possible to recognize genuine contingency in nature at the quantum level and at the same time hold that God's knowledge of such events is not limited ("maximal omniscience"). The neo-classical model I propose involves concepts of "transcendence-immanence complementarity" and a bilateral, a posteriori causal relation of the divine will and contingent events. It remains to consider some important objections to this point of view that have been raised by those who argue for limited divine omniscience.

Responding to Objections

According to Oxford theologian Keith Ward, God knows all that it is logically possible to know, but "no possible being can know as actual what is not yet actual."[41] Ward believes that the idea that God could "see" all creaturely choices and then determine the world to take account of them is incoherent, because "such choices do not actually exist unless the world exists in time up to that point," and once the world exists, one cannot subsequently change it.[42]

Ward's objections may be telling in relation to the concept of a purely "timeless" God, but not in regard to the model being proposed here. While Ward would seem to be correct in arguing that no being can know *as actual* what is not yet actual, he does not give adequate weight to the ontological category of *potentiality*. Various states of (physical) potentiality may have less ontological weight than actual states, but they constitute, in the physical order,

---

[40]Theologically this proposal stands in the Calvinistic tradition, as expressed in the 1647 Westminster Confession of Faith 5.2, which in its statement "Of Providence" holds that "although in relation to the foreknowledge and decree of God, the first cause, all things come to pass immutably and infallibly, yet by the same providence he ordereth them to fall out, according to the nature of second causes, either necessarily, freely, or contingently." This statements affirms both infallible divine foreknowledge of contingent events and genuine contingency at the level of secondary causation. The present proposal attempts to give an account of how these two realities can be compatible. It shares the Calvinistic presupposition that God is free to change or redirect the preexisting tendencies and inclinations of the creature. It would appear to differ, however, from the traditional Calvinistic model in attempting to give greater place to creaturely causal initiatives through the concept of bilateral, a posteriori divine determination of (some) events. It would seem that the Confession statement just quoted has usually been understood as similar to the view of classical Thomism.

[41]Keith Ward, *Rational Theology and the Creativity of God* (Oxford: Basil Blackwell, 1982), p. 130.

[42]Ibid., p. 152.

real states of being distinct from mere logical possibility and full actuality, and as such can be objects of divine knowledge. God can fully know both physical potentialities and physical actualities.[43] In the model proposed here, God is not only outside space-time in his transcendent aspect but also immanent within space-time—and so immanent within each instant of the time dimension itself—such that each creaturely essence, together with its potentialities and tendencies, is immediately present to the divine vision. The model's appeal to divine immanence within time, I suggest, relieves some of the difficulties associated with the picture of a static "block universe" that comes from stressing only the divine transcendence of time, as in the traditional Boethian and Thomistic concepts of a "timeless" God. God's middle knowledge of the creature, then, is based both on divine knowledge of all actualities and potentialities internal to the creature and on knowledge of the causal nexus external to the creature.[44] God "sees" that a given nucleus is about to disintegrate, and is free either to concur—and so make certain—or not concur in the creature's propensities and tendencies.

It might also be noted at this point that this defense of maximal divine omniscience of quantum-mechanical realities assumes the validity of a "causal principle" that could be stated in a proposition such as "Everything that begins to exist has a cause of its existence."[45] Quantum-mechanical events may not have classically deterministic causes, but they are not thereby uncaused or acausal. The decay of a nucleus takes place in view of physical actualities and potentialities internal to itself, in relation to a spatiotemporal nexus governed by the laws of quantum mechanics. The fact that uranium atoms consistently decay into atoms of lead and other elements—and not into rabbits or frogs—shows that such events are not acausal but take place within a causal nexus and lawlike structures. Accordingly, it seems plausible to

---

[43] An illustration of the notion of potentiality as an ontological reality distinct from pure actuality and mere logical possibility is found in the quantum-mechanical formalism of the wave function, which can describe the probability of finding the electron at a given distance from the nucleus of a hydrogen atom. Such "probability waves" are not fully actual, but neither are they merely logical possibilities, because they refer to existing features of the space-time universe.

[44] The foregoing observations, I suggest, also help to meet classical Thomists' objection to middle knowledge: that it has no real object, since only actual determinations of the divine will or actually existing states in the world can be known with certainty. I argue that physical states of potentiality do have ontic reality and can be known as such by God.

[45] For a discussion of issues of causality in relation to cosmology, see William Lane Craig and Quentin Smith, *Theism, Atheism and Big Bang Cosmology* (Oxford: Clarendon, 1993), and John Leslie's review of this work in *Zygon* 30, no. 4 (December 1995): 653-56.

assume the validity of some causal principle in such cases. God, knowing both the states internal to the nucleus and its external environment and governing laws, can at any given moment "see what the nucleus is about to do."

Finally, I should clarify that my purpose here has not been to argue that Peacocke's "self-limited omniscience" proposal is either impossible or incoherent. It seems quite possible to conceive a world as described by Peacocke, in which quantum-mechanical "fuzziness" and contingency really do obtain and in which God has chosen not to know certain states of affairs in advance. Whether such a proposal is consistent with biblical theism is another matter. My argument here is that the realities of quantum physics do not *require* an abandonment of the concept of maximal divine omniscience, and a model of the relationship of the divine will to contingent events postulating principles of transcendence-immanence complementarity and bilateral, a posteriori determination has been advanced in support of this view.

3

The "Copenhagen" Interpretation of Quantum Mechanics & "Delayed-Choice" Experiments

New Perspectives on the Doctrine of Predestination

*I*n *Space, Time and Incarnation* (1969) and *Space, Time and Resurrection* (1976)[1] the Scottish theologian Thomas F. Torrance explored the implications of twentieth-century physics's new understandings of space and time for the Christian understanding of the incarnation and resurrection. In a similar vein, here I will seek to relate concepts drawn from quantum physics to the biblical doctrine of predestination. I will make a case that (1) the emphasis of the Copenhagen school of interpretation of quantum mechanics on the role of experimental measurement in specifying the dynamic attributes[2] of a quantum

---

[1]Thomas F. Torrance, *Space, Time and Incarnation* (Oxford: Oxford University Press, 1969), and *Space, Time and Resurrection* (Edinburgh: Handsell, 1976). Torrance has also given extensive attention to issues arising in scientific and theological method in *Theological Science* (London: Oxford University Press, 1969).

[2]With respect to a quantum entity such as an electron, "dynamic" attributes are those such as momentum and position that change over time; "static" attributes such as mass and charge are constant.

entity and (2) the "delayed-choice" experiments proposed by John Wheeler provide new perspectives that can help resolve some longstanding difficulties associated with traditional formulations of the doctrine of predestination.

It has long been recognized in theological circles that the nature of time and the relationship of time to eternity are crucial elements in any formulation of the doctrine of predestination. Theologians in general, however, have not attempted to reexamine traditional formulations of this doctrine in light of the new understandings of the nature of time arising from quantum physics. This chapter proposes such a reformulation, with special reference to the problem of "fatalism"—the charge that a "pretemporal" divine decree of predestination from eternity inevitably renders insignificant and illusory the choice of the human will in time. In my new formulation, election is seen as a dynamic rather than as a static attribute in time, integrally tied to the "experimental measurement" context of faith and conversion which gives it its full actuality and definition.

The Problem

In the minds of many, the doctrine of predestination as traditionally understood seems to inevitably entail some form of fatalism. A secret, pretemporal decree of God before the creation of the universe (cf. Eph 1:4), determining the ultimate destiny of all human beings, appears to make the human response in time to the preaching of the gospel in the last analysis insignificant. Human "decisions" ultimately do not matter; the outcome has already been unilaterally determined by God in advance. The human response is more apparent than real. God even appears to be insincere, going through the motions of making an offer of salvation to the nonelect even though he knows in advance that these nonelect individuals will not and cannot respond.

The concept of the pretemporal decree of predestination has received classic creedal formulation in Calvinistic documents such as the Canons of the Synod of Dort (1619) and the Westminster Confession of Faith (1647).[3] At the Synod of Dort, Dutch Reformed divines sharpened their formulation of the sovereignty of God in redemption and predestination in response to the criticisms raised by Jacob Arminius and his followers. Under the "First Head of Doctrine" the Synod addressed the issue of divine predestination. In article 7

---

[3]For texts, translations and discussion of these creeds, see Philip Schaff, *The Creeds of Christendom,* 4th ed. (New York: Harper & Brothers, 1884).

election is defined as the "unchangeable purpose of God, whereby, before the foundation of the world, he hath, out of mere grace . . . chosen . . . a certain number of persons to redemption in Christ." According to article 11, the number of the elect is immutably fixed: "neither can the elect be cast away, nor their number diminished."

The Westminster Confession of Faith, formulated in the midst of the English Civil War by Puritan divines, speaks in a very similar fashion. Chapter 3, "Of God's Eternal Decree," states that "God from all eternity did, by the most wise and holy counsel of his own will, freely and unchangeably ordain whatsoever comes to pass." As for those who are predestined to salvation, "their number is so certain and definite that it cannot be either increased or diminished." The Confession asserts that by God's eternal decree the genuine contingency of secondary causes and the liberty of the human will are not taken away "but rather established," though how this can be the case has not been apparent to many readers.

For both the Synod of Dort and the Westminster Assembly, election or predestination is a static category, having a fixed and determinate meaning prior to the faith response (or lack of it) to the preaching of the gospel in history. This crucial assumption will be examined in this chapter in light of other strands of the biblical tradition and perspectives arising from modern physics.

It should also be noted that traditional formulations of the pretemporal, determinate decree of election have given rise to problems in systematic and pastoral theology, such as the sincerity of the offer of the gospel to the reprobate and the basis of the believer's assurance of salvation. If God knows in advance, on the basis of his own unilateral sovereign decree, who will actually believe, how can the offer of salvation to the nonelect really be meaningful and sincere? And if salvation ultimately depends on a secret, pretemporal decree of God prior to faith, how can a believer really know that she is among the elect?[4] These questions have continued to confront the tra-

---

[4]The problem of assurance of salvation in relation to the Reformed doctrines of predestination and limited atonement (the view that Christ intended to die for the sins of the elect alone, not for the world generally) is discerningly discussed in R. T. Kendall, *Calvin and English Calvinism to 1649* (Oxford: Oxford University Press, 1979). For further background on the history of theological discussions of the doctrine of predestination see Paul K. Jewett, *Election and Predestination* (Grand Rapids, Mich.: Eerdmans, 1985); Karl Barth, *Church Dogmatics* 2/2, *The Doctrine of God,* ed. G. W. Bromiley and T. F. Torrance (Edinburgh: T&T Clark, 1957), pp. 3-506; and Otto Weber, *Foundations of Dogmatics,* trans. Darrell L. Gruder, vol. 2 (Grand Rapids, Mich.: Eerdmans, 1983), esp. pp. 414-37, "The Problem Areas of the Doctrine of Election in Its Historical

ditional Calvinistic understandings of predestination in the centuries since
their formulations.

"Copenhagen" Quantum Mechanics and "Delayed-Choice" Experiments

Certain concepts drawn from two areas of modern quantum physics, the dominant Copenhagen interpretation of quantum mechanics and John Wheeler's
delayed-choice experiments, may shed light on the matter. The Copenhagen
school of interpretation, associated with Danish physicist Niels Bohr and his
followers, emphasizes the crucial role of experimental measurement in speaking about the attributes of a subatomic reality such as an electron or photon.[5]
Delayed-choice experiments proposed by John A. Wheeler indicate that certain quantum events normally considered as already in the past may not in fact
be fully actualized and determined until the experimental measurements have
been completed in the present.[6]

Before proceeding with the argument, I should make a few comments
concerning the validity of applying categories drawn from modern physics
to the task of constructive theology.[7] Admittedly both areas—the theological

---

Development." For the development of the doctrine of predestination in the Calvinistic tradition,
see John Calvin, *Concerning the Eternal Predestination of God* (1552), trans. J. K. S. Reid (Lon-
don: James Clarke, 1961); John Calvin, *Institutes of the Christian Religion,* trans. John Allen
(Philadelphia: Presbyterian Board of Christian Education, 1936), 3.21-24; and Richard A.
Muller, *Christ and the Decree: Christology and Predestination in Reformed Theology from
Calvin to Perkins* (Durham, N.C.: Labyrinth, 1986).

[5]Nontechnical yet accurate discussions of the Copenhagen and other schools of interpretation
of quantum mechanics may be found in P. C. W. Davies and J. R. Brown, *The Ghost in the
Atom: A Discussion of the Mysteries of Quantum Physics* (Cambridge: Cambridge Univer-
sity Press, 1986), and Nick Herbert, *Quantum Reality: Beyond the New Physics* (London:
Rider, 1985). Niels Bohr's views were developed in a series of famous debates with Albert
Einstein; the most important of these scientific papers have been reprinted in John A.
Wheeler and Wojciech H. Zurek, eds., *Quantum Theory and Measurement* (Princeton, N.J.:
Princeton University Press, 1983), pp. 3-151. For further exposition of Bohr's views see
John Honner, *The Description of Nature: Niels Bohr and the Philosophy of Quantum Phys-
ics* (Oxford: Clarendon, 1987), chap. 2, "Quantum Theory and Its Interpretation," pp. 25-70,
provides a helpful survey of the historical development of quantum theory and Bohr's role in
this development.

[6]John Archibald Wheeler, "The 'Past' and the 'Delayed-Choice' Double-Slit Experiment," in
Mathematical Foundations of Quantum Theory, ed. A. R. Marlow (New York: Academic Press,
1978), pp. 9-48. For experimental evidence supporting the Copenhagen interpretation and
Wheeler's notion of the "past," see Thomas Hellmuth et al., "Delayed-Choice Experiments in
Quantum Interference," *Physical Review* A35, no. 6 (March 1987): 2532-40.

[7]Helpful observations on the relationship of quantum physics and systematic theology may be
found in the essay by R. J. Russell, "Quantum Physics in Philosophical and Theological Perspective," in *Physics, Philosophy and Theology: A Common Quest for Understanding,* ed. Robert J.

doctrine of predestination and modern quantum physics—are complex and subject to diverse interpretations. Any new theological construction is bound to be somewhat speculative in nature. Any analogies drawn between the two fields must be done with great care and circumspection, especially since the two disciplines deal with such different subject matters: physics with the impersonal, theology with the personal. Nevertheless, the attempt is not without theological justification: the same God is the ultimate source of both nature (the laws of quantum mechanics) and Christian religious experience (faith, conversion, election). Nature rightly understood will be seen to be consistent with religious experience and Scripture rightly understood, and new insights from one area may shed helpful light on the other.[8] As will be argued below, biblical texts such as Romans 11:7, 23 provide warrant for the analogical application of concepts from quantum mechanics to the doctrine of predestination. This proposal is presented in an exploratory spirit, subject to the further critical scrutiny of both the theological and scientific communities.

As already noted, in the Copenhagen interpretation of quantum mechanics, which is the predominant view among working physicists today, measurement is assigned a crucial role in defining the attributes of a quantum system. According to Bohr, "isolated material particles are abstractions, their properties being definable and observable only through their interaction with other systems."[9] For example, in Bohr's view, it is not meaningful to ask, "Is an electron 'really' more like a particle or a wave?" Bohr would answer, "It depends on the type of experiment that you perform. In some situations the wavelike properties of the electron are manifested, in others the particlelike. You can't say what an electron is 'really' like in isolation from the concrete experimental situation."

Nick Herbert explains the Copenhagen point of view this way: "Although an electron is always *measured* to have a particular momentum, it is a mistake . . . to imagine that *before* the measurement it possessed some definite momentum. The Copenhagenists believe that when an electron is not being measured,

---

Russell, William Stoeger and George V. Coyne (Vatican City: Vatican Observatory, 1988), pp. 343-74.

[8]The complementary relationship of God's revelation through nature and God's revelation in Scripture and religious experience is presupposed in biblical texts such as Psalm 19; Romans 1:18-20; Acts 14:14-17; 17:22-26.

[9]Niels Bohr, quoted in Herbert, *Quantum Reality,* p. 161.

it has no definite dynamic attributes."[10]

The Copenhagen understanding of the nature of quantum reality might be called "contextual realism." *Realism* signifies the view that the existing entity denoted by the word *electron* is not created by the observer; the electron has a reality external to the observer's subjectivity. The term *contextual,* however, qualifies this by signifying that certain *attributes* of the electron have a definite meaning, value and existence only in the context of a specific experiment and set of measurements.

The Copenhagen view is thus quite paradoxical and counterintuitive when compared to commonsense notions of reality. In what could be called "ordinary realism," billiard balls and baseballs have definite attributes such as position and momentum even when no one is looking. In the strange world of quantum phenomena, whether an electron looks like a wave or a particle depends on how and when the observer chooses to look. For the Copenhagen view accepted by most physicists, and presupposed here, such attributes of the electron cannot be defined in isolation, only within an experimental context that connects electron, measuring device and observer. Attributes such as "particle" or "wave" are joint possessions of the entity and the measuring device.

The notion of contextual realism might be illustrated by the experience of looking at a rainbow.[11] The rainbow is not some figment of the observer's imagination; it is based in an external reality, sunlight that is being refracted by countless drops of water in the sky. The position of the rainbow in the sky—where it might appear to touch the ground—depends, however, on where the observer is standing. When the observer moves, the position of the rainbow moves. The "position" of the rainbow can have definite meaning only when the position of the observer has been specified.

In the discussion to follow, this notion of contextual realism drawn from the Copenhagen interpretation will be applied to the concept of predestination. I will argue that election should be viewed not as a timeless, fixed "static" attribute (as in the traditional view) but as a *dynamic* attribute that has a definite and fully actualized meaning for the believer only in the context of the conversion experience and faith.

---

[10]Herbert, *Quantum Reality,* p. 159. Similarly, Paul Davies states the essence of the Copenhagen interpretation this way: "Bohr's position . . . is that it is meaningless to ascribe a complete set of attributes to some quantum object prior to an act of measurement being performed on it" (Davies and Brown, *Ghost in the Atom,* p. 21).

[11]This illustration is used by Herbert, *Quantum Reality,* p. 164.

It is now widely recognized that twentieth-century physics has dramatically challenged traditional commonsense understandings of the physical universe. Einstein's Special Theory of Relativity transformed earlier understandings of the nature of space and time.[12] Countless experiments confirming the theory of quantum mechanics have demonstrated that our normal notions of cause and effect are inadequate to describe the realities of the subatomic world.[13] Less well known are the so-called delayed-choice experiments in quantum physics that challenge our commonsense notions of how the past is related to the present. Experiments proposed by the physicist John Archibald Wheeler, and subsequently performed in the 1980s and 1990s, indicate that in certain circumstances events that are normally understood to have occurred in the past are not fully actualized and determined until experimental measurements in the present have been completed.[14] The main features of Wheeler's delayed-choice experiment are indicated schematically in figure 2.

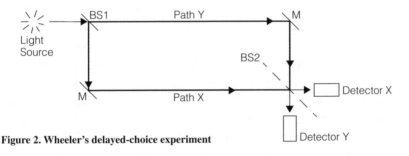

Figure 2. Wheeler's delayed-choice experiment

---

[12]The philosophical implications of Special Relativity are discussed in Hans Reichenbach, *The Philosophy of Space and Time,* trans. Maria Reichenbach and John Freund (New York: Dover, 1958); G. J. Whitrow, *The Natural Philosophy of Time* (London: Thomas Nelson & Sons, 1961), and Adolf Grunbaum's very technical *Philosophical Problems of Space and Time* (Dordrecht, Netherlands: D. Reidel, 1973).

[13]In addition to the references noted in n. 5 above, see Max Jammer, *The Philosophy of Quantum Mechanics* (New York: Wiley, 1974), and Bernard d'Espagnat, *Foundations of Quantum Mechanics,* 2nd ed. (Reading, Mass.: W. A. Benjamin, 1976).

[14]See the references in n. 6 above. Nontechnical explanations of delayed-choice experiments are also found in Herbert, *Quantum Reality,* pp. 164-67. For readable summaries of recent experiments consistent with this point of view, see Andrew Watson, " 'Eraser' Rubs Out Information to Reveal Light's Dual Nature," *Science* 270 (November 10, 1995): 913-14 (experiments by a team at the University of Innsbruck, Austria, showed that the "photon's wavelike nature can be resurrected even after they have been encouraged to behave in a particlelike way"); James Glanz, "Measurements Are the Only Reality, Say Quantum Tests," *Science* 270 (December 1, 1995): 1439-40 (discussion of recent experiments indicating that a physical attribute—such as "an electron's position or a photon's polarization—has no reality, or 'being,' until an experimenter measures its value"). For original experimental reports, see P. G. Kwiat et al., "Observations of

A pulse of light enters the experimental apparatus at the left and travels through the first beam splitter *(BS1)*, which sends the light along either path *x* or path *y*. Mirrors *M* reflect the light toward detectors *x* and *y*, which indicate which path the light beam has taken. In this mode, the light appears to behave like a particle that has taken a definite path, either *x* or *y*, but not both. However, if a second beam splitter *(BS2)* is interposed in the path even after the light has passed through *BS1*, an interference pattern appears, indicating that the light has apparently taken both paths *x* and *y*, behaving like a wave.[15]

This experiment indicates that an attribute such as the particle nature of light, which we normally would think of as having been "already" determined in the "past" when the beam passes through *BS1*, is actually fully determined only when *BS2* has (or has not) been interposed and the experimental measurement completed in the present. According to Wheeler, this paradoxical state of affairs means that, in a manner of speaking, "we choose what *shall* have happened after 'it has already happened.' It has not really happened, it is not a phenomenon, until it is an observed phenomenon."[16]

As Thomas Hellmuth argues, such experiments "have far-reaching consequences for our picture of the past." In the quantum world, an event is not fully actual until it has been brought to a close by an irreversible act of measurement. The past is not carved in stone or fully determined and actualized until the experiment is over. Or as Wheeler has stated, "the past has no existence except as it is recorded in the present."[17]

In the discussion to follow, I will argue that events traditionally understood to have been fixed and determined in the past—the divine choice in predestination (e.g., Eph 1:4)—become fully actualized in the present experience of conversion.

Election as a Dynamic Attribute
Whereas traditional formulations of the doctrine of predestination have treated election as a static category, I propose to understand it as a *dynamic*

---

a 'Quantum Eraser': A Revival of Coherence in a Two-Photon Interference Experiment," *Physical Review* A45 (1992): 7729-39; and T. J. Herzog et al., "Complementarity and the Quantum Eraser," *Physical Review Letters* 75 (1995): 3034-37.

[15]Figure 2 and its description are adapted from Hellmuth et al., "Delayed-Choice Experiments," p. 2532.

[16]Wheeler, "The 'Past' and the 'Delayed-Choice' Double-Slit Experiment," p. 14.

[17]Hellmuth et al., "Delayed-Choice Experiments," p. 2540.

one, inextricably related to the experiential and historical context of conversion and faith. It has been seen that in the Copenhagen interpretation of quantum mechanics, dynamic attributes of quantum phenomena, such as the position or momentum of the electron, or its wavelike or particlelike properties, have no fixed and determinate meaning apart from and prior to the actual experimental measurement. The "wave" attribute of the electron passes from potentiality to full actuality only in the context of the whole experimental situation, involving the present interaction of electron, measuring device and observer.

By way of analogy, it should be noticed that in the New Testament predestination is discussed not in an a priori but in an a posteriori context. That is, the categories of election and predestination do not appear in the context of speculations as to which individuals may be elect before the kerygma is preached; they are brought up in a postconversion context, addressing those who have already responded in faith to the message.[18] Having responded in faith to the kerygma, the believer can use concepts of election and predestination to see faith as ultimately grounded in the divine initiative and in the sovereign will of God. The New Testament texts on predestination are presented as clarifications and explanations of faith already existing, not as the basis for speculation concerning the eternal destinies of those who have not yet heard the Christian message.

Earlier streams of the Reformed tradition reflect this New Testament link between predestination and faith. In the 1559 edition of the *Institutes,* for example, Calvin discusses predestination in the context of soteriology, in the conclusion of book 3, "The Way We Receive the Grace of Christ," chapters 21-24. As noted by Otto Weber, Calvin "did not view the doctrine of predestination as an *a priori,* in a speculative fashion, but saw it as an *a posteriori,* as established in the experience of the salvation-event."[19]

In the later Reformed tradition the doctrine of predestination is removed from its soteriological context and treated in a more a priori fashion as part of the doctrine of the eternal, divine decrees. The Canons of the Synod of Dort

---

[18]Texts such as Acts 13:48; Romans 9:6-24; 1 Corinthians 1:27-28, 1 Thessalonians 1:4-5; Ephesians 1:4; 2 Timothy 1:9; 1 Peter 1:1-2 are illustrative. In each case the text is addressed to members of the community of faith, giving theological reflection on the ground of their faith and conversion in the divine will, presented as theologically prior to the human response.

[19]Weber, *Foundations of Dogmatics,* p. 425. Weber notes that this or a similar placement of the doctrine of predestination is found in Peter Martyr (1500-1562), Wolfgang Musculus (1497-1563), and the Belgic and Gallican confessions.

and the Westminster Confession of Faith are notable and influential examples in this regard. In the case of the Westminster Confession this means, as James Torrance has observed, a movement toward a view where "election precedes grace, so that the interpretation of the Person and Work of Christ is subordinated to the doctrine of the decrees . . . [and] grace is limited to the redemption of the elect."[20]

The history of theology has shown that such an abstracting of the doctrine of predestination from its soteriological context and placement into the a priori context of the eternal decrees inevitably gives rise to problems of fatalism and the sincerity of the offer of the gospel (to the "nonelect"). From the perspective of the Copenhagen analogy being argued here, such an abstraction is illegitimate, since election and predestination are categories that have full actuality and definition only in the "experimental" context of conversion and faith. By keeping the categories of predestination and election more closely tied to their New Testament contexts of conversion and faith, the problems of fatalism and sincerity of the offer can be mitigated if not avoided altogether.

The next step in the argument is to relate Wheeler's delayed-choice experiment and his proposition that "the past has no existence except as it is recorded in the present" to the concept of dynamic predestination. The significance of Romans 11:7, 23 for the present discussion has generally not been noticed by theologians and exegetes: "What then? What Israel sought earnestly [i.e., a righteous standing with God] it did not obtain, but the elect *[he ekloge]* did. The others *[hoi loipoi]* were hardened. . . . And if they [the others, hoi loipoi] do not persist in unbelief, they will be grafted in again, for God is able to graft them in again."

The "elect" in verse 7 are the minority of Jews who have responded to the apostolic kerygma and recognized Jesus as the Messiah. Paul's attribution of election to these individuals is subsequent to their faith and conversion. The "others" who have not believed are presumably among the "nonelect," but the crucial point to be noticed here is that while history continues, and while the gospel is still being preached, *the category of election is fluid and dynamic*

---

[20]James B. Torrance, "Strengths and Weaknesses of the Westminster Theology," in *The Westminster Confession in the Church Today,* ed. Alasdair I. C. Herron (Edinburgh: St. Andrews Press, 1982), pp. 45-46. Torrance also notes that the structure of the Westminster Confession is "no longer the Trinitarian one of the creeds or of Calvin's *Institutio* of 1559, but is dominated by the eternal decrees and the scheme of Federal Theology" (p. 45).

rather than fixed and determinate. According to verse 23, the "others," presumably nonelect in light of their present unbelief, can still become "elect" if they do not continue in their unbelief, "for God has the power to graft them in again." In the apostle's mind the election of Israel is not simply an a priori determination of the divine will in some eternal past; the dynamics of election continue to work immanently within history as divine grace interacts with human sin and unbelief. Once faith has been actualized, the "nonelect" become "elect," and quite paradoxically, what is *now* true (election) *becomes* "always" true (as in "chosen . . . before the foundation of the world," Eph 1:4). The "past" becomes concrete and fully actual, as does election, at the moment of conversion. The category of election in biblical thought expresses the unconditional priority of the divine will to the human will, and the unconditional priority of divine grace to human merit or effort in the process of redemption.

A few commentators have hinted at the dynamic nature of the category of election in Romans 11:7, 23, but the insight has not been systematically developed. Charles Hodge, representing a very traditional Calvinistic predestinarian tradition, observed in relation to verse 23 that there is "no inexorable purpose in the divine mind . . . which prevents their [unbelieving Israel's] restoration."[21] Karl Barth in commenting on this verse called attention to the continuing freedom and sovereignty of God in history: "God has not ceased to dispose but is free to dispose again . . . this is the . . . consoling truth in relation to every contemporary situation."[22] For Franz Leenhardt, the text shows that in the mind of the apostle history is not a process of "mechanical unfolding of external and immutable divine decrees." God does indeed direct history toward his chosen ends, but "He takes into account the obstacles which the freedom of man opposes to His will."[23]

In a more pastoral context, intimations of this concept of dynamic predestination can be found in the words of a prayer attributed to Charles Spurgeon: "Lord, hasten to bring in all thy elect, and then elect some more."[24] For Spurgeon, the sovereign God who has elected continues to elect in history.

---

[21]Charles Hodge, *Romans* (1835; reprint Wheaton, Ill.: Crossway, 1993), p. 332.

[22]Barth, *Church Dogmatics* 2/2, p. 294.

[23]Franz J. Leenhardt, *The Epistle to the Romans,* trans. Harold Knight (London: Lutterworth, 1961), p. 291.

[24] Cited in David L. Edwards, *Christian England*, rev. ed., 3 vols. (London: Collins, 1989), 3:259.

Some New Perspectives on Some Old Debates

I have argued that the contextual realism of the Copenhagen interpretation of quantum mechanics and the delayed-choice experiments of John Wheeler provide a conceptual framework within which predestination and election can be viewed as dynamic rather than static categories. In this perspective, "election" becomes a determinate attribute for a given individual at conversion, not before. All who hear the gospel are potentially elect prior to conversion; those who believe become actually elect at the moment of conversion.[25] Biblical texts such as Ephesians 1:4 that stress the temporal and eternal priority of the divine will in redemption are understood to be true in a potential and provisional sense prior to conversion; at the moment of saving faith this "already" aspect of sovereign grace in the "past" becomes actually and determinately true for the believer. Once conversion has taken place, it becomes the case that God has "already" chosen the believer from "eternity past."[26]

It remains to sketch out—of necessity, only briefly—some of the implications of this concept of dynamic election. With regard to fatalism, the perspective proposed here clearly places the matter in a different light. While the gospel is still being preached, the matter of election or nonelection remains a genuinely open question (cf. Rom 11:7, 23). Even hardened unbelief may yet be softened by the divine mercy which continues to work immanently in history, "for God has the power to graft them in again." The problem of fatalism does not arise, because election and reprobation are not determinate or etched in stone prior to conversion.

Similarly, on this view there is no problem of insincerity in the offer of the gospel to the reprobate. Texts such as John 3:16 can be taken in a most straightforward sense as full and sincere declarations of the divine desire to provide salvation for the sinner on condition of faith. None are excluded a priori; all who hear the gospel are potentially elect. Only persisting unbelief prevents an individual from entering the circle of the actually elect.

This proposal provides a different perspective on some of the intractable debates that historically have arisen in regard to the extent of the atonement.

---

[25]It should be noted that in the categories of historical theology this proposal stands within the Reformed rather than Arminian tradition in soteriology, in that the decisive and distinguishing factor in conversion is understood to be the divine rather than the human will.

[26]This is by way of analogy to the delayed-choice experiment where the past states of the quantum entity become fully determinate and actual only in context of the present, when the experimental measurements have been completed.

The question as traditionally stated is "Did Christ intend to atone for the sins of all people, or for the sins of the elect only?" When "elect" and "election" are seen as categories that have an open and provisional character prior to conversion—that is, when election is understood dynamically rather than statically—the question can be seen in quite a different light. In a potential sense the design of the atonement is universal prior to conversion, in that all who hear the gospel are potentially elect. Upon conversion, the benefits of the atonement become actual for the believer, as the category of election itself becomes actual and concrete. To paraphrase the prayer of Spurgeon, in this perspective, which might be termed "dynamically particular atonement," it would be true to say that "Christ died for the sins of the 'elect'—but God is still electing in history."[27]

Finally, the concept of dynamic predestination avoids some of the pastoral problems that have arisen historically in the matter of assurance of salvation. A secret, pretemporal decree and "limited atonement" can give rise to nagging doubts and unhealthy introspection as the believer wonders, "Am I really one of the elect for whom Christ died?"[28] This proposal returns the doctrine of predestination to its New Testament and early Reformed context of Christology and soteriology. In a real sense John 3:16 is the only decree with which the believer needs to be concerned. Assurance of election comes as the believer responds in faith to Christ offered in the preaching of the gospel.

This point of view is consistent with the wise theological and pastoral insights of the father of the Reformed tradition, who wrote, "I do not send men

---

[27]In some respects this proposal of dynamic predestination and a dynamically particular atonement has resemblance to the "hypothetical universalism" of the French Reformed theologian Moyse Amyraut (1596-1664). On the system of Amyraut, see Roger Nicole, *Moyse Amyraut: A Bibliography with Special Reference to the Controversy on Universal Grace* (New York: Garland, 1981), esp. pp. 1-21 for a helpful overview of Amyraut's life, works and chief points of the controversy; and Brian G. Armstrong, *Calvinism and the Amyraut Heresy: Protestant Scholasticism and Humanism in Seventeenth-Century France* (Madison: University of Wisconsin Press, 1969). According to Armstrong (p. 266), Amyraut was being true to Calvin in seeing predestination as an ex post facto explanation of the work of God in salvation; in not placing the doctrine of predestination immediately after the doctrine of God; in seeing in texts such as John 3:16, 2 Peter 3:9 and Ezekiel 18:33 a universal aspect in God's will to save, while not denying the particularism of actual redemption. The present proposal shares these concerns but differs from the Amyraldian scheme in viewing election as a *dynamic* category. Despite their differences, the parties in the traditional debates on the extent of the atonement—orthodox Calvinists, Arminians, Amyraldians—all tacitly agreed in seeing election in static rather than dynamic terms, as a category that was determined pretemporally, prior to the preaching of the gospel in history.

[28]As discussed in Kendall, *Calvin and English Calvinism.*

off to the secret election of God to await with gaping mouth salvation there. I bid them make their way directly to Christ in whom salvation is offered us. . . . Whoever does not walk in the plain path of faith can make nothing of the election of God but a labyrinth of destruction."[29] This essay has attempted to retrieve this emphasis in Calvin with the aid of concepts drawn from modern quantum physics.

---

[29]Calvin, *Concerning the Eternal Predestination of God,* cited in Weber, *Foundations of Dogmatics,* p. 425.

4

Theological Reflections on Chaos Theory

*W*e collectively wish to apologize for having misled the general educated public by spreading ideas about the determinism of systems satisfying Newton's laws of motion that, after 1960, were proved to be incorrect." James Lighthill, then president of the International Union of Theoretical and Applied Mechanics, made this remarkable public apology exactly three hundred years after Newton's great *Principia Mathematica* was presented to the Royal Society of London. "Modern theories of dynamical systems," Lighthill went on to say, "have clearly demonstrated the unexpected fact that systems governed by the equations of Newtonian dynamics do not necessarily exhibit the 'predictability' property."[1]

In his presidential address Lighthill was reflecting on a new field of scien-

---

[1]James Lighthill, "The Recently Recognized Failure of Predictability in Newtonian Dynamics," *Proceedings of the Royal Society of London* A407 (1986): 35, 38.

tific research that has come to be known as *chaos theory*—a body of theoretical concepts and experimental results that have changed the way scientists think about determinism, predictability and a broad variety of phenomena in the natural world ranging from the weather to the beating of the human heart to the growth and decline of animal populations.

In this chapter I shall review the historical origins of chaos theory and some of its key features, and then reflect theologically on its implications for a Christian view of the world. Does chaos theory provide new perspectives on the vexing question of determinism and free will, as some commentators have suggested? If chaos research has undermined the predictable, "clockwork" universe of Newtonian science, what implications does this have for our understanding of the limitations of human knowledge and human control of nature? Does chaos theory open up new ways to understand the relationship of "chance" events to the providence of God, and the ways God creates new forms of life in the natural world? These are some of the questions that call for theological reflection. My underlying conviction is that not only does chaos theory not represent a threat to Christian faith, but in fact it provides new ways of understanding the richness and complexity of God's creative work and providential ordering of the physical universe.

Chaos Theory: Historical Origins and Key Features

In 1963 Edward Lorenz, a meteorologist at the Massachusetts Institute of Technology, published an article, "Deterministic Nonperiodic Flow," which was destined to become a classic in the newly emerging field of chaos research.[2] Using mathematical models and computer simulations of flow patterns in the atmosphere, Lorenz concluded that for weather forecasting, "prediction of the sufficiently distant future is impossible by any method." In view of the inevitable incompleteness of weather observations, "precise very-long-range weather forecasting would seem to be non-existent."[3] As Lorenz's results became known, most scientists came to agree that earlier optimism about human ability to control the weather or even forecast it in the longer term was scientifically unfounded. Systems like global weather were simply

---

[2]Edward N. Lorenz, "Deterministic Nonperiodic Flow," *Journal of the Atmospheric Sciences* 20 (1963): 130-41. Lorenz's work is discussed in James Gleick, *Chaos: Making a New Science* (London: Abacus, 1993), pp. 11-31. Gleick's work is one of the most readable popular presentations of chaos theory currently available.

[3]Lorenz, "Deterministic Nonperiodic Flow," p. 141.

too complex to admit of long-range predictability.

Lorenz's studies of weather forecasting gave rise to a concept in chaos research that is popularly known as the "butterfly effect." The rather remarkable idea expressed in this term is that a very small change in the initial conditions of some physical system—such as the fluttering of a butterfly's wing in Beijing—as it cascades unpredictably through a complicated system, can have very large effects later in time, producing a thunderstorm in New York.

The butterfly effect is a general characteristic of chaotic systems, more abstractly characterized as "sensitive dependence on initial conditions." If one were able to balance a pencil on its point, obviously the slightest touch from any direction would produce a much larger effect—the fall of the pencil to the surface. This is a very simple and crude illustration of a feature—*sensitive dependence on initial conditions*—of a great variety of complex systems in the physical world: the flow of gases and liquids through the atmosphere and pipes, the behavior of certain chemical solutions, electronic circuits, human heartbeats, the spread of diseases through a population, the dripping of water droplets from a faucet, the formation of patterns and fractures in metallic and crystalline surfaces, the formation of snowflakes, the behavior of the stock market, and so on. In each of these cases, and many more like them, very small changes in the system at the beginning can be multiplied so as to produce erratic and unpredictable behavior at some later point in time. Even the swinging of a pendulum—long thought to be the paradigm of Newtonian predictability—is now known to exhibit "chaotic" and irregular motion under certain conditions.[4]

Chaotic behavior is associated with systems that are termed "dissipative" by physicists—that is, systems where friction is a significant factor. Water flowing through a pipe or a hockey puck moving across the ice are examples of dissipative systems. In such cases a *nonlinear equation* is needed to describe the behavior of the system. In contrast to linear equations—represented by a straight line on a graph—nonlinear equations are very difficult to solve and in many cases have no exact solutions. Such equations are "messy," and as a result mathematicians and physicists have tended to give them less attention until relatively recently. The research in chaos theory that began emerging in the 1960s established the remarkable result that systems described by such nonlinear equations, while in principle being deterministic

---

[4]Lighthill, "Recently Recognized Failure," pp. 42-47.

and obeying the laws of classical Newtonian physics, are characterized by long-term unpredictability. One researcher in the field, David Ruelle, has in fact suggested that the essence of chaotic systems is the paradoxical combination of "determinism—yet long-term unpredictability."[5] The surprising thing is, as James Crutchfield has noted, that "simple deterministic systems with only a few elements"—for example, a swinging pendulum—"can generate random behavior." This randomness is fundamental, observes Crutchfield; "gathering more information does not make it go away."[6]

In 1975 biologist Robert May published an important article in the journal *Nature* in which the concepts of chaos theory were applied to the growth of animal populations.[7] May demonstrated that a relatively simple equation of the form X [next] $= kX(1-x)$, used to model the growth and decline of an animal population in a given environment, could display very erratic and unpredictable behavior over time. May's application of chaos theory to biological and ecological systems challenged biologists to look at population growth in a different way. Traditionally biologists had tended to assume that erratic fluctuations in, say, the number of deer in a certain habitat simply reflected fluctuations in the environment such as drought or disease. May's analysis demonstrated that such fluctuations could be built into the very mathematical laws that describe population growth.

In his seminal article May also drew attention to the fact that traditional scientific textbooks focused on simple systems with predictable behaviors. Consequently students were poorly equipped to confront the nonlinear and "chaotic" systems that are common in the real world outside the laboratory. "Not only in research, but also in the everyday world of politics and economics," May observed, "we would all be better off if more people realized that

---

[5]David Ruelle, *Chance and Chaos* (London: Penguin, 1993), p. 45.
[6]James Crutchfield et al., "Chaos," *Scientific American* 255, no. 6 (December 1986): 38. This article is a good introduction to chaos theory for the general reader. Other introductions that use little mathematics include William Ditto and Louis Pecora, "Mastering Chaos," *Scientific American* 269, no. 2 (August 1993): 62-83; Ian Stewart, *Does God Play Dice? The Mathematics of Chaos* (Oxford: Basil Blackwell, 1989), esp. chaps. 5-11; J. T. Houghton, "New Ideas of Chaos in Physics," *Science and Christian Belief* 1 (1989): 41-51; Paul Davies, *The Cosmic Blueprint* (London: Unwin Hyman, 1989), chap. 4, "Chaos," pp. 35-56. Technical treatments for scientists and engineers include A. J. Lichtenberg and M.A. Lieberman, *Regular and Stochastic Motion* (New York: Springer Verlag, 1983), especially chap. 7, "Dissipative Systems"; M. V. Berry et al., "Dynamical Chaos," *Proceedings of the Royal Society* A413 (1987): 1-199; Jong Hyun Kim and John Stringer, eds., *Applied Chaos* (New York: John Wiley & Sons, 1992).
[7]Robert M. May, "Simple Mathematical Models with Very Complicated Dynamics," *Nature* 261 (1976): 459-67.

simple nonlinear systems do not necessarily possess simple dynamical properties."[8] He was, in effect, calling for a paradigm shift in biology that would recognize and take seriously a body of unpredictable behavior that had been there all along. The fact that May was trained in theoretical physics and applied mathematics before becoming involved in biology "through the back door"[9] exemplified the frequently cross-disciplinary interests of many workers in this new field—quite in contrast to the trend toward narrow specialization that had come to dominate science since the nineteenth century.

During the 1960s and 1970s developments in chemistry, thermodynamics (the study of heat) and pure mathematics contributed significantly to the newly emerging field of chaos research. In 1977 the Belgian scientist Ilya Prigogine was awarded the Nobel Prize for his work in nonequilibrium thermodynamics. Classical thermodynamics, developed in the nineteenth century, studied the flow of heat in systems that were tending toward thermal equilibrium: if the door between one room with air at 80 degrees and an adjoining room with air at 60 degrees is opened, over time the air temperature will tend toward an equilibrium temperature of 70 degrees. Prigogine discovered that chemical solutions and heated fluids can display both oscillations and erratic, unpredictable behaviors, quite unlike the phenomena studied in traditional chemistry and thermodynamics. He argued that in many cases these nonlinear, chaotic systems can give rise to order and new complexity at higher levels in the system, and so might provide a way of understanding the emergence of life itself from its chemical and physical substrates.[10]

Developments in pure mathematics also spurred chaos research. In the 1970s Bernard Mandelbrot, a somewhat eccentric mathematician working in IBM's pure research division in New York, pioneered a whole new field of mathematics which came to be known as fractal geometry.[11] Mandelbrot coined the term *fractal* for the irregular, jagged patterns that occur in an astonishing variety of forms in nature: snowflakes; clouds; a flash of lightning; the

[8]Ibid., p. 467.

[9]Gleick, *Chaos,* p. 69.

[10]Ilya Prigogine, *Order out of Chaos: Man's New Dialogue with Nature* (New York: Bantam, 1984). Prigogine believes that discoveries in nonequilibrium thermodynamics, which emphasize the importance of time and irreversible events in nature, can provide a new paradigm that can reunite the physical, biological and human sciences, often seen as fundamentally bifurcated since the time of Newton.

[11]The seminal work here is Bernard Mandelbrot, *The Fractal Geometry of Nature* (New York: Freeman, 1977).

coastline of England; fractures in metal or the crust of the earth. Traditional Euclidean geometry had predisposed the human eye to see nature in terms of straight lines and smooth curves; Mandelbrot provided a new geometrical lens that could help human beings to see nature in all its rough complexity. Scientists and engineers gained a powerful mathematical tool to study the rough and jagged surfaces of metals, the tiny holes and channels in oil-bearing rocks, the intricate network of capillaries in the human body, to mention a few of the many applications of the new geometry in the physical and life sciences.

Some have raised the question why "chaos" was not discovered sooner, given the fact that many of the phenomena—such as the possibly erratic motions of a simple pendulum—were, in principle, known long before the field emerged in the 1970s. Very early in the twentieth century, for example, the great French mathematician Henri Poincaré had pointed to "chaotic" possibilities lurking in the equations of Newtonian science.[12] Part of the answer may lie in the fact that not until the 1960s did scientists have the powerful computers that could perform the laborious number crunching involved in solving the non-linear equations used to model chaotic behaviors. For much of the twentieth century the energy and attention of physicists was absorbed in exploring the new vistas opened by quantum theory and special relativity. And until Mandelbrot and other mathematicians developed mathematical tools for conceptualizing and rigorously describing these irregular and erratic phenomena, scientists tended not to "see" realities that had been there all along.

The Reality of Chaos: Theological Reflections

At the time of this writing there has been only limited response from the theological community to discoveries in chaos research. This is not surprising, given the rather technical nature of much of this work and the recentness of these developments. The first international scientific conference on chaos theory was held only in 1977 in Como, Italy, and many of the most significant among the original scientific papers are hidden away in obscure journals not easily accessible to the general public.

As early as the 1950s, however, some Christian theologians were giving

---

[12]In 1903 Henri Poincaré wrote, "It may happen that small differences in the initial conditions produce great ones in the final phenomena. A small error in the former will produce an enormous error in the latter. Prediction becomes impossible, and we have the fortuitous phenomenon" (quoted in Crutchfield et al., "Chaos," p. 40).

attention to issues of chance and unpredictability in relation to God's providential government of the world. As we shall see, these reflections do have relevance to the issues later raised by chaos research. These early reflections were in large measure attempts to come to grips theologically and philosophically with the issues raised by the strange and unpredictable phenomena of quantum physics, which began to penetrate the public consciousness in the 1920s. In his 1958 book *Chance and Providence* the priest-physicist William Pollard stated that the Christian can answer yes to Einstein's famous question, "Does God throw dice?" According to Pollard, "only in a world in which the laws of nature govern events in accordance with the casting of dice [i.e., probability] can the biblical view of a world whose history is responsive to God's will prevail."[13] For Pollard biblical and scientific descriptions of the same events were complementary, and "chance" was encompassed within the divine providence.

Similarly, Donald M. Mackay, writing in 1978, defined "chance" as "what defies determination on the basis of precedent." *Chance* refers to events that may be unforeseeable, but they are not therefore meaningless. From a Christian perspective, apparently chance events are subsumed under the wider providence of God.[14] Both Pollard and Mackay were dealing with "quantum" uncertainties rather than "chaotic" uncertainties, but their observations have analogical relevance to the unpredictable phenomena that burst upon the scientific world subsequent to their writings.

In his 1979 article "God and the Contingent Order," Scottish theologian Thomas F. Torrance reflected on the new awareness of temporality and irreversibility in science, alluding to big bang cosmologies and the nonequilibrium thermodynamics of Prigogine. Writing at a time when awareness of chaos research was beginning to extend beyond the boundaries of the scien-

---

[13]William G. Pollard, *Chance and Providence: God's Action in a World Governed by Scientific Law* (London: Faber and Faber, 1958), p. 97.

[14]Donald M. Mackay, *Science, Chance and Providence* (Oxford: Oxford University Press, 1978), p. 39. Compare the similar viewpoint of Peter Geach, *Providence and Evil* (Cambridge: Cambridge University Press, 1977), p. 116: "chance" events may not be determined by humanly knowable causes, but they do not "escape from the knowledge and control of Divine Providence," citing Proverbs 16:33. Geach also observes on p. 120 that "if men are to act freely there must be both some determinism [law, regularity, predictability] and some indeterminism [unpredictability] in the world." An "Alice in Wonderland" world in which pink-flamingo croquet rackets were not dependably rigid would be chaotic; a clockwork world of iron-clad determinism would be boring, oppressive and destructive of genuine human freedom and moral responsibility.

tific community, Torrance attempted to incorporate these new perspectives into Christian understandings of God's relationship to the world.[15]

The 1984 book by statistician D. J. Bartholemew, *God of Chance,* is one of the most significant attempts to relate chance in the natural world to a Christian understanding of providence. Thinking primarily of quantum uncertainties, but with some awareness of the newer chaos theory, Bartholemew posits that "since chance is such an integral part of creation, it must be part of God's plan." Chance should be seen as "grist for the providential mill rather than as an obstacle to providential action." Chance can in fact play a very positive role in God's creative work, since the variety and uncertainty it introduces provide a stimulating and challenging environment for the full scope of human development.[16] Like Pollard and Mackay before him, Bartholemew sees chance and unpredictability as consistent with rather than antithetical to the providential purposes of God.

Writing in the 1980s and early 1990s, Philip Hefner and Stuart Chandler discussed the notion of chaos in ancient religious mythologies, but with little or no interaction with scientific research in chaos theory.[17] In a 1989 article British meteorologist J. T. Houghton suggests that chaos theory represents a significant challenge to reductionistic views of the world; he believes that nature uses chaos constructively to provide biological systems with access to new forms.[18]

In August 1993 a cross-disciplinary group of twenty scholars and scientists met at the Center for Theology and the Natural Sciences in Berkeley, California, to explore the implications of chaos theory for philosophical and theological understandings of God's action in the world. The conference papers, representing both scientific and theological perspectives, were subsequently

---

[15]T. F. Torrance, "God and the Contingent World," *Zygon* 14:4 (1979): 329-48.

[16]D. J. Bartholemew, *God of Chance* (London: SCM Press, 1984), pp. 118, 138, 143.

[17]Philip Hefner, "God and Chaos: The Demiurge Versus the *Urgrund*," *Zygon* 19, no. 4 (1984): 469-85, contrasting the negative role of chaos in Plato's *Timaeus* and the Babylonian Enuma Elish with the creative role of chaos in the philosophy of Nicolas Berdyaev; Stuart Chandler, "When the World Falls Apart: Methodology for Employing Chaos and Emptiness as Theological Constructs," *Harvard Theological Review* 85 (1992): 467-91, discussing chaos in religious mythology and "emptiness" in the Buddhist tradition. J. W. Stines, in "Time, Chaos Theory and the Thought of Michael Polanyi," *Perspectives on Science and Christian Faith* 44 (1992): 220-27, attempts to relate chaos theory to the notion of "tacit knowledge" in the philosophy of Michael Polanyi but apparently does not clearly see chaotic uncertainty as a new *tertium quid* distinct from quantum uncertainty and the "classical" uncertainty (e.g., a coin toss) of Newtonian physics.

[18]J. T. Houghton, "New Ideas of Chaos in Physics," *Science and Christian Belief* 1 (1989): 41-51.

published under the title *Chaos and Complexity: Scientific Perspectives on Divine Action.*[19] This volume represents the most substantial philosophical and theological response to chaos theory so far. Most of the contributors, however, concluded that chaos theory does not provide any easy answers to the question of exactly how God's action in the world is to be understood in relation to scientific laws.

Further Theological Reflections

Some writers have suggested that chaos theory provides a way of resolving the vexing problem of determinism and free will. If the behavior of matter is determined by physical laws, and human beings (including their brains) are at least in part material beings, how can the exercise of free will be consistent with these physical laws? Crutchfield has suggested that inasmuch as underlying chaotic processes selectively magnify small fluctuations, "chaos provides a mechanism that allows for free will within a world governed by deterministic laws."[20] In a similar vein, Doyne Farmer, a scientist then working at the Los Alamos National Laboratory, observed that chaos theory might provide "an operational way to define free will," a way to reconcile free will and determinism. "The system is deterministic, but you can't say [exactly] what it is going to do next."[21]

However attractive such suggestions might initially appear, further reflection reveals them to be seriously problematic. The basic problem is that these suggestions are essentially reductionistic, attempting to explain a human and personal reality (freedom) in terms of entities that are impersonal and subpersonal. Thus this approach makes a fundamental category mistake: physical realities can be explained by appealing to physical substances and laws, but personal realities lie in a higher dimension of reality—the personal—that subsists within the natural order but transcends it. Such a standpoint is indicated by the biblical conception of humankind as being both "dust"—and so part of the natural order—and "image of God," and so transcending the natural order. From a Christian viewpoint, the biblical doctrine of the *imago Dei* places a fundamental barrier against all attempts to explain the human person completely or exclusively in terms of scientific laws. The suggestions noted above,

---

[19] Robert John Russell, Nancey Murphy and Arthur R. Peacocke, eds., *Chaos and Complexity: Scientific Perspectives on Divine Action* (Vatican City: Vatican Observatory, 1995).
[20] Crutchfield et al., "Chaos," p. 49.
[21] Quoted in Gleick, *Chaos*, p. 251.

while well intended, have the irremediable defect of reducing a human and spiritual reality to a phenomenon explainable by the behavior of material objects and forces.

There is yet another sense in which the suggestions of Crutchfield and Farmer represent serious category mistakes. In the attempt to find a space for human freedom in a deterministic world, there is an implicit identification of freedom with randomness or unpredictability. The problem with this implicit identification is that it overlooks the crucial fact that genuine human freedom is connected with the *purposes* of human agents acting for the realization of certain ends.

I choose a certain career or to marry or not to marry in light of my values and purposes. Genuinely free choices of human agents take place within this purposive or *teleological* context. It makes no sense to say that a spinning roulette wheel is exercising "free will" simply because its behavior appears to be random and unpredictable. The appearance of randomness or unpredictability may be associated with a free choice, but such randomness is not of the essence of freedom. The purposive dimension of human choices, directed toward the realization of certain ends among a number of alternatives, cannot be reduced to the categories of physics—whether the physics in question is Newtonian, quantum-mechanical or "chaotic."

A substantial consensus has emerged among scientists, philosophers and theologians that the new discoveries in chaos research have shattered forever the Newtonian image of a predictable "clockwork universe" that has dominated the popular imagination for the last three hundred years. It is now known that in chaotic systems, though they are in principle governed by laws that are deterministic in form, small uncertainties are amplified so radically that in practice, as Robert J. Russell has noted, "their behavior rapidly becomes unpredictable."[22] Arthur Peacocke, a trained biochemist and Anglican priest, emphasizes that such unpredictability is "ineradicable" and is not removable by even an "absolutely accurate knowledge of the initial conditions, if this were attainable."[23]

In chaotic systems there is an inescapable "predictability horizon" (for the weather, about two weeks) beyond which exact prediction is impossible. "We are able to come to this conclusion without ever having to men-

---

[22]Russell, Murphey and Peacocke, *Chaos and Complexity*, p. 14.
[23]Arthur Peacocke, *Theology for a Scientific Age* (London: SCM Press, 1993), p. 51.

tion quantum mechanics or Heisenberg's uncertainty principle," notes James Lighthill. "A fundamental uncertainty about the future is there, indeed, even on the supposedly solid basis of the good old laws of motion of Newton."[24]

These startling scientific perspectives are just beginning to penetrate the general public's consciousness, but informed scientists realize that the Enlightenment dream of a thoroughly predictable and controllable world is now dead and in the process of being buried. This dream was given classic expression in a famous series of lectures in 1795 at the Écoles Normales in Paris by the great French mathematician Pierre-Simon Laplace, an apostle of the Newtonian world system. Imagine, said Laplace, that we could look at the world, with all its objects, planets and individual atoms, from the perspective of an infinite intelligence, having a comprehensive knowledge of all the initial positions and velocities. "We ought then to consider the present state of the universe as the effect of its previous state and as the cause of that which is to follow," said Laplace, expressing the determinism of physical law. "For such an [unlimited] intelligence nothing would be uncertain, and the future, like the past, would be open to its eyes."[25] In this Laplacean clockwork universe an "infinite intelligence"—or a quasi-omniscient scientist—could presumably predict the headlines appearing on tomorrow's *New York Times!*

This Laplacean dream has been shattered forever; scientists now realize that it was never true. It is apparent that even the paradigm of regularity and predictability—the simple pendulum—can exhibit chaotic behavior under certain conditions. Astonishingly, it has been recently recognized that the solar system, long considered to be the model of regularity, exhibits chaotic behavior as well. The motion of the planet Pluto is chaotic, and the orbits of Venus and the Earth exhibit substantial irregularities. The known instabilities in the orbit of Mercury are such that this planet may cross the orbit of Venus within five billion years. According to French astronomer Jacques Laskar, "Without the Moon, the tilt of the Earth would be highly unstable, which would probably have strongly disturbed the development of organized life on its surface." The rotation of Mars on its axis is chaotic; it can wobble

---

[24]Lighthill, "Recently Recognized Failure," p. 47.

[25]Pierre-Simon Laplace, *Philosophical Essay on Probabilities,* 5th French ed. (1825), trans. Andrew I. Dole (New York: Springer Verlag, 1995), p. 2.

between 0 and 60 degrees.[26]

The larger universe is not a simple, linear Newtonian mechanical system; in many respects it behaves as a chaotic system. "No finite intelligence, however powerful," physicist Paul Davies has concluded, "could anticipate what new forms or systems may come to exist in the future."[27]

This "death of the dream of unlimited predictability" points to fundamental limitations on human knowledge that have been encountered by science during the last century. Einstein's Special Theory of Relativity stated that the speed of light places an absolute limit on the speed of travel of any physical object or message. Heisenberg's Uncertainty Principle pointed to fundamental limitations on human ability to measure quantities in the subatomic world. The second law of thermodynamics pointed to inherent limitations on the efficiency of heat devices and the impossibility of ever constructing a perpetual-motion machine. Now chaos theory has demonstrated the inherent limitations on the human ability to predict and control the future.

From a Christian perspective, such an encounter with limits should remind us of the fundamental distinction between an infinite Creator and a finite and limited creation, including humankind. The discoveries of chaos theory give us further reason to adopt a stance of epistemic humility in the face of a complex and unpredictable world.

Chaos theory also has important philosophical implications for the reductionism implicit in much of the modern scientific agenda. Now that it is increasingly being realized that even simple systems can give rise to complex and unpredictable behavior, more scientists are beginning to acknowledge that the entire range of physical and personal reality cannot be adequately explained in terms of the motions and interactions of atoms, molecules and elementary particles. These scientists have begun to see the limitations of studying parts in isolation from the whole. "For them," notes James Gleick, "chaos was the end of the reductionist program in science."[28]

Crutchfield concludes that the hope that physics could offer a complete description of physical reality through an increasingly detailed understanding of fundamental particles and forces is unfounded. The fact is that the interac-

---

[26]The astronomical data in this paragraph are from Jacques Laskar, "Large-Scale Chaos in the Solar System and Planetological Consequences," paper summary in *Sciences de la terre et des planetes* (Paris) 322, series 2a, no. 3, item 163.
[27]Davies, *Cosmic Blueprint*, p. 56.
[28]Gleick, *Chaos*, p. 304.

tion of components on one scale "can lead to complex global behavior on a larger scale that in general cannot be deduced from knowledge of the individual components."[29] Davies states flatly that "reductionism is nothing more than a vague promise founded on the . . . discredited concept of determinism."[30]

This growing recognition of the inadequacy of reductionism as a master paradigm for science implies that the realities of living organisms, including human beings, cannot be exhaustively understood in the categories of physics and chemistry. Living beings subsist within the material order, of course, and are subject to—and to a considerable extent analyzable in terms of—material categories. But these physical and chemical processes give rise to new levels of organization, complexity, sentience and value that transcend the purely physical and that should be accorded "ontic recognition" together with the elementary particles of physics.

Again, I am *not* claiming that one can draw a straight logical inference from chaos theory to, say, human freedom. To attempt to do so would be to fall back into the same reductionistic approach that is being criticized: the notion that at the end of the day human freedom is really nothing but a product of the motion of material particles. Rather, my point is that the new perspectives arising from chaos research help to make cultural and epistemic space for the human sciences, including religion. Any scientific work that highlights the untenable nature of the Laplacean Enlightenment vision is, at least indirectly, a significant contribution to a more adequate worldview that acknowledges the complex, multileveled and less predictable nature of the world that God has created. If science now acknowledges the impossibility of predicting the future behavior of even a simple pendulum in all cases, then how much more impossible to reduce human behavior and values to the mere motion of material particles! To the extent that chaos research provides a check on the epistemic hubris of a Laplacean agenda for science, a new sensibility is made possible and a new cultural space can open for more fruitful interactions between the natural sciences and religious communities.

Chaos theory also provides new perspectives for understanding God's works of creation and providence. In particular, these discoveries make it pos-

---

[29]Crutchfield et al., "Chaos," p. 48; see also Houghton, "New Ideas," p. 50.

[30]Davies, *Cosmic Blueprint,* p. 140. Davies does not claim that "reductionistic" techniques in science are never justified, only that reductionism is not adequate as a global scientific paradigm or metaphysical framework.

sible to see some of the issues in the historic creation-evolution controversies
in a different light. As a case in point, in his 1874 attack on Darwinism, the
Princeton theologian Charles Hodge saw the fundamental threat to Christian
faith to be the denial of purpose and design in nature. "The denial of final
causes is the formative idea of Darwin's theory," Hodge believed, "and therefore no teleologist can be a Darwinian." In Hodge's view, the denial of design
in nature was tantamount to a denial of God. Darwin was personally not an
atheist, but his theory was "virtually atheistical": God may have called the
universe into existence and created the first germ of life; but afterward he
"abandoned the universe itself to be controlled by chance and necessity, without any purpose on his part as to the result." It was this denial of divine providence, as Hodge understood Darwin's theory of evolution, that led him to
conclude, as the answer to the question posed in the title of his book: "What is
Darwinism? It is atheism."[31]

In Hodge's view, Darwinism is completely incompatible with Christian
theism because "pure chance" is inconsistent with divine providence. But
today the perspectives provided by chaos research have opened up other ways
of understanding the relationship between "chance" events and lawlike behaviors. As Bartholemew and others have pointed out, it is now recognized that
apparently random behaviors can lead to orderly results; order can be a consequence of "chaos." For example, the behavior of any given individual and her
age of death are highly uncertain, but the actuarial tables of life insurance
companies can give very accurate forecasts of mortality for the population at
large. Bartholemew helps us see that "the mere existence of chance processes
in nature is not a sufficient ground for inferring the absence of purpose."[32] Just
as human agents can use chance mechanisms for their own purposes—in a lot-
tery, in a game of Monopoly or to distribute a limited number of kidney dialy-
sis machines—so it is certainly possible to conceive of God's using apparently
random processes to achieve his own creative purposes.

Writing from this perspective, Peacocke argues that the discoveries of
chaos and complexity suggest a new paradigm for understanding nature in
terms of a creative interplay of chance and law. Chance operates within a lawlike framework that limits possible outcomes. Chance allows for new forms of
life and organization to emerge, while deterministic laws provide the stability

---

[31]Charles Hodge, *What Is Darwinism?* (New York: Scribner, Armstrong, 1874), pp. 173-77.
[32]Bartholemew, *God of Chance,* pp. 78, 82.

for these new forms to endure. "It is the combination of the two [law and chance] which makes possible an ordered universe capable of developing within itself new modes of existence."[33] In this perspective, chance is not an autonomous metaphysical principle opposed to divine purpose but is in fact part of a larger lawful structure and one of the mechanisms used by God in the process of creation. Viewed in this light, the role of chance in evolutionary theory is not necessarily a threat to Christian theism as Hodge supposed.[34]

This way of viewing the relationship of chance events to the providence of God has significant precedent in the history of Christian theology. In the *Summa Contra Gentiles* Thomas Aquinas states that while all events are subject to divine providence, not all "will be necessary, but a good many are contingent." God is the cause of all things, and just as an animal cares for its young, so God takes care of all that he has made. His divine providence applies to contingent singulars such as the fall of a sparrow (Mt 10:29) as well as to those things that happen by necessity.[35]

The Westminster Confession of Faith (1647), perhaps the single most influential confessional document in English-speaking Christianity, addresses the issue of providence (5.2). The Westminster divines, speaking from a Puritan and Calvinistic theological perspective, state that "although in relation to the foreknowledge and decree of God, the first cause, all things come to pass immutably and infallibly, yet by the same providence he ordereth them to fall out, according to the nature of second causes, either necessarily, freely, or contingently." The confession here uses the Thomistic distinction between *pri-*

---

[33]Peacocke, *Theology for a Scientific Age,* p. 65. Similarly, Prigogine argues as one of the main conclusions of his research that "nonequilibrium is the source of order" (*Order out of Chaos,* p. 287).

[34]Hodge was, of course, correct in seeing an *autonomous* "blind chance," understood as an independent metaphysical principle, as incompatible with Christian theism. No doubt he would have reached similar conclusions with respect to modern antiteleological presentations of evolutionary theory such as Jacques Monod, *Chance and Necessity* (London: Collins, 1972); Richard Dawkins, *The Blind Watchmaker* (Harlow, U.K.: Longman, 1986); and Stephen Jay Gould, *Wonderful Life: The Burgess Shale and the Nature of History* (New York: W. W. Norton, 1989). The point being made here is that placing chance and chaos within the larger law structures created by God gives an entirely fresh perspective for understanding the issues of the creation-evolution debate. The "random variations" of evolutionary biology then may be seen as providential means ordained of God in the process of creation. For the variety of Christian responses to Darwinian evolution in the nineteenth century, see James R. Moore, *The Post-Darwinian Controversies* (Cambridge: Cambridge University Press, 1979).

[35]Thomas Aquinas, *Summa Contra Gentiles,* trans. Vernon J. Bourke (Notre Dame, Ind.: University of Notre Dame Press, 1975), 3.1.72, 74, pp. 242-44, 250-53.

mary and *secondary* causes. God is the primary and ultimate cause of all that happens, whether the fall of a sparrow, the fall of an empire, the rising of the sun or the crucifixion of the Messiah. God's primary causation is usually mediated, however, through the agency of secondary causes—either human choices or the operation of natural laws. These secondary causes can act "necessarily," as in the falling of a stone to the ground; "contingently," as in the casting of a lot; or "freely," as in King David's decision to commit adultery with Bathsheba. Although the seventeenth-century Westminster divines understood the term *contingently* in terms of what we would now call "classical" uncertainty (such as a coin toss) rather than "quantum" or "chaotic" uncertainty, which were of course unknown at the time, their basic point can be extended to encompass the phenomena of chaos theory. "Secondary causes" can be expanded to include the phenomena described by quantum mechanics and chaos theory as well as those described by Newtonian (or Aristotelian) physics. All events of history and nature are embedded within a lawful, coherent structure ultimately ordered by the providence of God.

It is important to note that the biblical understanding of the relationship of God to chaotic phenomena is quite different from that found in many of cosmologies of the ancient world. In a creation myth from the ancient Near East such as the Enuma Elish, the so-called Babylonian Genesis, Marduk battles for supremacy among the gods by defeating Tiamat, the personification of the forces of chaos.[36] In Plato's *Timaeus* the Demiurge gives form to a preexisting chaotic matter rather than calling all things into being by a sovereign act of *ex nihilo* creation.[37] In biblical thought the chaotic forces of nature and history are not divine beings or metaphysical principles that have independence over against God. The God of the Bible is the sovereign Creator, Sustainer and Redeemer who uses the humanly unpredictable and uncontrollable forces of the natural world for his own purposes.

In a textbook on chaos theory written for scientists and engineers, Francis

---

[36]For translation and commentary on the Enuma Elish, see Alexander Heidel, *The Babylonian Genesis: The Story of Creation* (Chicago: University of Chicago Press, 1951); and Stephanie Dalley, *Myths from Mesopotamia: Creation, the Flood, Gilgamesh and Others* (New York: Oxford University Press, 1989). For illuminating discussion of the Genesis creation narrative in the context of ancient Near Eastern religions, see Claus Westermann, "Creation in the History of Religions and in the Bible," in *Genesis 1-11: A Commentary,* trans. John J. Scullion (London: SPCK, 1984), pp. 19-47.
[37]Plato *Timaeus* 30a, in *Plato,* trans. R. G. Bury (Cambridge, Mass.: Harvard University Press, 1929), 9:55.

C. Moon notes that the paradigm that is beginning to supplant the Newtonian clockwork image is a "concept of chaotic events resulting from orderly laws, not a formless chaos, but one in which there are underlying patterns, fractal structures, governed by a new mathematical view of our 'orderly' world."[38] Moon's observation that chaotic phenomena are embedded in deeper underlying structures accords remarkably well with a biblical theology of creation and providence. There is a "logos structure" (Jn 1:1, 3; cf. Col 1:15-20) in God's created order which encompasses the turbulent and unpredictable events studied by chaos theorists. These phenomena are chaotic but do not represent a lawless or unbounded chaos; they are embedded within deeper structures of order.

In one of the closing chapters of the book of Job God speaks out of the whirlwind: "Where were you when I laid the earth's foundation?" (Job 38:4). In a long series of questions about the creation, God leads Job to realize that a deeper awareness of the features of the natural order can arouse wonder and humility in the face of the Almighty's creative work. Ilya Prigogine marvels, "Everywhere we look, we find a nature that is rich in diversity and innovations."[39] The discoveries of chaos theory represent one of the more exciting recent chapters in the history of humankind's encounters with God's creation. Far from being a threat to a biblical understanding of providence, chaos theory can be seen as a new avenue for appreciating both the limitations of human ability to predict the future and the complexity and richness of God's creative power.

---

[38]Francis C. Moon, *Chaotic and Fractal Dynamics: An Introduction for Applied Scientists and Engineers* (New York: John Wiley & Sons, 1992), pp. 42-43.
[39]Prigogine, *Order out of Chaos,* p. 208.

5

Does Gödel's Proof
Have Theological Implications?

*H*e has been called "the greatest logician since Aristotle." His striking fundamental results during the decade 1929-1939 established him as "the most important logician of the twentieth century," transformed the field of mathematical logic and influenced all subsequent work in the area of foundations of mathematics.[1]

These high accolades were paid to Kurt Gödel (1906-1978), an obscure German-speaking mathematician and logician largely unknown to the general public. In an epochal paper of 1931 he demonstrated that "it can be proved rigorously that in every consistent formal system . . . there exist undecidable . . . propositions and . . . moreover, the consistency of any such system cannot be

---

[1]Solomon Feferman, "Gödel's Life and Work," in Kurt Gödel, *Collected Works,* ed. Solomon Feferman (Oxford: Clarendon, 1986), 1:1, 8.

proved in the system."[2] Gödel's fundamental result challenged the way that the notions of logical proof and provability had been understood since the days of Aristotle and Euclid.

Who was Kurt Gödel, and why is his famous "incompleteness proof" considered such an important milestone in the history of human thought? Does his work have theological implications for such questions as free will versus determinism, divine omniscience, biblical authority, and the limitations of human reason? Has Gödel's work contributed to the rise of the postmodern sensibility? These are some of the issues to be explored in this chapter.

A Brief Biographical Sketch

He was described as "deeply private and reserved," a man of slight build and frail-looking, very cautious about his food and anxious about illness to the point of hypochondria. He became a familiar sight at the Institute for Advanced Study in Princeton, New Jersey, walking home after a day's work bundled up in a heavy black overcoat, even in warm weather.[3]

This shy mathematical genius was born in 1906 in Brno, Czechoslovakia, then part of the Austro-Hungarian empire, of German-speaking parents. At the age of eighteen Kurt Gödel went to the University of Vienna to study physics, but his interests quickly turned to mathematics and mathematical logic. He became an Austrian citizen in 1929 and was awarded the Ph.D. in 1930 at the age of twenty-four. His famous incompleteness proof was published in 1931, and the next year he became a *Privatdozent* (unsalaried lecturer) at the University of Vienna. In January 1940, after the Nazi takeover of Austria, Gödel and his wife Adele, whom he had married in 1938, left Vienna to emigrate to the United States. They traveled through eastern Europe by train, continuing across Siberia to Yokahama, by boat across the Pacific to San Francisco, and finally by train to Princeton, never to return to Europe.

---

[2]Kurt Gödel, "Uber formal unentscheidbare Satze der *Principia mathematica* und verwandter Systeme I" (On formally undecidable propositions of *Principia mathematica* and related systems I; 1931), in *Collected Works* 1:195. In a "formal system," as understood by Gödel, "reasoning in them, in principle, can be completely replaced by mechanical devices" such as a computer (ibid., n. 70). This article was originally published in the scientific journal *Monatshefte für Mathematik und Physik* 38 (1931): 173-98.

[3]This biographical information is largely drawn from Feferman, "Gödel's Life and Work," pp. 1-36. Further background information is provided in Hao Wang, "Some Facts About Kurt Gödel," *Journal of Symbolic Logic* 43, no. 3 (1981): 653-59, and Hao Wang, *Reflections on Kurt Gödel* (Cambridge, Mass.: MIT Press, 1987).

Gödel was invited to take up residence at the Institute for Advanced Study in Princeton, an elite academic think tank, where he remained for his entire academic career. He became a close friend of Albert Einstein, also a resident of the institute, and the two could often be seen walking on the grounds engaged in intense conversation. Gödel was awarded the National Medal of Science by President Gerald Ford in 1975. In poor health from the 1960s onward, Gödel died in 1978 at the age of seventy-two, his physical condition aggravated by depression and paranoia. He and his wife had no children.

The Meaning of Gödel's Proof

Gödel's fundamental result can be summarized in the following way: Arithmetic and other more complex mathematical systems cannot establish their own internal consistency and must contain propositions that are undecidable—that is, propositions that can be neither proved nor disproved within the system.[4] This result can be stated more precisely in the form of two theorems.

First theorem: "Every formal axiomatic system S, large enough to contain arithmetic, contains statements which are not provable in S."

Second theorem: "If such a system S is consistent, then it is impossible to prove it consistent by methods within the system S."[5]

To appreciate the significance of Gödel's work, we need to understand a number of technical terms. A "formal axiomatic system" is a system in which some principles (axioms) are assumed to be true and other propositions (theorems) are proved using these principles. A familiar example of such an axiomatic system is Euclidean geometry. Euclid began with a set of axioms (e.g., "Between any two points only one straight line can be drawn") that were considered to be self-evidently true, and on the basis of these axioms he proved many theorems (e.g., the Pythagorean theorem: "The square of the hypotenuse of a right triangle is equal to the sum of the squares of the other two sides").

---

[4]H. Martyn Cundy, "Gödel's Theorem in Perspective," *Science and Christian Belief* 3, no. 1 (April 1991): 35. Other expositions of Gödel's work may be found in Ernest Nagel and James R. Newman, *Gödel's Proof* (London: Routledge and Kegan Paul, 1959); Harry J. Gensler, *Gödel's Theorem Simplified* (Lanham, Md.: University Press of America, 1984); and J. Van Heijenoort, "Gödel's Theorem," in *Encyclopedia of Philosophy,* ed. Paul Edwards (New York: Macmillan, 1967), 3:348-57. See also Douglas R. Hofstadter, *Gödel, Escher, Bach* (New York: Basic Books, 1979), esp. chap. 4, "Consistency, Completeness and Geometry," and chap. 14, "On Formally Undecidable Propositions." Despite its age, the work by Nagel and Newman remains the best treatment for the nonspecialist.

[5]These formulations are from Cundy, "Gödel's Theorem in Perspective," p. 35.

Euclid's axiomatic system became the paradigm of logical rigor and strict proof in Western civilization.

In the context of this discussion, *arithmetic* has a somewhat different meaning from its use in ordinary discussion. *Arithmetic* here means something more like high school algebra, limited to positive whole numbers and signs for variables, such that it would include statements such as "$2 + 2 = 4$" and "If $xy = 18$, and $x = 2y$, then $x = 6$ and $y = 3$."[6]

Gödel's proof showed that there are fundamental limitations to any formal system in the areas of *completeness* and *consistency*. Any reasonably interesting and complex axiomatic system is inherently "incomplete" in that there are true statements that can be formulated within the language of the system but cannot be proved (or disproved) given the axioms of the system. They are "undecidable." These statements can be proved if the original system is enlarged by the addition of further axioms, but then the same problem arises: there are new propositions that are unprovable within the new, enlarged system.

A famous problem in the history of mathematics known as "Goldbach's Conjecture" may be a good example of this property of incompleteness and undecidability. In 1742 the German mathematician Christian Goldbach conjectured that "every even number can be written as the sum of two prime numbers." A prime number, such as 3, 5 or 17, is divisible only by itself and by 1. An even number such as 8 can be written as the sum of 3 + 5; 10 can be represented as 7 + 3; and so on. The mathematical challenge is contained in the term *every*. Mathematicians have been unable to either prove or disprove Goldbach's conjecture; it could be true but it is not known to be true. Consequently, it could represent an interesting case of the incompleteness of number theory.

As for consistency, Gödel demonstrated that it is impossible to prove the complete internal consistency of any formal system using methods that are available within the system. A system is internally inconsistent if, from the given set of axioms, both a proposition ("Socrates is a man") and its negation ("Socrates is not a man") can be proved. A system may be consistent, but it cannot prove its own consistency.

Ernest Nagel and James R. Newman summarize the basic significance of Gödel's astonishing proof this way: Gödel demonstrated "an inherent limitation in the axiomatic method." The mathematician's dream of finding unshak-

---

[6]These examples are from Gensler, *Gödel's Theorem*, p. 2.

able foundations for the discipline of mathematics "by way of specifying once for all a fixed set of axioms from which all true arithmetical statements would be formally derivable" has been irreversibly shattered.[7] The epistemological implications of Gödel's work are still being debated by philosophers, and the general public remains largely unaware of this astonishing intellectual achievement.

Gödel's Proof and Christian Theology

Some writers have argued that Gödel's theorems have important implications for Christian theology. In an influential article published in 1961, "Minds, Machines and Gödel," Oxford philosopher J. R. Lucas advanced the claim that Gödel's work had important consequences for the debate on free will versus determinism. "Gödel's Theorem," wrote Lucas, "seems to me to prove that Mechanism is false, that is, that minds cannot be explained as machines."[8] Gödel's proof has been generally understood by logicians and philosophers as demonstrating the impossibility of constructing and programming a computer that by purely mechanical means could decide the truth or falsity of any and every statement that could be written in a given formal system. Lucas argued that no machine or computer can be a complete or adequate model of the mind; "minds are essentially different from machines." Unlike computers and other mechanical devices, human beings are not confined to making deductive inferences. The human mind, with its powers of imagination and creativity, can devise new modes of reasoning and argument that go beyond the rules and procedures that may exist at a given moment—as Gödel's own groundbreaking work demonstrated. Furthermore, human minds are self-conscious and

---

[7]Nagel and Newman, *Gödel's Proof,* p. 86. These authors present a relatively accessible explanation of how Gödel was able to prove his results using a mathematical technique known as "mapping." They also give valuable historical perspectives on how Gödel's work arose naturally out of developments in the nineteenth century: the development of modern symbolic logic by George Boole; the rise of non-Euclidean geometries, which implied that some of the "self-evident" axioms of Euclid might not be self-evidently true and mutually consistent; the attempt of Bertrand Russell and Alfred North Whitehead, *Principia Mathematica* (1910) to establish the consistency of arithmetic by reducing it to symbolic logic. For further discussion of the background of these discussions concerning the foundations of mathematics, see Heijenoort, "Gödel's Theorem"; Stephen Cole Kleene, *Introduction to Metamathematics* (Amsterdam: North-Holland Publishing, 1952); and Raymond L. Wilder, *Introduction to the Foundations of Mathematics* (New York: John Wiley & Sons, 1952).

[8]J. R. Lucas, "Minds, Machines and Gödel," *Philosophy* 36 (1961): 112. Lucas's arguments are also contained in J. R. Lucas, *The Freedom of the Will* (Oxford: Clarendon, 1970), pp. 124, together with responses to some of his critics.

self-reflective as computers are not.[9]

Lucas believed that these conclusions are inescapable, because Gödel's theorem applies to "all reductive analyses of human behavior in terms of rule-bound descriptions and regularity explanations."[10] All mechanistic explanations of the human mind as a computer, no matter how powerful, would be subject to the Gödelian limitations, according to Lucas. Since the human mind can transcend these limitations, in Lucas's view, the human mind can never be completely reduced to a computer, and determinism must be false. This conclusion is of great consequence philosophically, because no longer is it necessary "to deny freedom in the name of science. . . . No longer will the moralist feel the urge to abolish knowledge to make room for faith."[11]

It is not easy to assess the force of Lucas's argument. Some philosophers have questioned his use of Gödel's theorem on technical grounds,[12] and others would argue that the growing power and sophistication of computer technology could overcome some of the limitations that Lucas considered inherent, perhaps leading to computers that in some sense are "creative" and even "self-conscious." Lucas's claim that the human mind has powers that transcend the rule-bound behavior of computers certainly seems plausible, but if there is to be a resolution of the debate between Lucas and his critics, it will have to await further developments both in the philosophical analysis of Gödel's proof and the mind-body problem, and in the areas of computer science and technology.

Gödel's Proof and Divine Omniscience

One American philosopher, Patrick Grim, has suggested that Gödel's theorem has consequences for the doctrine of divine omniscience. Within the limits of any logic that we know about, he thinks, "omniscience appears to be simply impossible." In fact, given Gödel's results, the very notion of omniscience does not appear to have any coherent meaning.[13]

How does Grim arrive at this rather bold and unsettling conclusion? He begins with a simple definition of omniscience: "Any omniscient being will

[9]Lucas, "Minds, Machines," pp. 112, 119, 125.
[10]Lucas, *Freedom of the Will*, p. 166.
[11]Lucas, "Minds, Machines," p. 127.
[12]I. J. Good, "Gödel's Theorem Is a Red Herring," *British Journal for the Philosophy of Science* 19 (1969): 357-58; see also Hofstadter, *Gödel, Escher, Bach,* chap. 15, for other criticism of the Lucas thesis.
[13]Patrick Grim, "Logic and Limits of Knowledge and Truth," *Nous* 22 (1988): 341, 359.

believe all [truths] and only truths."[14] A key implication of Gödel's theorem, according to Grim, is that there does not exist a "set of all truths." Since an omniscient being must know all truths, there can be no omniscient being.[15]

Grim thinks this conclusion follows from Gödel's proof that any moderately complex formal system is "incomplete," in the sense of containing true statements that cannot be proved within the system. Just as there is no highest natural number, so knowledge has no "intrinsic maximum"; for every formal system and every body of knowledge there is some knowledge beyond it. There is no such thing as a "totality of facts" that even an "omniscient" being could know; the universe and any description of it are essentially open and incomplete.[16]

What are we to make of this rather bold argument? Does Gödel's theorem really overturn the Christian understanding of God's omniscience? It is clear that the *definition* of omniscience is critical to the answer. Grim's definition is significantly different from the traditional one, which can be stated in the following way: "A being X is omniscient if, at a given time T, X knows every true proposition."[17] The qualification "at a given time" is significant. At any given time there is a finite number of true propositions that can be stated within the language of a given formal system. While it is true that there are additional true statements within an enlarged system, it still remains the case that at a given future time $T2$ there are only a finite number of true propositions that can be stated (and hence known) within the language of the enlarged system. Given the inclusion of the reference "at a given time," Grim's objection to the concept of omniscience fails.

There is yet another way of stating a definition of omniscience that avoids Grim's objection: A being X is omniscient if X knows all true propositions that

---

[14]Ibid., p. 361, n. 1. Grim does admit the somewhat speculative nature of his argument: "As noted in the introduction, philosophical speculation regarding metalogical results is a notoriously risky business" (p. 359).

[15] Ibid., p. 356

[16]Ibid., p. 361.

[17]Richard Swinburne, *The Coherence of Theism* (Oxford: Clarendon, 1977), p. 162. Swinburne himself presents a nontraditional view of "limited omniscience" in which God does not know the future choices of free beings. For a defense of a more traditional view of divine omniscience, see William Lane Craig, *Divine Foreknowledge and Human Freedom* (Leiden, Netherlands: E. J. Brill, 1991), in which, on the basis of an appeal to the notion of "middle knowledge" of Luis Molina, Craig argues that divine sovereignty, human freedom and God's knowledge of future contingent events can be reconciled.

are logically possible to know. This is a qualification that is implicit in traditional understandings of divine omniscience. Thus it makes no sense to say that God could know the proposition "2 + 2= 5"; such a statement is logically impossible to know, just as the question "Could God make a stone so heavy that he could not lift it?" is self-contradictory and meaningless. Such qualifications are no real limitations on the genuine knowledge of God, which implies a maximal and perfect knowledge of all things actual and all things possible. Thus it is in principle no problem for Christian theology to incorporate into some definition any *logical* consequences that follow from Gödel's theorem; such a qualification is no more a limitation on God than the "inability" to know "2 + 2 = 5."

Implications for Biblical Authority

H. Martyn Cundy has suggested that Gödel's theorem has implications for the Protestant understanding of biblical authority. The Bible should not be treated as a "formal system" of propositions intended to give exhaustive truths covering all human situations. In every age the church needs the illuminating presence of the Holy Spirit to apply the principles of Scripture to new circumstances and issues that are not explicitly addressed by the categories and language of the Bible. If even formal mathematical systems are incomplete, we should not expect the Bible to be an exhaustive compendium of every conceivable truth needed by the church.[18] Cundy is suggesting, in effect, that Gödel's proof implies a significant limitation on the Protestant notion of "sola scriptura."

Is Cundy's inference a plausible one? The answer to this question, of course, hinges on the extent to which there is a valid analogy and substantial correspondence between the Bible and formal axiomatic systems. One can certainly find in the history of Christian theology statements by systematic theologians suggesting that the Bible is to be treated in a logically rigorous and even "scientific" way. In the nineteenth century Princeton theologian Charles Hodge, in a discussion of theological method, stated that the "Bible is to the theologian what nature is to the man of science."[19] The Scriptures contain all the "facts" of theology, and it is the theologian's task, using an inductive method, to collect, arrange and exhibit in their

---

[18]Cundy, "Gödel's Theorem in Perspective," pp. 48-49.
[19]Charles Hodge, *Systematic Theology,* 3 vols. (New York: Charles Scribner, 1878), 1:10.

internal relations all the facts of the Bible.[20]

In the post-Reformation period, the Reformed and Lutheran orthodox theologians of the seventeenth century, sometimes called "Protestant Scholastics," were known for massive, closely argued theological systems defending the Protestant faith against the claims of Rome. These theologians made substantial use of the logic and dialectics of the day.[21] However, it would be a mistake to understand these theological systems merely as a "Protestant Aristotelianism"; the biblical doctrine of justification by faith remained the central core and driving force of these theological works.[22]

Even with Hodge and the seventeenth-century orthodox, the similarity of their theologies to formal axiomatic systems is rather slight. The *differences* between theology and formal logical systems would be even more emphatically stressed by modern theological writers. In his influential essay *The Nature of Doctrine,* George Lindbeck, for example, characterizes religion as a "cultural-linguistic framework" that shapes the entirety of life and thought. Theology uses a vocabulary of both discursive and nondiscursive symbols and has its own distinctive "logic" and "grammar" that have meaning within the context of a particular faith community. Theological discourse involves not only doctrine but also stories, myths, rituals and ethical directives; it is a particular "language game" (Wittgenstein) reflecting specific "forms of life."[23] Theological discourse is related to the affective and behavioral dimensions of human experience in ways that the systems of formal logic are clearly not.

Other recent theological writing has drawn attention to the *narrative* basis of Christian doctrine. David F. Ford, for example, notes that in Christian systematic theology "story" has a key role. The content and structure of Christian theology are inseparable from the form and content of the Christian stories, especially the Gospels. The main relationship of the classical theological loci (God, election, creation, providence, fall, Christ, salvation, church, eschatology) is not in the first instance systematic but an ordering in an "overarching

[20]Ibid., 1:1, 17.

[21]For representative sources of seventeenth-century Reformed orthodoxy, see Heinrich Heppe, *Reformed Dogmatics, Set Out and Illustrated from the Sources,* rev. and ed. Ernst Bizer, trans. G. T. Thomson (London: Allen & Unwin, 1950).

[22]Otto Weber, *Foundations of Dogmatics,* trans. Darrell L. Gruder (Grand Rapids, Mich.: Eerdmans, 1983), 1:113.

[23]George Lindbeck, *The Nature of Doctrine: Religion and Theology* (London: SPCK, 1984), p. 33.

story."[24] A system of Christian doctrine is less like a formal logical system and more like a story whose basic elements are creation, fall, redemption and consummation. The logic involved does involve some use of formal inferences, but the plausibility and coherence of a story are more central to the theological project than rigorous deductions from any set of axioms.

The upshot of these observations is that the dissimilarities between formal logical systems and systems of Christian theology seem more significant than any similarities. Cundy's conclusion about the need for the Spirit's illumination to apply Scripture to new situations is true enough, but the appeal to Gödel's proof in support of this conclusion does not appear to be either necessary or convincing.

Gödel and the Postmodern Sensibility

According to the philosopher John Kadvany, mathematics as a discipline today is a "fragmented and bifurcated intellectual activity," a notable and important example of the intellectual skepticism that characterizes much of the postmodern world. He sees the intellectual legacy of Kurt Gödel for logic and the foundations of mathematics as "mathematical skepticism in an age of postmodernism."[25] Gödel demonstrated that the quest for complete consistency and completeness in the foundations of mathematics is unattainable. Pure mathematics was left as a disparate set of subdisciplines with arbitrary starting points and little connection to the real world outside the mathematician's mind. Since mathematics, with its deductive systems and logical rigor, has generally been regarded as the standard of knowledge to which other disciplines should strive to attain, it would seem that Gödel's results have implications for the entire range of human knowledge.[26]

The work of Kurt Gödel can be seen in the larger cultural context of the shift from the modern to the postmodern sensibility. His elegant incompleteness theorems are both symptomatic of this shift and significant contributing

---

[24]David F. Ford, "System, Story, Performance: A Proposal About the Role of Narrative in Christian Systematic Theology," in *Why Narrative? Readings in Narrative Theology,* ed. Stanley Hauerwas and L. Gregory Jones (Grand Rapids, Mich.: Eerdmans, 1989), pp. 191, 207. See also Mark Ellingson, *The Integrity of Biblical Narrative: Story in Theology and Proclamation* (Minneapolis: Fortress, 1990), which relates narrative theology to homiletics from a theological perspective informed by the work of Hans Frei, George Lindbeck and Brevard Childs.

[25]John Kadvany, "Reflections on the Legacy of Kurt Gödel: Mathematics, Skepticism, Postmodernism," *Philosophical Forum* 20, no. 3 (1989): 162, 178.

[26]Heijenoort, "Gödel's Theorem," p. 356.

factors to it. According to Stephen Toulmin, the Enlightenment project of modernity was characterized by a "drive for certitude and universality"; it was in large measure a reaction to disunity and bloodshed in Europe following the Reformation. The philosophers of the Enlightenment were seeking indubitable rational foundations for knowledge, in hopes that such knowledge would bring peace to a war-torn Europe. A scientific-logical rationalism emerged in the seventeenth century as the ideal of human knowledge.[27]

Philosopher of science Nancey Murphy argues that "modernity" has been characterized by foundationalism in epistemology, referentialism in philosophy of language and atomism in metaphysics.[28] Foundationalism in epistemology asks the questions, "What beliefs ought to serve as the 'foundations' or indubitable starting points for justifying other beliefs? What is the proper method of 'construction' [inference] for building on the 'foundations' to the higher levels of the 'superstructure'?" Foundationalism in epistemology suggests the image of a building, where basic beliefs form the foundation, and beliefs supported by the foundation form the "superstructure." Euclidean geometry, with its axioms (foundation) and theorems (superstructure), is a classic paradigm of such a foundationalist project.

In the modern period the rationalist epistemology of René Descartes epitomized the foundationalist approach. His famous statement "Cogito ergo sum" ("I think, therefore I am") expressed the hoped-for undoubtable starting point for human knowledge in the "clear and distinct ideas" of the human mind. Descartes's foundationalist approach was formalized in his *Discourse on Method* of 1637, in which he sought to unify and give certitude to the whole range of human knowledge through a rational method. The essentials of Descartes's method can be distilled into four propositions: (1) accept only what is so clear to the mind as to exclude all doubt, (2) split large problems into smaller ones, (3) argue from the simple to the complex, (4) check and verify when done.[29] Descartes's dream was to develop a universal method whereby all human problems—whether in science, law, politics or philosophy—could

---

[27]Stephen Toulmin, *Cosmopolis* (New York: Free Press, 1990), quoted by Nancey Murphy, "Postmodern Non-relativism: Imre Lakatos, Theo Meyering and Alasdair MacIntyre," *Philosophical Forum* 27, no. 1 (1995): 37.

[28]See Murphy, "Postmodern Non-relativism," p. 38, for discussion of these terms; cf. also Nancey Murphy, "Scientific Realism and Postmodern Philosophy," *British Journal for the Philosophy of Science* 41 (1990): 291-303.

[29]As summarized in Philip J. Davis and Reuben Hersh, *Descartes' Dream: The World According to Mathematics* (New York: Harcourt Brace Jovanovich, 1986), p. 4.

be worked out rationally and systematically, by logical computation. Some would call him the first truly modern man.[30]

The work of Gödel has shown that foundationalist programs like that of Descartes promised more than they could ever deliver. There can be no logical system in any area of human thought that can claim to have achieved a final completeness and consistency on the basis of indubitable "foundations." This does not mean, of course, that formal axiomatic systems are of no value; it simply means that the inherent limitations of such systems have become more apparent.

As part of the shift from the modern to the postmodern sensibility, philosophers have moved away from various foundationalist epistemologies toward what has been called "epistemological holism."[31] In epistemological holism the image of knowledge as a web or a net replaces the image of a building with its foundation.[32] The fabric of human knowledge is like a web or net with many interconnected strands and nodes; no single strand may be able to carry the entire weight of a particular object, but each strand contributes to the overall strength of the net. The net as a whole is connected to human experience in its various forms, and this experience forms the boundary conditions for human knowledge. In theology such a holistic or "postfoundationalist" approach could mean, for example, that the claims of theism rest not on any one airtight proof for the existence of God but on multiple strands of argument and evidence drawn from the entire range of human experience which, when taken together, make theism plausible.[33]

It seems, then, in relation to the question posed in the title of this paper, that Gödel's proof may have more indirect than direct significance for Christian theology. Because neither the Bible nor systematic theologies are formal axiomatic systems in the Gödelian sense, one must be very cautious in attempting

---

[30]Ibid., pp. 7, 5.

[31]Murphy, "Postmodern Non-relativism," p. 40.

[32]Influential here have been W. V. O. Quine, "Two Dogmas of Empiricism," *Philosophical Review* 40 (1951): 20-43, and W. V. O. Quine and J. S. Ullian, *The Web of Belief*, 2nd ed. (New York: Random House, 1978).

[33]Such an approach is found in the work of Oxford philosopher of religion Richard Swinburne, *The Existence of God*, rev. ed. (Oxford: Clarendon, 1991). A "web of belief" approach in religious epistemology is also developed in William P. Alston, *Perceiving God: The Epistemology of Religious Experience* (Ithaca, N.Y.: Cornell University Press, 1991), speaking of a "cumulative case" and "mutual support" perspective on the grounds of Christian belief: "though no single strand is sufficient to keep the faith secure, when combined into a rope they all together have strength to do the job" (p. 306).

to draw theological and philosophical conclusions directly from Gödel's proof. On the other hand, the indirect significance seems great. Because Gödel has demonstrated the inherent limitations of all formal systems, thinkers who are aware of his work are less likely to regard the logical-scientific methods of mathematics and the natural sciences as the norm by which all valid claims to knowledge must be measured and justified. Gödel's proof can, in effect, be seen as making greater cultural space in the postmodern world for disciplines such as theology that have sources, canons and methods quite different from those of the natural sciences. As one writer has observed, Gödel's theorem has helped to make it more clear than ever that the notion of truth cannot be reduced to the notion of *provability*.[34] Theology has its own distinctive voice and need not forever be preoccupied with justifying itself in the language of Euclid and Einstein.

Finally, if the postmodern context and the work of Gödel bring some benefit by way of greater cultural and epistemic space, it should be noted that there are also some potential dangers for Christian theology. It would be quite easy to overreact to the Enlightenment in the name of the postmodern and to misinterpret the significance of Gödel. Gödel's proof demonstrated that axiomatic systems are inherently limited—not that reason per se is useless or that the search for logical rigor and clarity is without value. "Reason" and the natural sciences may rightly be chastened by Gödel's work for epistemic hubris, but it would be a grave mistake for evangelical thinkers to uncritically embrace the relativistic and irrational aspects of postmodernity, for to do so would be to compromise the universal and normative claims of the Christian message.

---

[34]Nigel J. Cultand, "What Does Gödel Tell Us?" *Science and Christian Belief* 3, no. 1 (1991): 54.

More specifically, here I advance two theses: first, that the progress of AI research challenges Christian theology to retrieve in its own traditions the *relational* as opposed to *functional* understandings of the nature of personhood, and second, that the progress of AI research challenges the AI community to develop an ethical framework for the social application of its results—a framework that *cannot be supplied by the scientific method itself.* Finally, I will suggest that AI research may be opening up a promising new front for the emerging science-religion dialogue in our culture.

Historical Context

A two-month workshop on "thinking machines" held on the campus of Dartmouth University during the summer of 1956 is generally regarded as the beginning of the modern artificial intelligence research program. Marvin Minsky, Claude Shannon and Ray Solomonoff, all from MIT, together with six other participants crafted a statement known as the "physical system hypothesis" that has remained a cornerstone of AI research down to the present day: "Every aspect of learning or any other feature of intelligence can in principle be so precisely described that a machine can be made to simulate it."[8] The assumption was that human intelligence is essentially the ability to process symbols and that this symbol-processing power can, in principle, be replicated by the arrays of switches inside a digital computer.

Six years prior to the Dartmouth conference, English mathematician Alan Turing had proposed in the philosophical journal *Mind* a famous thought experiment that ever since has been known as the "Turing Test." Imagine, proposed Turing, an investigator isolated in a room and communicating only through a keyboard with a human subject and a computer in another room. The investigator has only five minutes to pose questions to the human and to the computer and to evaluate the responses. If it were possible to program the computer so well that the investigator had only about a 70 percent chance of distinguishing the human from the computer, then the computer would be deemed "intelligent." Writing in 1950, Turing thought

---

[8]Cited in Crevier, *AI,* p. 48. For historical overviews of the development of AI research, see also Hans Moravec, *Mind Children: The Future of Robot and Human Intelligence* (Cambridge, Mass.: Harvard University Press, 1988), pp. 1-74, and David F. Noble, *The Religion of Technology: The Divinity of Man and the Spirit of Invention* (New York: Alfred A. Knopf, 1997), chap. 10, "The Immortal Mind: Artificial Intelligence."

that in about fifty years computers might reach such a level of sophistication.[9]

In the years following the Dartmouth conference, Carnegie-Mellon University, MIT and its Lincoln Laboratory, and, to a lesser extent, Stanford and IBM emerged as the leading centers of AI research.[10] Computers continued to double in information-processing power approximately every two years, continuing a sixty-year trend. By the late 1980s the largest supercomputers had processing power roughly equivalent to the one-gram brain of a mouse.[11] According to one estimate computers would reach human equivalence around the year 2025,[12] give or take seventeen years, but this estimate could turn out to be too conservative. Deep Blue's victory over world chess champion Garry Kasparov in May 1997 confounded the critics and gave further impetus to the AI project.

The Challenge of AI to the Theological Community

My first thesis is that the progress of artificial intelligence research challenges the theological community to retrieve from its own traditions a *relational* as opposed to a *functional* understanding of the nature of personhood. Such a retrieval would involve a reexamination of traditional understandings of foundational concepts found in the Jewish and Christian Bibles such as "the image of God" in the light of other biblical categories such as election and adoption, with a view to recovering their relational implications for the current discussion.[13] The chapter's concluding section will suggest that such a relational concept of person, rather than functional concepts based on cognitive or information-processing abilities, can provide a more adequate basis for safeguarding the human rights of marginalized members of the social order.

In both the Jewish and Christian traditions the biblical concept of the image of God has been foundational for understandings of the nature of personhood. Early Christian writers such as Irenaeus, Clement of Alexandria and Augus-

---

[9]Cited in Noble, *Religion of Technology,* pp. 150-51; the original reference is A. M. Turing, "Computing Machinery and Intelligence," *Mind* 59, no. 236 (1950).

[10]Crevier, *AI,* p. 51.

[11]Moravec, *Mind Children*, p. 61.

[12]Cited in Crevier, *AI,* p. 303.

[13]The biblical concept of humans being made in (or "as") the "image of God" is found in texts such as Genesis 1:26-27; 5:3; 9:6; James 3:9; and Colossians 1:15; 3:10. The concept of "image of God" is a focus of the present study rather than the concept of "soul," since the former is judged to be more helpful in recovering a relational understanding of the person.

tine identified the "image" with human intellect and the power of reason, distinguishing humans from the lower creation.[14] Many scholars have suggested that Platonic and Neo-Platonic philosophy exerted a significant influence on early Christian interpretation at this point.

For Thomas Aquinas, human beings are said to be the image of God by reason of their intellectual nature. The mind distinguishes humankind from the lower creation, and the intellectual nature imitates God chiefly in this, "that God understands and loves himself." Human beings, through their intellectual nature, have a "natural aptitude for understanding and loving God."[15]

Protestant Reformer Martin Luther understood the image of God to be humans' "moral substance, or nature" by which we know God and believe him to be good. As a result of humankind's sin and the Fall, our intellect and will, aspects of the image, have been corrupted, though not destroyed, but they can be restored through faith in Christ.[16]

For John Calvin, the image of God was essentially spiritual in nature, extending "to the whole excellence by which man's nature towers over all the kinds of living creatures." Because of human sin, this image is now "confused" and "mutilated." It is partially restored through conversion and faith but will regain its full splendor only in heaven.[17]

In the post-Reformation and modern periods scholars have suggested a variety of meanings for the "image," usually seeing in this concept a reference to some quality intrinsic to humans, such as a "feeling" or sense of the transcendent, or even humanity's bipedalism or upright walking.[18] Karl Barth, considered by many to be one of the most influential Christian theologians of

---

[14]Irenaeus, *Against Heresies* 4.4.3; Clement of Alexandria *Protreptikos* 124.3; Augustine *De trinitate* 14.4. On the history of interpretation in the early church, see David Cairns, *The Image of God in Man* (London: Collins, 1973), pp. 116-19; and Karl Barth, *Church Dogmatics* 3/1, *The Doctrine of Creation,* ed. G. W. Bromiley and T. F. Torrance (Edinburgh: T & T Clark, 1958), pp. 192-93.

[15]Thomas Aquinas, *Summa Theologica,* trans. Fathers of the English Dominican Province (New York: Benziger Bros., 1947), 1:471 (1.q93.a4). Aquinas clearly continues the intellectualistic understanding of Augustine and the Greek fathers, but significantly sees in the image the basis for man's *loving relationship* to God.

[16]Martin Luther, *Commentary on Genesis,* in *A Compend of Luther's Theology,* ed. Hugh T. Kerr (Philadelphia: Westminster Press, 1966), pp. 82-83.

[17]John Calvin, *Institutes of the Christian Religion,* trans. Ford Lewis Battles (Philadelphia: Westminster Press, 1960), 1:186 (1.15).

[18]These modern interpretations are helpfully reviewed in Gunnlaugur A. Jonsson, *The Image of God: Genesis 1:26-28 in a Century of Old Testament Research* (Lund, Sweden: Almqvist & Wiksell, 1988), covering the period 1882-1982.

the twentieth century, identified the image with the relationship of humankind as male and female: "The fact that he was created man and woman will be the great paradigm of everything that is to take place between him and God."[19]

In recent years Old Testament scholars have argued that the context of ancient Near Eastern religions is important for understanding the meaning of the image. Religious texts from ancient Egyptian and Mesopotamian sources, for example, portray the king as the "image" of the god(s), his royal represen- tative on earth, or an image or idol as the place on earth where the spirit and authority of the god is localized.[20]

These parallels from ancient Near Eastern religions are significant, but my central point is a *relational* understanding of humanity as the image of God. That is to say, humans are the image of God in view of a unique capacity for a personal relationship to God as the transcendent ground of their being. In this view humans are unique not so much in terms of innate capacities as through being uniquely gifted and capacitated for relationship with the transcendent personal being called "God" in the traditions of Jewish, Christian and Islamic theism. Such a perspective has been expressed by the Dutch theologian G. C. Berkouwer: "The relation of man's nature to God is not something which is added to an already complete, self-enclosed, isolated nature; it is essential and constitutive for man's nature, and man cannot be understood apart from this relationship."[21] There is no abstract or innate defining essence of the human such as intelligence or rationality; the nature of the human is understood in terms of relationship to God, and this relationship is *constitutive* of human nature.[22]

---

[19]Barth, *Church Dogmatics* 3/1, p. 186. Many of Barth's critics have pointed to a fundamental problem with this view: male-female sexual differentiation as the basis of relationship does not distinguish humanity from the animals—whereas in Genesis 1:26, the image, however it is to be understood, is that which distinguishes humankind from the lower creation.

[20]See, for example, the texts cited in D. J. A. Clines, "The Image of God in Man," *Tyndale Bulletin* 19 (1968): 53-103.

[21]G. C. Berkouwer, *Man: The Image of God*, trans. Dirk W. Jellema (Grand Rapids, Mich.: Eerd- mans, 1962), p. 23.

[22]The point can be illustrated from the context of marriage and family relationships. A person is not *inherently* a "husband" or "wife"; one is constituted as husband or wife by *entering into the marriage relationship*. The relationship is constitutive of the role. While it is true, as noted by Jonsson, *Image of God*, p. 224, that the dominant trend in modern scholarship has been to understand the image functionally in terms of "dominion," it is still the case that in the Genesis texts the function of dominion is understood within the context of God's *relationship* to human beings, a relationship that defines and constitutes humanity's true meaning and purpose. An attempt to link a relational understanding of the image of God to artificial intelligence research

The implication of such a relational understanding of the person is that Christian theology need not, in principle, see as a fundamental threat to its view of the person the successful development of a computer that actually exceeds the human brain in computational power, that perhaps can feel or even replicate itself. Human uniqueness is to be found in the relationship with God, in itself a gratuitous capacitating of the person, rather than in the innatist, cognitive, mechanistic and functional categories that have tended to dominate thinking about the nature of personhood from the time of René Descartes down to the present.[23]

This relational understanding of the image of God is consistent with other fundamental concepts of Christian theology such as election and adoption. In both these instances the individual (or Israel as a nation) is constituted, capacitated, for a special personal relationship with God and given value not in view of an innate quality or achievement but in virtue of the divine initiative in establishing the relationship. The identity, purpose and value of the "elect" person or nation is constituted and defined by the electing or choosing purposes of God[24] rather than by the inherent characteristics, merits or achievements of the elect ones.

The practice of adoption was well known both in the ancient Near Eastern and Greco-Roman cultures. The biblical writers use this concept to illustrate the redemptive action of God. Israel is depicted as being chosen by God as his "son" (e.g., Is 1:2; Hos 11:1; Jer 3:19). The term *adoption* ("sonship") is significant in Pauline theology (Rom 8:15, 23; 9:4; Gal 4:5; Eph 1:5). Salvation

---

is also found in Anne Foerst, "Cog, a Humanoid Robot, and the Question of the Image of God," *Zygon* 33, no. 1 (March 1998): 91-105.

[23]In an interesting sociological and historical observation, David Wells has noted that at the beginning of the nineteenth century the typical newspaper obituary made some mention of the character of the deceased; occupation was rarely mentioned. By 1990 occupation had become the key means of identification, and the deceased's character was rarely mentioned. Wells suggests that this substitution of function for character is consistent with the rise of anonymous, complex urban societies in which there is less and less social consensus about what might constitute "good character" (David Wells, *God in the Wasteland* [Grand Rapids, Mich.: Eerdmans, 1994], p. 11).

[24]See, for example, in the Hebrew Scriptures, a text such as Deuteronomy 7:6-8: "You are a people holy to the LORD your God. . . . The LORD did not . . . choose you because you were more numerous than other peoples [on the basis of inherent qualities]. . . . But it was because the LORD loved you and kept the oath he swore to your forefathers" (the patriarchs Abraham, Isaac and Jacob). For surveys of theological discussion of the biblical themes of election and predestination, see Karl Barth, *Church Dogmatics* 2/2, *The Doctrine of God,* ed. G. W. Bromiley and T. F. Torrance (Edinburgh: T & T Clark, 1957), pp. 3-506, and Otto Weber, *Foundations of Dogmatics,* trans. Darrell L. Gruder (Grand Rapids, Mich.: Eerdmans, 1983), 2:414-37.

or redemption involves being made part of the family of God, being delivered from the past, given a new status and way of life in the present and a new hope for the future.[25] As is the case with election, so in adoption the emphasis is on the benevolent and gratuitous initiative of God, not any innate qualifications of the person. In both cases the divinely grounded relationship is the fundamental basis of personhood.

The Challenge to the AI Community

The second thesis of this essay is that prospects of success for the "strong" AI project inevitably challenge the AI community to confront the *ethical limitations* of the scientific method. While the scientific method must guide AI research, neither the scientific method per se nor a specific scientific concept such as natural selection can generate the ethical framework that is needed for the social application of such technology. Some of the implications of this argument for the current science-religion dialogue will be noted.

Before considering scientific method in the context of the history of science, perhaps this second thesis can be more immediately focused if we consider two specific examples of the application of scientific method and knowledge: the atomic bomb and the Human Genome Project. With respect to the atomic bomb, one can say that the Manhattan Project during World War II was the (successful) attempt to realize in weapons technology the scientific truth expressed in Einstein's famous equation $E=mc^2$, the equivalence and interchangeability of mass and energy. The point here is that the scientific method does not generate the moral criteria for the humane application of its discoveries: the scientific method can give us the knowledge necessary to build an atomic bomb, but it does not tell us whether it is right or wrong to drop such a bomb on Hiroshima. Equations such as $E=mc^2$ are neither "right" nor "wrong"; they are descriptive and not normative statements.

Similarly, the success of the Human Genome Project will give us a complete genetic mapping of the human person and will presumably give information that could be used for projects of human enhancement genetic

---

[25]P. H. Davids, "Adoption," in *Evangelical Dictionary of Theology,* ed. Walter A. Elwell (Grand Rapids, Mich.: Baker, 1984), p. 13. On the theology and social background of adoption, see also Robert Alexander Webb, *The Reformed Doctrine of Adoption* (Grand Rapids, Mich.: Eerdmans, 1947); J. van Seters, "The Problem of Childlessness in Near Eastern Law and the Patriarchs of Israel," *Journal of Biblical Literature* 87 (1968): 401-8; Francis Lyall, "Roman Law in the Writings of Paul—Adoption," *Journal of Biblical Literature* 88 (1969): 458-66.

engineering or human cloning. However, such genetic information does not contain the ethical framework for its social application. Whether human beings *should* be cloned or have their average height and intelligence increased involves normative judgments that cannot be determined by scientific method alone.

The success of the strong AI project would presumably produce machines that can think and feel and have computational abilities that exceed that of *Homo sapiens*. The desirability of such an outcome and how humans should view such entities and relate to them, however, are questions that transcend the ability of the scientific method to answer.

The inadequacy of the scientific method to generate the ethical values needed for the proper social application of its results can be seen in the historical context of the positivist philosophy that came to dominate science after the middle of the nineteenth century.[26] Positivism excluded reference to teleology or purpose in scientific discourse, limiting legitimate discourse to efficient and material causes. Natural objects and physical laws are neither "good" nor "bad" with respect to the final purposes of some Designer; natural law simply "is." For the positivist, facts are simply facts from which no value-laden inferences can be made. Ordinary, "commonsense" thought, on the other hand, inevitably operates with teleological assumptions of some sort. A hammer, for example, is judged to be a good, bad or indifferent tool in relation to the purpose for which a designer intended it to be used. The present dilemma for a positivist philosophy of science is that modern technologies such as human-enhancement genetic engineering or the strong artificial intelligence project, since they impinge quite directly on human agents and not just impersonal objects, inevitably raise issues of the purpose and nature of human existence—questions that are excluded a priori by the positivist methodology.

Furthermore, it is almost true by definition that the concept of natural selection is inadequate to supply the ethical framework for future applications of AI technologies. Natural selection is a blind, random process of nature; in the foreseeable future, human agents must take up responsibility to make con-

---

[26]On the development of a positivist philosophy of science in the nineteenth century, see David C. Lindberg and Ronald Numbers, eds., *God and Nature: Historical Essays on the Encounter Between Christianity and Science* (Berkeley: University of California Press, 1986), esp. pp. 351-68, "Christianity and the Scientific Community in the Age of Darwin"; and Nancy R. Pearcey and Charles B. Thaxton, *The Soul of Science: Christian Faith and Natural Philosophy* (Wheaton, Ill.: Crossway, 1994), pp. 47-49, "Science According to Positivism."

scious, intentional choices about the use of such technologies, within the context of whatever ethical frameworks they choose to adopt.

The issue was clearly articulated by evolutionary biologists such as George Gaylord Simpson. Natural selection excludes considerations of purpose, plan or design. The recognition that the universe "lacked any purpose or plan has the inevitable corollary that the workings of the universe cannot provide any automatic, universal, eternal, or absolute criteria of right and wrong."[27] The possibility of humankind's influencing the direction of its future evolution involves our assuming the ethical responsibility for doing so.[28] If humans are to make ethical choices concerning the future direction of the evolutionary process, those ethical values cannot be supplied by a nonteleogical or antiteleological concept of natural selection.

In conclusion, the progress of artificial intelligence research programs challenges both the religious and the AI communities to seek understandings of the nature of personhood that have grounding in a transcendent frame of reference. The Christian tradition is challenged to reemphasize the relational aspects of its theological heritage inherent in such concepts as the image of God, election and adoption. The AI community is challenged to face the philosophical limitations of a positivistic understanding of the scientific method and of the concept of natural selection, insofar as these might be considered sources for ethical frameworks for the appropriate social applications of such technology. It is to be hoped that the growing science-religion dialogue in areas such as artificial intelligence research, astronomy and cosmology, and genetics will continue, as the various communities in our postmodern culture seek adequate ethical frameworks for the responsible management of the human future.

---

[27]George Gaylord Simpson, *The Meaning of Evolution,* rev. ed. (New Haven, Conn.: Yale University Press, 1949), p. 346.

[28]Ibid., p. 331. This strong insistence on the nondirective, nonprogressive nature of the evolutionary process is found also in the work of Stephen Jay Gould, e.g., *Wonderful Life: The Burgess Shale and the Nature of History* (New York: W. W. Norton, 1989). See also Richard Dawkins, *The Blind Watchmaker* (London: Penguin, 1988), for a similar antiteleological emphasis.

7

Is "Progressive Creation" Still a Helpful Concept?

Reflections on Creation, Evolution &
Bernard Ramm's Christian View
of Science and Scripture

*I*n the estimation of one historian of science, Bernard Ramm's 1954 book *The Christian View of Science and Scripture* "profoundly influenced the way in which many orthodox Christians answered the questions posed by creation and evolution."[1] Twenty-five years after the book's publication, John W. Haas Jr., a member of the American Scientific Affiliation (an association of evangelicals in the natural and biological sciences), called Ramm's book "a pivotal event" in the modern history of science and religion.[2]

In his discussion of the biological sciences Ramm proposed the concept of

---

[1]Ronald L. Numbers, *The Creationists* (Berkeley: University of California Press, 1992), p. 187.
[2]John W. Haas Jr., "*The Christian View of Science and Scripture:* A Retrospective Look," *Journal of the American Scientific Affiliation* 31 (1979): 117.

"progressive creation" as an alternative to both theistic evolution and the "fiat creationism" of those who understood creation almost exclusively in terms of instantaneous, supernatural acts of God. According to Ramm, progressive creation was the means by which the Spirit of God, as "World Entelechy," brought to pass the divine will in nature. Under the direction of the Holy Spirit, the laws of nature, over a long period of time and through a variety of processes, actualized the plan of God.[3] Because he believed in several acts of sudden, fiat creation in the history of the earth—in view of the discontinuities in the fossil record—Ramm considered his view to be clearly differentiated from theistic evolution. In Ramm's mind, "progressive creation" avoided the arbitrariness of fiat creationism while preserving its emphasis on the transcendence of God, and also avoided the "uniformitarianism" of theistic evolution while affirming its emphasis on progress and development.[4]

Ramm expressed the rather grandiose and somewhat naive hope that his concept of progressive creation could form the basis of "a new biological synthesis" that would be for biology what relativity theory was for physics.[5] Quite contrary to Ramm's intentions, his proposal in fact sparked a renewal of the "flood geology" and "young-earth creationist" tradition in American fundamentalism, a tradition Ramm had hoped to lay to rest.[6]

In this chapter I propose that "progressive creation" is still a useful category for interpreting the biblical and scientific data relating to origins. Much has transpired in both biblical scholarship and scientific research since Ramm published his work. After reviewing significant developments in the theological and scientific areas, I will attempt to relate a modified version of Ramm's concept of progressive creation to current discussions of creation and evolution in English-speaking Christianity.

Trends in Biblical Scholarship

Biblical scholars have increasingly drawn attention to the fact that the agendas

---

[3]Bernard Ramm, *The Christian View of Science and Scripture* (Grand Rapids, Mich.: Eerdmans, 1954), p. 116.

[4]Ibid., pp. 113, 116.

[5]Ibid., p. 272.

[6]Numbers, *Creationists,* pp. 187-88. Numbers traces the responses by John C. Whitcomb Jr. and Henry Morris, and the launching of the modern "creation science" movement, signaled by the 1961 publication of Whitcomb and Morris, *The Genesis Flood* (Philadelphia: Presbyterian & Reformed, 1961), defending (against Ramm) a young earth, a literal six-day creation and a universal flood as causal explanations for the earth's major geological features.

that modern interpreters have tended to bring to the text of the early chapters of Genesis—issues of "science and Scripture"—are at best secondary to the primary interests of the biblical writers. Evangelical scholars such as Gordon Wenham, for example, stress that Genesis is to be seen in the first instance against the background of its ancient Near Eastern religious environment, rather than in terms of the issues of "Genesis and modern science" that have occupied much attention in the West since the eighteenth century. According to Wenham, Genesis 1—11 is best seen as a "tract for the times," challenging the ideas of the polytheistic religions of the ancient Near East about the nature of God, the world and humankind. Genesis is concerned with affirming the unity of God in the face of polytheism and the justice of God rather than caprice; "scientific" issues in the modern sense of the word are related only indirectly to the primary purpose of the text.[7]

In a similar vein, Gerhard Hasel has argued for the "polemic nature of the Genesis cosmology."[8] A primary concern of the text is to criticize the polytheistic nature religions of the ancient Near East which identified the sun, moon, stars and forces of nature as deities. The Genesis cosmology forcefully asserts that the heavenly bodies are not gods and goddesses to be worshiped but creatures of the one holy God who created the world and who rules it according to his righteous laws. The Genesis cosmology represents a complete break with the mythological cosmologies of Israel's neighbors in the Fertile Crescent.[9]

Shortly after Ramm published *The Christian View*, evangelical theologian J. I. Packer made the valuable observation that interpreters must draw distinctions between "the subjects about which the scripture speaks and the terms in which it speaks of them." The writers of Scripture spoke about the natural world in an ordinary, nontechnical language shared with their contemporaries. Their concern was not primarily the inner structure of the world and of human beings but with the *relationship* of both to God.[10]

---

[7]Gordon Wenham, *Genesis 1—15* (Waco, Tex.: Word, 1987), pp. xlv, l.

[8]Gerhard F. Hasel, "The Polemic Nature of the Genesis Cosmology," *Evangelical Quarterly* 46 (1974): 81-102. The ancient Near Eastern religious context of Genesis and ancient religious ideas of creation are masterfully reviewed in Claus Westermann, "Creation in the History of Religions and in the Bible," in *Genesis 1—11: A Commentary,* trans. John J. Scullion (London: SPCK, 1984), pp. 19-46. Further helpful discussion of the background and theological purposes of the creation accounts in Genesis may be found in Bruce K. Waltke, "The Creation Account in Genesis 1:1-3, Part 1: Introduction to Biblical Cosmogony," *Bibliotheca Sacra* 132 (1975): 25-36.

[9]Hasel, "Polemic Nature," p. 91.

[10]J. I. Packer, *Fundamentalism and the Word of God* (London: InterVarsity Fellowship, 1958), pp. 96-98.

This point concerning the relational rather than scientific focus of Genesis has also been made in another way by British geneticist R. J. Berry. Since the end of the eighteenth century, in Berry's view, liberal and conservative interpreters alike have erred in approaching the biblical accounts of creation "as if they were primarily concerned with origins rather than with relationships."[11] The preoccupation with questions of origins has deflected attention away from the primary biblical concerns: the relationship of nature to God and humankind's proper relationship to the creation. As a result, evangelicals have failed to develop an adequate theology and practice of environmental stewardship.

Discussions of "creation and evolution" have at times suffered from a lack of attention to the range of possible meanings of the biblical terms used to describe God's creative work. For example, the primary sense of the crucial word *bara* ("create"), used forty-nine times in the Old Testament including ten times in Genesis, is that through God's command something comes into being that had not existed before. The word is used exclusively of divine action and implies a creative work that is beyond human power. Since the word never occurs with the object of the material, the primary emphasis of the term is on the newness of the created object. The concept of *ex nihilo* creation, while it may be implied in a given case, is not necessarily inherent in the meaning of the word.[12]

It is important to notice here that the focus of *bara* is not so much on the physical *processes* used by God as on the *results* of the divine action and the *relationship* of these results to God's redemptive purposes. Modern science is primarily concerned with physical processes; Scripture is primarily concerned with results and relationships.[13] *Bara* can be used to refer to a clearly supernatural, *ex nihilo* creative act that brings the universe into being (Gen 1:1), or to the divine power working through natural processes to "create" the winds (Amos 4:13) or to bring animals to birth through normal processes of gesta-

---

[11] R. J. Berry, "Creation and the Environment," *Science and Christian Belief* 7 (1995): 21. The references in this article provide a comprehensive review of historical and theological literature relating to environmental issues.

[12] Helmer Ringgren, *"bara,"* in *Theological Dictionary of the Old Testament,* ed. G. Johannes Botterweck and Helmer Ringgren, trans. John T. Willis (Grand Rapids, Mich.: Eerdmans, 1975), 2:242-49; and Thomas E. McComiskey, *"bara,"* in *Theological Wordbook of the Old Testament,* ed. R. Laird Harris (Chicago: Moody Press, 1980): 1:127-28.

[13] In Aristotle's terminology of the four types of causes, modern science, in its concern with quantitative understanding of physical processes, focuses on "material" and "efficient" causes; the Bible and Christian theology, concerned with the meaning and purpose of God's creative work, focus on "formal" (issues of design, designer) and "final" (issues of purpose, teleology) causes.

tion (Ps 104:30). Whether God's creative work in any given case involves natural or supernatural means, or long periods of time rather than instantaneous effects, cannot be judged in advance but must be determined in light of the particular biblical texts and specific features of the natural order. This distinction between process and results will be noted again in the reflections on progressive creation and theistic evolution in the closing section of this chapter.

Scientific Developments Since Ramm

The biological sciences have developed dramatically since Ramm wrote *The Christian View of Science and Scripture* in 1954.[14] Some of the most explosive growth has been in the disciplines of genetics and molecular biology. The discovery of the double-helix structure of the DNA molecule by James Watson and Francis Crick in 1953 and the subsequent deciphering of the genetic code were watershed events in the history of biology, opening up new frontiers of scientific research.[15] Biologists have since been able to study living forms not only externally but internally as well, at the genetic and molecular levels.

According to Stephen Jay Gould, the most important event in evolutionary biology during the 1970s was the "development of electrophoretic techniques for the routine measurement of genetic variation in natural populations."[16]

---

[14]Surveys of current trends in evolutionary biology may be found in standard texts such as Douglas J. Futuyma, *Evolutionary Biology,* 2nd ed. (Sunderland, Mass.: Sinauer Associates, 1986), and Mark Ridley, *Evolution* (Boston: Blackwell Scientific, 1993). Historical studies of the development of modern biological thought are presented in Ernst Mayr, *The Growth of Biological Thought: Diversity, Evolution and Inheritance* (Cambridge, Mass.: Harvard University Press, 1982), and David Young, *The Discovery of Evolution* (Cambridge: Cambridge University Press, 1992). Young traces the historical development of evolutionary thought from the seventeenth century to the late twentieth against the background of the growth of the disciplines of botany, zoology and geology, in a clearly written and helpfully illustrated text.

[15]For the historical development of the discipline of genetics and reviews of basic concepts, see John B. Jenkins, *Genetics* (Boston: Houghton Mifflin, 1975); George W. Burns and Paul J. Bottino, *The Science of Genetics,* 6th ed. (New York: Macmillan, 1989); David Suzuki and Peter Knudston, *Genetics: The Clash Between the New Genetics and Human Values* (Cambridge, Mass.: Harvard University Press, 1989); Gunther Stent, *Molecular Genetics: An Introductory Narrative* (San Francisco: W. H. Freeman, 1971). D. J. Weatherall, *The New Genetics and Clinical Practice,* 3rd ed. (Oxford: Oxford University Press, 1991), is considered the definitive work on genetics and clinical ethics. The impact of new genetic research on evolutionary biology is discussed in Christopher Wills, *The Wisdom of the Genes: New Pathways in Evolution* (New York: BasicBooks, 1989). For the original discovery of the structure of the DNA molecule, see James D. Watson, *The Double Helix: A Personal Account of the Discovery of the Structure of DNA,* ed. Gunther S. Stent (London: Weidenfeld and Nicolson, 1981).

[16]Stephen Jay Gould, *Ontogeny and Phylogeny* (Cambridge, Mass.: Harvard University Press, 1977), p. 406.

These techniques allow biologists to compare the sequences of the bases in the chains of genetic material (DNA and RNA) and the amino-acid sequences of proteins that are characteristic of each organism. The quantitative differences in these sequences are interpreted as measures of the degree of the remoteness of two organisms from a common ancestor. These discoveries in genetics and molecular biology provide ways for biologists to check hypotheses about the relationships between living forms previously limited to studies of morphology and embryology.[17]

During the last two decades of the twentieth century there were important new discoveries in the field of paleontology, especially in the fossil record of vertebrates. New groups of jawless fishes, sharks, amphibians and dinosaurs have come to light, and major transitions between amphibians and reptiles, reptiles and mammals, and dinosaurs and birds have been extensively studied.[18]

In the 1970s two paleontologists, Niles Eldredge of the American Museum of Natural History and Stephen Jay Gould of Harvard University, sparked a major controversy in evolutionary biology and paleontology with their concept of "punctuated equilibria." According to this view, evolution proceeds in fits and starts rather than in small, gradual Darwinian steps. Evolution proceeds very rapidly when new species are being formed, and then these forms typically remain unchanged for long periods of time ("stasis"). According to the "punctuationists," the well-known gaps in the fossil record are real and are to be expected if speciation occurs rapidly in small, geographically isolated populations that would leave few fossil remains.[19]

Defenders of orthodox Darwinian gradualism argue that the punctuationists have overstated their case. The coarse time resolution of most fossil studies

---

[17]Colin W. Stearn and Robert L. Carroll, *Paleontology: The Record of Life* (New York: John Wiley & Sons, 1989), p. 29.

[18]Robert L. Carroll, *Vertebrate Paleontology and Evolution* (New York: W. H. Freeman, 1988), preface. For readable introductions to the field of paleontology, see Stearn and Carroll, *Paleontology;* Steven M. Stanley, *Earth and Life Through Time* (New York: W. H. Freeman, 1986; combines historical geology and paleontology); and Richard Fortey, *Fossils: The Key to the Past* (London: Heinemann, 1982; well illustrated).

[19]The case for punctuated equilibria is argued by Steven M. Stanley, *The New Evolutionary Timetable: Fossils, Genes and the Origin of Species* (New York: Basic Books, 1981), and by Niles Eldredge, *Time Frames: The Rethinking of Darwinian Evolution and the Theory of Punctuated Equilibria* (London: Heinemann, 1986). The latter work includes as an appendix, pp. 193-223, the original 1972 paper by Eldredge and Gould, "Punctuated Equilibria: An Alternative to Phyletic Gradualism."

biases the observer toward a perception of stasis. Some cases seem to fit the punctuationist model fairly well, but other groups, such as the mammals, seem to have adapted and changed in very gradual and piecemeal ways.[20]

As late as 1953, when paleontologist George Gaylord Simpson published his classic book on macroevolution, *The Major Features of Evolution,*[21] the major evolutionary transitions between the larger taxonomic groups were still, for the most part, inadequately documented from the fossil record.[22] Charles Darwin himself had been quite aware of the major gaps in the fossil strata and attributed them to the "imperfections" of the geological record.[23] Since the 1950s new fossil discoveries have given evidence of some transitional forms that are clearly intermediate between fishes and amphibians and between reptiles and mammals.

Beginning in 1952 Erik Jarvik and other paleontologists have given extensive attention to a primitive extinct amphibian, *Ichthyostega,* discovered in the sedimentary rocks of eastern Greenland; it has anatomical features that are intermediate between the more advanced amphibians and the crossopterygian (lobe-finned) lungfishes from which amphibians are believed to have evolved. The extinct lungfishes *Eusthenopteron* and *Ichthyostega* share many features, including the ability to breathe air, the shape of the body, and skeletal features of the upper limbs and skull. *Ichthyostega* had a genuine fishlike tail, and its skin was protected by small fishlike scales. Its compressed body

---

[20]Jeffrey Levington, *Genetics, Paleontology and Macroevolution* (Cambridge: Cambridge University Press, 1988), pp. 407-8. The orthodox, neo-Darwinian "gradualist" paradigm is also defended by Antoni Hoffman, *Arguments on Evolution: A Paleontologist's Perspective* (New York: Oxford University Press, 1989). It should be noted that this debate is an intramural dispute within evolutionary biology, not an abandonment of the evolutionary paradigm itself.

[21]George Gaylord Simpson, *The Major Features of Evolution* (New York: Columbia University Press, 1953).

[22]Robert L. Carroll, "Revealing the Patterns of Macroevolution," *Nature* 381 (May 2, 1996): 19. Simpson and Carroll were aware, of course, of the famous series of horse fossils documented by Marsh and others in the nineteenth century, and the notable *Archaeopteryx,* intermediate between dinosaurs and birds, but had in mind the relative absence of forms clearly intermediate between major groups such as fishes and amphibians or reptiles and mammals.

[23]Awareness of major discontinuities in the fossil record was a significant factor in the development of the punctuated equilibria hypothesis by Eldredge and Gould. Today many paleontologists would prefer to describe the fossil record as "biased" rather than as "inadequate." They point out that the process of fossilization is inevitably biased in favor of the preservation of hard-bodied rather than soft-bodied organisms, and in favor of those animals that die near large, shallow bodies of water rather than at higher elevations, and so on. When these biases are taken into account, paleontologists "can make corrections for them in order to arrive at a balanced view of the life of the past" (Stearn and Carroll, *Paleontology,* p. 12).

shape was typical of the fishes. Yet in spite of its strange mixture of fish and amphibian characteristics, *Ichthyostega* was clearly a full-fledged tetrapod and can be placed among the early amphibians, of which it is a primitive representative.[24]

More recently Per Ahlberg, a paleontologist working at the British Museum of Natural History, has reported new findings related to *Panderichthys*, an extinct lobe-finned fish that shows a mosaic of fishlike and amphibianlike characteristics.[25] These fossils indicate that changes in the skull roof, braincase and fins occurred in a relatively rapid period (geologically speaking) of nine to fourteen million years, and provide further evidence of transition between strictly aquatic lobe-finned fishes and four-legged amphibians.[26]

The fossil sequence from the reptiles to the earliest mammals "is the most fully documented of the major transitions in vertebrate evolution," according to Robert Carroll, a paleontologist at McGill University.[27] The transformations in the fossil record can be traced over a period of 150 million years, from "small, cold-blooded scaly reptiles to tiny, warm-blooded, furry mammals."[28] Here rather than "gaps in the fossil record" we have an abundance of riches. According to T. S. Kemp of the University Museum and Department of Zoology at Oxford, "this is the one known example where the evolution of one class of vertebrates from another class is well documented by the fossil record."[29]

Paleontologists generally agree that the ancestry of the mammals is to be sought among a group of extinct mammal-like reptiles known as cynodonts.[30]

---

[24]This information on *Ichthyostega* and the fish-amphibian transition is from Edwin H. Colbert and Michael Morales, *Evolution of the Vertebrates: A History of the Backboned Animals Through Time,* 4th ed. (New York: John Wiley & Sons, 1991), pp. 67-69; I. I. Schmalhausen, *The Origin of the Terrestrial Vertebrates,* trans. Leon Kelso (New York: Academic Press, 1968), p. 34; and Robert L. Carroll, *Vertebrate Paleontology and Evolution* (New York: W. H. Freeman, 1988), pp. 158.

[25]Per E. Ahlberg, Jennifer A. Clack and Ervins Luksevics, "Rapid Braincase Evolution Between *Panderichthys* and the Earliest Tetrapods," *Nature* 381 (May 2, 1996): 61-63.

[26]Carroll, "Revealing the Patterns of Macroevolution," p. 20.

[27] Carroll, *Vertebrate Paleontology and Evolution,* p. 361.

[28]Ibid., p. 362.

[29]T. S. Kemp, *Mammal-like Reptiles and the Origin of Mammals* (London: Academic Press, 1982), p. 1. Kemp's statement implies, of course, that the transitions between other major vertebrate classes are less well documented and based on inferences from small numbers of fossil remains.

[30]Colbert and Morales, *Evolution of the Vertebrates,* p. 228.

The fossil record of mammal-like reptiles (synapsids) is the most complete of any group of terrestrial vertebrates with the exception of the mammals themselves.[31]

By way of illustration we may examine the case of *Cynognathus*, an extinct cynodont about the size of a large dog, displaying a blend of reptilian and mammalian characteristics. *Cynognathus* had a rather large skull that was doglike in appearance. Its teeth were differentiated and specialized, unlike the undifferentiated teeth of a reptile. Small, peglike incisors were adapted for biting and nipping, while the postcanines were suited for chewing food—an indication that this animal cut its prey into small pieces before eating it rather than swallowing it whole as do many reptiles. The vertebral column was differentiated into cervical, dorsal and lumbar regions. The limbs were held beneath the body with the knee pointing forward and the elbow pointing backward, giving efficiency of locomotion. These and other specializations of *Cynognathus* show that it was an active, carnivorous reptile that was approaching a mammalian stage of development in many respects.[32] *Cynognathus* is only one example from a very large class of extinct tetrapods that display characteristics that are intermediate between the reptiles and the mammals.

It is also worth noting that some *living* forms—the monotremes, or egg-laying mammals of Australia—also exhibit features intermediate between reptiles and the more advanced mammals. The echidna and the platypus or duckbill are very primitive mammals that reproduce by laying eggs and suckle their young on milk secreted by modified sweat glands.

The skeletons and soft anatomies of these animals display certain reptilian characteristics.[33] The cervical ribs are not fused, and certain reptilian characteristics can be seen in the skull. The urogenital system and rectum open into a common cloaca as in the reptiles rather than separately as in mammals. In many respects monotremes such as the platypus and the echidna serve as excellent living examples of "mammals intermediate in their stage of evolution between the mammal-like reptiles and the higher mammals."[34]

Any discussion of intermediate forms in the geological record must include the fossil evidence of hominid forms that are believed to be the precursors of

---

[31]Kemp, *Mammal-like Reptiles,* p. 1.
[32]The above description is from Colbert and Morales, *Evolution of the Vertebrates,* pp. 123-25.
[33]Ibid., p. 241.
[34]Ibid.

modern *Homo sapiens.*[35] Much new evidence has come to light since Ramm wrote in 1954. The hominid fossil record shows that the anatomical and behavioral characteristics that we associate with the "human" have emerged and developed over long periods of time. For example, the Australopithecines, extinct hominids that flourished in Africa approximately three to four million years before the present, were capable of upright walking, like modern humans, but in brain capacity and other anatomical features were more like chimpanzees. The Australopithecines in these respects are intermediate forms between modern humans and the great apes. As the hominid fossil record is followed over a four-million-year period from the Australopithecines to *Homo habilis* to *Homo erectus* to *Homo neanderthalensis* to modern *Homo sapiens,* one can see changes in brain capacity and dentition (tooth structure) and skeletal structures that move from forms that are more apelike to those more characteristic of modern humans. This evidence of transitional forms in the fossil record, together with evidence from comparative anatomy and molecular biology,[36] leads modern biologists and anthropologists to believe that modern humans and the great apes shared a common ancestor some five million years ago, probably on the African continent.

One of the most notable features of the fossil record is the sudden, almost "explosive" appearance of the major phyla during the late Precambrian and early Cambrian periods. Since that time extensive changes have occurred *within* the phyla, but few new animal phyla have appeared. It is also quite notable that, according to Don L. Eicher and A. Lee McAlester, "there is no fossil record of the origin of these phyla, for they were already clearly separate and distinct when they first appeared as fossils."[37] Complex, multicellular organisms such as the trilobites, corals and crustaceans appear fully formed in the fossil record with no obvious ancestral forms.

---

[35]The hominid fossil evidence is reviewed and analyzed in works such as Michael H. Day, *Guide to Fossil Man,* 4th ed. (Chicago: University of Chicago Press, 1986); Richard G. Klein, *The Human Career: Human Biological and Cultural Origins* (Chicago: University of Chicago Press, 1989); Roger Lewin, *Human Evolution: An Illustrated Introduction,* 3rd ed. (Boston: Blackwell Scientific, 1993); Ian Tattersall, *The Fossil Trail* (New York: Oxford University Press, 1995); John Reader, *Missing Links: The Hunt for Earliest Man* (New York: Penguin, 1988).

[36]Anatomically, modern humans are more similar to the great apes (the gorillas and chimpanzees) than to any other living forms. At the molecular level of DNA sequences, humans and chimpanzees share an approximately 98 percent degree of similarity.

[37]Don L. Eicher and A. Lee McAlester, *History of the Earth* (Englewood Cliffs, N.J.: Prentice-Hall, 1980), p. 236. The beginning of the Cambrian is generally dated approximately 570 million years (Myr) before the present.

Various explanations have been offered for the "Cambrian explosion," which has been called the big bang in the history of life on earth. Some have alleged that increases in oxygen levels in the oceans could have promoted the rapid development of life. Other suggestions have included increases in the calcium or phosphorous content of the oceans, enabling the rapid development of organisms with skeletons; the advent of predators providing selection mechanisms for diversification; the evolution of regulatory genes making possible the rapid appearance of new body plans.[38] All these suggestions are rather speculative, and no single explanation has won general acceptance within the scientific community.

Prior to 1947 almost nothing was known about the nature of multicellular life prior to the Cambrian. During that year an extensive fossil deposit of soft-bodied organisms, dating to about 640 million years (Myr) before the present, were discovered in the Ediacara Hills of southern Australia. These fossils, which have since come to be known as the Ediacara fauna, fall into four main categories: jellyfishes, soft corals, segmented worms and other organisms of unknown affinities.[39] These animals did not possess shells or skeletons.

In recent years a rich and varied fauna from the lower Cambrian-Precambrian boundary has been discovered in Siberia. These tiny fossils, many of which have phosphatic shells, are generally known as the "Tommotian fauna." Similar fossils have since been found in Australia, England and Scandinavia. Many of these forms continue up into the lower Cambrian, where they appear with the trilobites.[40]

It is not clear how either the soft-bodied Ediacara fauna or the small shelly Tommotian fauna could plausibly be seen as ancestral to complex organisms such as the trilobites. In the words of E. N. K. Clarkson of the University of Edinburgh, these fossils testify to "an explosive development of life at this most critical point in life's history."[41]

---

[38]T. Peter Crimes, "The Period of Evolutionary Failure and the Dawn of Evolutionary Success: The Record of Biotic Changes Across the Precambrian-Cambrian Boundary," in *The Paleobiology of Trace Fossils,* ed. Stephen K. Donovan (New York: John Wiley & Sons, 1994), pp. 125. Richard Fortey says that "the acquisition of shells and skeletons is one of the great milestones in the history of the biosphere, and the difficulty of finding a single neat explanation only adds to the fascination" (*Fossils: The Key to the Past* [London: Heinemann, 1982], p. 148).

[39]E. N. K. Clarkson, *Invertebrate Paleontology and Evolution,* 2nd ed. (London: Allen & Unwin, 1986), p. 48.

[40]Ibid., pp. 51-52.

[41]Ibid., p. 52.

Some of the most extensively studied animals from the Cambrian period are the trilobites, hard-shelled creatures somewhat like modern horseshoe crabs, which are abundantly represented in the fossil record from the lower Cambrian, 570 Myr before present, until their final extinction during the Permian, about 250 Myr ago. The trilobites appear in the fossil record abruptly and fully formed. Their origins are one of the major mysteries in the history of life. According to H. B. Whittington, a leading authority in this field, to the questions of how and where the trilobites arose "unequivocal answers cannot be given"; no transitional series of fossils have been found.[42] Candidates for the presumed ancestors of the trilobites have been found among the annelid worms or the Ediacara genus *Spriggina*, but as Clarkson has admitted, "this is only speculation."[43]

Since the 1960s the remarkable compound eyes of the trilobites have been extensively studied.[44] The eyes of trilobites are the most ancient visual system known in the entire history of life. Like the eyes of insects and crustaceans, they are compound eyes composed of radially arranged visual units that give a wide-angled visual field. The number of optical elements could range from about one hundred to more than fifteen thousand in a single eye. It is believed that with such eyes the trilobite could form an image of a nearby object and even estimate its distance. The problem, from a purely evolutionary perspective, is how to explain the origin of such a complex and abruptly appearing organ through a process of small, gradual changes and natural selection. No living forms prior to the trilobites give evidence of having even rudimentary eyes, much less complex eyes like those of the trilobites.

When Ramm published *The Christian View,* experimental research on the origins of life was in its infancy. In 1953 Stanley Miller and his associates at the University of Chicago had just completed the first successful prebiotic

---

[42]H. B. Whittington, *Trilobites* (Woodbridge, U.K. : Boydell, 1992), pp. 84-85.

[43]Clarkson, *Invertebrate Paleontology and Evolution,* p. 331.

[44]See Riccardo Levi-Setti, *Trilobites: A Photographic Atlas* (Chicago: University of Chicago Press, 1975), pp. 23; Richard S. Boardman, ed., *Fossil Invertebrates* (London: Blackwell Scientific, 1987), pp. 227; Whittington, *Trilobites;* and Clarkson, *Invertebrate Paleontology and Evolution.* According to Levi-Setti (*Trilobites,* p. 23), the properties of the trilobite eye lenses "represent an all-time feat of function optimization"; the trilobites had apparently in some remarkable fashion "discovered" and applied sophisticated principles of optics scientifically described by Descartes and Huygens in the seventeenth century so as to be able to correct for spherical aberration of light and form sharp images (p. 38).

simulation experiments, synthesizing a variety of amino acids by passing electric sparks through a mixture of methane, ammonia, hydrogen and water vapor.[45] Four decades of intensive chemical experimentation since Miller's pioneering work of 1953 have shown that the synthesis of amino acids is rather easy to achieve, but the prebiotic synthesis of the more complex molecules necessary for life is extremely difficult.[46] The basic problem facing origins-of-life researchers is that life requires the presence of very complex molecules (proteins, enzymes) for metabolism and very complex molecules (RNA, DNA) for replication, and these molecules must occur together.[47] The enormous difficulties of creating such molecules under conditions similar to those obtaining in the early earth led Francis Crick, the codiscoverer of the structure of the DNA molecule, to propose the bizarre hypothesis that life was sent to earth by an advanced civilization in the form of bacteria on a spaceship ("directed panspermia").[48]

Some of the leading researchers in this field believe that RNA was the original molecule in the origins of life, somehow initially serving both as a metabolic catalyst and as an informational "template" for replication. Chemist Manfred Eigen has been able to synthesize an RNA molecule with the aid of an enzyme extracted from a living bacteria, and Leslie Orgel has been able to synthesize RNA from simpler molecules using a form of RNA as a template. But neither Eigen nor Orgel has been able to synthesize RNA without the presence of either an enzyme or a template, as would have been the case under

---

[45]These and subsequent experiments are described in Stanley L. Miller and Leslie Orgel, *The Origins of Life on the Earth* (Englewood Cliffs, N.J.: Prentice-Hall, 1974), pp. 83-102. Influential in origins-of-life research were the earlier speculations of Russian scientist A. I. Oparin, *The Origin of Life on the Earth*, 3rd ed., trans. Ann Synge (Edinburgh: Oliver and Boyd, 1957). Oparin, operating from the philosophical standpoint of Marxist-Leninist dialectical materialism, attributed self-organizing properties to matter: "Matter never remains at rest, it is constantly moving and developing. . . . [It] changes from one form of motion to another . . . each more complicated and harmonious than the last. Life thus appears as a particularly very complicated form of the motion of matter, arising as a new property at a definite stage in the development of matter" (p. xii). While not necessarily sharing Oparin's dialectical materialism, other workers in this area, recognizing the great improbability of the chance origins of life, have similarly attributed powers of "self-organization" to inanimate matter.

[46]A very helpful overview and analysis of origins-of-life research is provided by Freeman Dyson, *Origins of Life* (Cambridge: Cambridge University Press, 1985), esp. pp. 1-34.

[47]Metabolic processes are those by which a living organism converts nutrients from its environment into useful forms of energy; "replication," governed by the RNA and DNA molecules, refers to the processes by which the cell duplicates itself and its substructures.

[48]Francis Crick, *Life Itself: Its Origin and Nature* (London: Macdonald, 1981). Needless to say, Crick's suggestion has not been taken very seriously by the scientific community.

the actual conditions of the prebiotic earth.[49]

Other researchers, such as A. G. Cairns-Smith, a chemist at Glasgow University, believe that the problems of life's originating in the primeval ocean are overwhelming and have proposed as an alternative the "clay hypothesis." According to Cairns-Smith's speculations, the first organisms on earth had a different biochemistry from that of life at the present and evolved through natural selection from inorganic crystals. Complex molecules were built up on a substrate of clay, which in some fashion was presumably able to supply the information needed for replication now provided by RNA and DNA.[50] In one experiment researchers were able to build up long molecules on mineral surfaces, but these molecules were not able to replicate themselves, as in a living system.[51]

It would seem that the creation of life in the laboratory, if it is indeed possible, is a long way in the future. While investigators have proposed many models for the origins of life, Leslie Orgel, a leading authority in the field, has admitted that "evidence in favor of each of them is fragmentary at best." In a somewhat somber prognostication, Orgel concludes, "The full details of how . . . life emerged may not be revealed in the near future."[52]

Some Concluding Reflections

The foregoing survey has shown that momentous discoveries have occurred in the life sciences since Bernard Ramm wrote in the mid-twentieth century. Nevertheless, I am convinced that Ramm's concept of "progressive creation"

---

[49]On the work of Manfred Eigen, see Manfred Eigen, *Steps Toward Life: A Perspective on Evolution,* trans. Paul Woolley (Oxford: Oxford University Press, 1992), and Manfred Eigen et al., "The Origin of Genetic Information," *Scientific American* 244, no. 4 (April 1981): 78-94; for a good overview of Orgel's work and a review of research in the field, see Leslie E. Orgel, "The Origin of Life on the Earth," *Scientific American* 271, no. 4 (October 1994): 53-61.

[50]A. G. Cairns-Smith, *Genetic Takeover and the Mineral Origins of Life* (Cambridge: Cambridge University Press, 1982); a simplified layperson's account of this theory is presented in A. G. Cairns-Smith, *Seven Clues to the Origin of Life* (Cambridge: Cambridge University Press, 1985). Cairns-Smith believes that among the intractable problems faced by the more popular "primeval soup" model are contamination of early prebiotic molecules by other chemical substances, the difficulty of achieving sufficiently strong concentrations of the essential molecules in the primordial ocean, and the problem of hydrolysis: left to themselves, complex molecules in a watery solution would break down into the simpler constituent amino acids (*Genetic Takeover,* pp. 45-59).

[51]James P. Ferris et al., "Synthesis of Long Prebiotic Oligomers on Mineral Surfaces," *Nature* 381 (May 2, 1996): 59-61.

[52]Orgel, "Origin of Life," p. 61.

is still a helpful way of interpreting both biblical and scientific data relating to origins. Progressive creation, understood as an alternative to "fiat creation" and theistic evolution that incorporates the elements of truth in both, is here taken to mean that *God's creative action has occurred over long periods of time through a variety of means.*

The emphasis on "a variety of means" calls attention to the fact that the focus of the biblical terminology of creation is on the results of God's action, and the relationship of those results to the divine purpose, rather than on the details of the processes God used to achieve these results. Fiat creationism in both its older and more recent forms in American fundamentalism is based on an unnecessary dichotomy between natural and supernatural processes as possible methods of creation.[53] God is free to create through natural or supernatural means and by rapid processes or over long periods of time; no single type of process can be identified a priori as uniquely suited to the divine purpose.[54]

Progressive creation, like theistic evolution, recognizes that a Christian theory of origins must acknowledge and incorporate the evidence for the evolutionary changes that have occurred in the history of life. In some cases, such as the reptilian-mammalian transitions in the fossil record, the evidence for macroevolutionary change is stronger than Ramm supposed, and "theistic evolution" would seem to be an appropriate term.[55] In other cases, however, the

---

[53]For example, Henry Morris and Gary Parker, representing the "creation science" point of view (young earth, six-day creation, "flood geology"), state that "evolution purports to explain the origin of things by natural processes, creation by preternatural process; and it is semantic confusion to try to equate the two" (Henry Morris and Gary Parker, *What Is Creation Science?* [El Cajon, Calif.: Master Books, 1987], p. 300). This would seem to be an example of the *fallacy of the excluded middle:* "*X* must be explained in terms (and only in terms) of either *A* or *B*." Instead it may be the case that X can be explained by *C* or *D,* or by some combination of *A, B, C, D* and so forth. In the case of origins, it needs to be recognized that God is free to create through either natural or supernatural means, or through a combination of both.

[54]Rather than a twofold distinction between "natural" and "supernatural" means, it is in fact more biblically accurate to recognize a threefold distinction between God's works of ordinary providence, special providence and miracle. In ordinary providence God works immanently through the regular laws of nature (e.g., causing the grass to grow through the processes of photosynthesis [Ps 104:14] or creating animals through the normal processes of gestation [Ps 104:24, 30]); in extraordinary providence God redirects the forces and laws of nature (e.g., causing a wind to blow quail from the sea to feed the Israelites during the wilderness wanderings [Num 11:31]); in miracles God transcends the laws of nature for a redemptive purpose (e.g., the floating axhead [1 Kings 6:6], the feeding of the five thousand, the bodily resurrection of Jesus).

[55]In the perspective being argued here, theistic evolution is understood as a subcategory within the larger framework of progressive creation. Biblical texts such as Genesis 1:20-21, where God is said to create mediately by addressing the waters and the earth, can be seen as consistent with

evidence for discontinuity and the rapid emergence of novelty in the history of nature is strong, and the phrase "progressive *creation*" calls attention to this.[56] Notable cases here would be the *ex nihilo* creation of space-time, matter and energy at the big bang, the emergence of life from inanimate matter over 3.5 billion years before the present, the explosive appearance of the major animal phyla at the Precambrian-Cambrian boundary some 570 million years ago, and the sudden appearance of art and other expressions of behaviorally modern humanity some forty thousand years before the present.

"Progressive creation" is a broad enough term and concept to encompass both the immanent presence of God working within the laws of nature and the transcendent power of God above the laws of nature. From this perspective, the Christian working in the life sciences is free to recognize the variety of ways in which God's creative activity has been expressed, in the confidence that the "book of nature" rightly interpreted will ultimately be consistent with the "book of Scripture" rightly understood.

---

creation through natural processes. Texts such as Genesis 1:21, 24 ("kinds") and 1 Corinthians 15:39 ("all flesh is not the same"—birds, animals, fish) can be seen as statements concerning the *results* of God's creative work—the major groups of animals are distinct and not interfertile— rather than excluding descent from a common ancestor with modification as a possible process of origination.

[56]Some proponents of theistic evolution as the more inclusive category seem reticent to recognize special divine interventions in the natural order. Howard J. Van Till, for example, believes that the creation's "functional integrity" and the natural order's "God-given creaturely capacities" are " sufficiently robust so as not to require additional acts of special creation . . . to actualize the full array . . . of life forms that have ever existed" (Howard J. Van Till, "Basil, Augustine and the Doctrine of Creation's Functional Integrity," *Science and Christian Belief* 8, no. 1 [1996]: 29). See also by the same author *The Fourth Day: What the Bible and the Heavens Are Telling Us About the Creation* (Grand Rapids, Mich.: Eerdmans, 1986), esp. chaps. 1-5. "Progressive creation" seems to be a more adequate term for explicitly affirming the theological categories of miracle (e.g., the resurrection) and special providence (e.g., answers to petitionary prayer) that are essential for biblical faith.

8

The Anthropic Principle —
or "Designer Universe"?

*T*he more I examine the universe and study the details of its architecture," wrote the physicist Freeman Dyson, "the more evidence I find that the universe in some sense must have known that we were coming."[1] During the very year (1979) that Dyson was writing, astronomers B. J. Carr and M. J. Rees made a similar point in an article published in *Nature:* "The possibility of life as we know it . . . depends on the values of a few basic physical constants—and is . . . remarkably sensitive to their numerical values."[2]

These writers were calling attention to what has come to be known as the "anthropic principle"—a term used to refer to the fact that the universe appears to be "fine-tuned" in a most remarkable way. Our own existence, or the existence of any form of intelligent life anywhere in the cosmos, appears

---

[1]Freeman Dyson, *Disturbing the Universe* (New York: Harper & Row, 1979), p. 250.
[2]B. J. Carr and M. J. Rees, "The Anthropic Principle and the Structure of the Physical World," *Nature* 278 (1979): 612.

to depend very sensitively on a narrow range of values for basic constants in physics and astronomy.

The anthropic principle (AP) has generated a substantial volume of philosophical and theological discussion since the late 1970s. Some have dismissed it as a "mere tautology" or trivial observation: if the universe were not the way it is, we would not be here to talk about it; so why talk about it? Other writers have gone so far as to claim that the AP and the evidence on which it is based represent a "quiet revolution in scientific understanding" that has "radical implications for the modern world view." In this latter view, the AP represents the overthrow of the picture of a "random universe" and a newer, stronger scientific basis for resurrecting the design argument for the existence of God that most philosophers have dismissed in light of the criticisms of David Hume, Immanuel Kant and Charles Darwin.[3]

After a brief review of the historical origins of the AP and a presentation of some of the relevant data from physics and astronomy, this chapter will attempt to sort out some of the philosophical issues that have been raised in the debate and to assess the significance of the AP in light of Christian theology.

Historical Background

Current discussions of the AP arose in the context of scientific work in the mid-twentieth century which drew attention to a number of "cosmic coincidences" related to the values of basic constants in physics and astronomy. As early as 1937 physicist P. A. M. Dirac noticed that the large number 10 appears rather surprisingly in a number of ratios that can be formed from basic physical constants such as the speed of light (c), the gravitational constant (G), Planck's constant of quantum action (h), the masses of the electron and proton (mp) and the charge of the electron (e).[4] Was this large number just a coincidence, or did it have some deeper physical significance?

In 1961 astronomer Robert Dicke may have been the first to state what has now come to be known as the anthropic principle: he observed that only a certain range of basic physical constants would permit the existence of human life at certain stages of the universe's evolution.[5] The actual term "anthropic

---

[3]Patrick Glynn, "Beyond the Death of God," *National Review,* May 6, 1996, p. 28.
[4]P. A. M. Dirac, "The Cosmological Constant," *Nature* 139 (1937): 323-24.
[5]R. H. Dicke, "Dirac's Cosmology and Mach's Principle," *Nature* 192 (1961): 440-41.

principle" was coined in 1974 by Brandon Carter, a British astronomer. Carter was arguing for a "balanced intermediate attitude" within the astronomical community between the "primitive anthropocentrism" of a pre-Copernican, earth-centered cosmology and its equally unjustifiable antithesis: "our own situation in the universe is in no way privileged." According to Carter, our position in the universe may not be central, but it is privileged to the extent that "special conditions are necessary to our existence." The fact that "special conditions" were necessary for the existence of intelligent life was given the label "anthropic principle" by Carter.[6]

In 1986 John D. Barrow and Frank Tipler published a major work in this area, *The Anthropic Cosmological Principle,* with a comprehensive presentation of the scientific data, together with historical background and discussion of broader philosophical issues.[7] This book has remained a benchmark for all subsequent discussion of the anthropic principle.

In subsequent discussions some writers have made a distinction between "weak" and "strong" forms of the anthropic principle. The Weak Anthropic Principle (WAP), the earlier of the two, has been stated in this way: "Given the presence of human life, the physical conditions required by such life must obtain."[8] Stated in this way, the WAP amounts to a trivial truth: If X is a precondition for the existence of Y, and Y exists, then X in fact obtains. This is certainly true but not very interesting or illuminating. The Strong Anthropic Principle (SAP) can be stated as follows: "The universe is governed by a teleological, life-directed principle that ensures that the basic physical requirements of human life are met." The SAP seems to suggest, in effect, that "the universe must have known that we were coming." This latter interpretation of the anthropic principle implies that the future emergence of human life in some way predirected or preselected the values of the basic constants of nature such that the eventual emergence of intelligent life was possible.

---

[6]Brandon Carter, "The Anthropic Principle and Its Implications for Biological Evolution," *Philosophical Transactions of the Royal Society of London* A310 (1983): 347.

[7]John D. Barrow and Frank J. Tipler, *The Anthropic Cosmological Principle* (Oxford: Clarendon, 1986).

[8]This and the following formulation are from Patrick A. Wilson, "What Is the Explanandum of the Anthropic Principle?" *American Philosophical Quarterly* 28, no. 2 (1991): 167. Compare the formulations by Carter, "Anthropic Principle," pp. 347, 351: Our position in the universe is privileged to some extent inasmuch as "special conditions are necessary to our existence" (WAP); "our existence imposes restrictions . . . on the general properties of the universe . . . including the values of the fundamental parameters" (SAP).

The SAP is clearly more speculative than the WAP. The focus of this essay will be the AP in its "weak" form, especially in relation to the interest it has generated regarding the possibility of intelligent design in the universe.

Evidence of a Fine-Tuned Universe

The anthropic principle would hardly have merited the considerable volume of scholarly analysis generated since the 1970s were there not a substantial body of significant scientific data supporting it. The values of basic constants in physics and cosmology—the basic parameters that describe our universe at both its smallest and largest dimensions—seem remarkably "fine-tuned" so as to permit the existence of life.[9] If the strong nuclear force, which binds protons and neutrons together, had been slightly stronger, hydrogen would be a rare element in the universe. Stars like our sun, which exist for long periods of time by the slow burning of hydrogen in their cores, would not exist. On the other hand, if the strong nuclear force had been much weaker, then hydrogen would not burn at all and no heavier elements would have been generated in the cores of the stars. Life itself depends on a rather narrow range of possible values of the strong nuclear force. The weak nuclear force, which governs certain types of radioactive decay, is just weak enough so that the hydrogen in the sun burns at a slow and even rate. A significantly weaker or stronger value for the weak nuclear force would have been inhospitable to the existence of life.

Another basic law of physics, the Pauli Exclusion Principle, forbids two electrons to occupy exactly the same state. If this were not the case, some of the basic chemistry necessary for life would not obtain. Without such "lucky accidents" in atomic physics, water would not exist in a liquid state, carbon atoms would not form complex organic molecules, and hydrogen atoms would not form essential bridges between molecules.

If the electromagnetic force were much stronger, no planets would have formed and all stars would have been red dwarfs. If the ratio of the mass of the proton to the mass of the electron were much different from 1837, the replication of the DNA helix would be adversely affected. If the resonance levels in the nuclei of carbon and oxygen atoms had been much different, reactions in the cores of stars that synthesized elements neces-

---

[9]The following examples are drawn from Barrow and Tipler, *Anthropic Cosmological Principle,* p. 305; Dyson, *Disturbing the Universe,* pp. 250-51; and Joseph M. Zycinski, "The Weak Anthropic Principle and the Design Argument," *Zygon* 31, no. 1 (1996): 117-18.

sary for carbon-based life would not have occurred.

If the explosive force of the big bang had been slightly greater, the rate of expansion of the universe would have been such that galaxies would not have formed. On the other hand, if the rate of expansion had been a little less, the universe would have collapsed upon itself in a "big crunch," and life (had it arisen) would have been annihilated in a cosmic fireball. "Cosmic coincidences" such as these have led physicist Freeman Dyson to conclude that "the universe is an unexpectedly hospitable place for living creatures to make their home."[10] This remarkable fine-tuning of the universe cries out for a philosophical or theological explanation.

Is the Anthropic Principle an Explanation?
Does the anthropic principle provide an adequate explanation for the remarkable cosmic coincidences noted above? Some have seen the AP not so much as an "explanation" of the coincidences but rather as a way of denying the need for explanation. This type of reasoning could be paraphrased as follows: It does seem rather surprising, at least initially, that the basic constants of physics and cosmology are so delicately "fine-tuned" as to permit the existence of intelligent life. But the very fact that we are here and exist implies that these constants must be as they are. If they were not so "fine-tuned" we would not be here to discuss the matter. Therefore no further discussion or explanation is called for.

This way of appealing to the AP in the face of the cosmic coincidences is philosophically unsatisfactory. Such a response does not provide an adequate explanation of the universe's remarkable fine-tuning; it is rather a denial of the need to offer an explanation. While it is true—in fact, trivially true—that "if the constants were different, we would not be here to discuss the matter," this type of response begs the question of what caused the universe to be fine-tuned in the first place.

The question-begging nature of such a use of the AP has been illustrated by the firing-squad analogy offered by philosopher William Lane Craig and others.[11] Imagine, says Craig, that you have been sentenced to death by firing squad. On the morning of your execution, you have your back to the wall and

---

[10]Dyson, *Disturbing the Universe*, p. 251.
[11]William Lane Craig, "Barrow and Tipler on the Anthropic Principle vs. Divine Design," *British Journal for the Philosophy of Science* 39 (1988): 392. Craig credits John Leslie as the original source of the analogy.

are facing one hundred expert marksmen who have their rifles aimed at your heart from a distance of only twenty-five yards. The order to fire is given; one hundred shots ring out. Amazingly, all one hundred marksmen miss their target, and you are left standing alive! What are we to make of this state of affairs? Suppose an observer who was there that morning gave this "explanation": "It might, at least initially, seem remarkable that you are standing here alive now and that all one hundred marksmen missed the target. But if they had not missed, we would not be here having this discussion. Therefore no further discussion or explanation is necessary."

Few would consider that response an adequate explanation. It is trivially true that I would not be alive to raise the questions had not all one hundred marksmen missed, but the real question is, Why in fact did all one hundred miss their target? What causal conditions can account for the fact that I am still alive, when common sense and experience would have indicated that I should have been dead by now? While it is theoretically possible that all hundred expert marksmen missed the target merely by chance, most would reject this as highly improbable and would suspect that the outcome was in fact *prearranged*, a result of prior discussion and agreement among the marksmen and the authorities involved. The "anthropic" type of response quoted above is not an explanation of the fact that I am still alive but a way of begging the question and denying the need for a real causal explanation.

These points concerning the use of the AP as a pseudo-explanation can be generalized by stating this type of reasoning in a more abstract form: X (cosmic coincidences) are preconditions for the existence of Y (intelligent life); Y exists; therefore no explanation of X is called for. Both X and Y are *contingent* states of affairs. It is not logically necessary that human life exist; nor is it logically necessary that the basic constants of physics be what they are. X may be a precondition for Y, but the real questions are, Why should Y obtain at all? What causes X to be the way that it is? The entire set of affairs designated by $X+Y$ is contingent, and contingent states of affairs call for explanation by some principle that is noncontigent. Such an explanation is not provided by appealing to the AP in a way that shuts down further conversation and inquiry.

Alternatives to Anthropic Reasoning
If the anthropic principle is not an adequate explanation of the universe's remarkable fine-tuning, what alternatives are there to be considered? It would

seem that there are four possibilities: (1) the universe as "brute fact," (2) a "deeper physics," (3) the "many worlds" hypothesis and (4) intelligent design.

Could it be that the remarkable cosmic coincidences to which the AP points are to be accepted merely as "brute facts" for which no further explanation is to be sought? It could be argued that in every area of human experience the process of explanation must stop somewhere, that in every case the chain of explanation will finally terminate in assumptions, axioms, "self-evident truths" or "brute facts" which cannot be explained in terms more fundamental or elementary than themselves, and which are merely accepted as givens. This is bound to be the case, whether the field in question is Euclidean geometry, physics, theology or commonsense experience. But in the case of the cosmic coincidences, terminating discussion and accepting the universe's fine-tuning as an inexplicable brute fact would seem to be premature. Two of the major conversation partners in the current anthropic discussions—physics and theology—both, in their different ways, hope to show that the brute facts are rooted in a deeper reality. The physicist hopes to be able to show how the values of the basic constants of physics and cosmology are in fact explainable in terms of a more fundamental understanding of the laws of nature. The theologian hopes to argue that the universe's fine-tuning can be most plausibly understood as evidence of intelligent design. Both would consider an appeal to brute facts and a call to terminate the search for deeper explanation premature.

A second possible response to the cosmic coincidences is the search for a "deeper physics." It could be the case that the precise values of the fundamental constants and forces of physics which have made human existence possible are themselves consequences of more fundamental laws of nature that are yet to be discovered. Physicists are currently attempting to develop ambitious "theories of everything" that would bring together our understanding of the world of the very small (quantum mechanics, elementary particles) and the world of the very large (cosmology, gravitation, General Relativity). Presumably a theory of everything would show that the known values of the basic constants are not arbitrary but consequences of yet more fundamental laws of physics.

Would such a theory of everything or "superphysics" be the termination of the chain of possible explanation? At the level of physical explanation, the answer would appear to be yes; but at the level of metaphysics, the answer would appear to be no. As Carr and Rees point out in their 1979 article, even if the cosmic coincidences were shown to be the consequences of some future unified physical theory, "it would still be remarkable that the relationships dictated by physical theory happened also to be those propitious for life."[12] In other words, the questions would remain: Why is it that the laws of physics are of such a character as to be hospitable to life? Why do the laws of physics have this particular character and not another? If the laws of physics are not logically necessary—and few would wish to argue that they are—then have they been "designed" in such a way as to permit the existence of life? Must we accept the laws of physics as the ultimate brute fact, or could they have been designed by a superior intelligence so as to be hospitable to life? Even if a theory of everything were to be developed, such questions would still arise at the level of metaphysical and theological inquiry.

Another line of explanation that has been offered for the cosmic coincidences is the so-called many-worlds hypothesis. According to this highly speculative approach, our known universe is only one of a great (or possibly unlimited) number of universes that actually exist.[13] Such hypotheses have arisen in the contexts of quantum mechanics and cosmology. In 1957 physicist Hugh Everett hypothesized that the universe "splits" or "branches" at every quantum event (e.g., the decay of an atomic nucleus), so that our present observable universe is only one of many.[14] In the area of cosmological speculation, A. D. Linde and others have postulated "inflationary universe" scenarios: the universe rapidly "inflates" in the very earliest moments after the big bang, such that there are many "universes" that are causally disconnected from one another and between which no communication exists.[15]

The point of such many-worlds speculations is that if there were in fact many (or an unlimited number of) universes, then presumably in at least one

---

[12]Carr and Rees, "Anthropic Principle," p. 612.

[13]For a historical survey of philosophical speculations concerning other worlds (and the possibility of intelligent life in them) in ancient and modern times, see Steven J. Dick, *Plurality of Worlds: The Origins of the Extraterrestrial Life Debate from Democritus to Kant* (Cambridge: Cambridge University Press, 1982), and Michael J. Crowe, *The Extraterrestrial Life Debate, 1750-1900* (Cambridge: Cambridge University Press, 1986). See also Jay Wesley Richards, "Many Worlds Hypotheses: A Naturalistic Alternative to Design," *Perspectives on Science and Christian Faith* 49, no. 4 (1997): 218-27.

[14]Hugh Everett, " 'Relative State' Formulation of Quantum Mechanics," *Reviews of Modern Physics* 29 (1957): 454-62. Most working physicists do not view Everett's speculation with favor.

[15]For discussion of such inflationary many-worlds scenarios, see Barrow and Tipler, *Anthropic Cosmological Principle,* pp. 434-40. On pp. 437-38 the authors comment, "Only if such a scenario [as Linde's] could make a testable prediction would cosmologists take it seriously."

universe, such as ours, the precise combination of the values of the physical constants necessary for life would obtain, and the "coincidences" would be explained.

A fundamental problem with all such speculations, however, is that they are unverifiable and lacking in empirical evidence.[16] No physicist or astronomer can point to evidence for the existence of universes other than our own. The many-worlds hypothesis seems to be the very antithesis of Occam's Razor, the philosophical principle that states that simple and economical explanations are to be preferred to ones that are complex. In order to explain the features of one universe, the existence of many universes are postulated—apart from physical evidence![17] Furthermore, as physicist Paul Davies has pointed out, such speculations raise as many questions as they answer. Why should there be many worlds (or even one) in the first place? Why should the laws of physics be the same in all worlds?[18] Such are some of the considerations that show the inadequacy of the many-worlds hypothesis as an explanation of the cosmic coincidences.

The fourth way of responding to the cosmic coincidences is to see them as evidence for intelligent design. Even those who, like Davies, do not explicitly endorse the traditional design arguments for the existence of God nevertheless acknowledge the plausibility of interpreting the facts in this way. According to Davies, "the universe looks *as if* it is unfolding according to some plan or blueprint. . . . [The laws of physics] look *as if* they are the product of intelligent design. I do not see how that can be denied."[19]

In his evaluation of the evidence, William Lane Craig concludes that there are only two plausible alternatives: either an infinite number of other worlds or a cosmic designer. Given these options, writes Craig, "is not theism just as

---

[16]John Earman has noted that to be legitimate, "anthropic reasoning must be based on substantive reasons for believing in the required world-within-worlds structure. . . . Neither classical general relativity nor quantum mechanics provide any firm grounds for taking [such] models seriously" ("The SAP Also Rises: A Critical Examination of the Anthropic Principle," *American Philosophical Quarterly* 24, no. 4 [1987]: 316).

[17]Physicist John Polkinghorne comments, "It is enough to make poor William of Occam turn in his grave. Entities are being multiplied with incredible profusion. Such prodigality makes little appeal to professional scientists, whose instincts are to seek . . . a tight and economical understanding of the world" (*One World: The Interaction of Science and Theology* [London: SPCK, 1986], p. 49).

[18]Paul Davies, *The Mind of God: Science and the Search for Ultimate Meaning* (London: Simon & Schuster, 1992), p. 215.

[19]Ibid., p. 214.

rational a choice as other worlds?" There are no reasons, according to Craig, "a careful thinker may not . . . rationally infer the existence of a supernatural intelligence which designed the universe."[20]

Philosopher John Leslie, who has written extensively on the anthropic principle, agrees with Davies in concluding that the universe, which "religious thinkers believe to be created by God, does look very much as if it were created by God." Leslie, however, does not commit himself clearly to the intelligent design hypothesis. In his view "the God hypothesis has no advantage over multiple worlds."[21]

In his analysis of the evidence for the universe's fine-tuning, Oxford philosopher of religion Richard Swinburne concludes that the "existence of God is much more likely on the evidence . . . than the existence of 'many worlds.' "[22] Unlike Craig and Leslie, who appear to believe that the many-worlds and intelligent design hypotheses are equally plausible, Swinburne sees the evidence as clearly favoring design.

Swinburne would appear to have the better argument here. With reference to Everett's quantum-mechanical version of the many-worlds hypothesis, Swinburne is surely justified in his observation that "there are considerable philosophical difficulties in supposing that persons can be split."[23] Could this comment be seen as a fine example of British understatement? Splitting atoms into various branching universes may seem plausible to some physicists, but splitting minds and persons is quite a different matter.

Swinburne's decision for the design option also seems justified in that the many-worlds hypothesis is ad hoc, unverifiable, inconsistent with Occam's principle and not supported by independent lines of evidence. The hypothesis of divine design, on the other hand, not only is consistent with the evidence of cosmic fine-tuning but also coheres with a broad range of other considerations—religious experience, moral awareness, providence and miracle—that

---

[20]Craig, "Barrow and Tipler," p. 395.

[21]John Leslie, "How to Draw Conclusions from a Fine-Tuned Universe," in *Physics, Philosophy and Theology: A Common Quest for Understanding,* ed. Robert John Russell, William R. Stoeger Jr. and George V. Coyne (Vatican City: Vatican Observatory, 1988), pp. 309-10. See also John Leslie, "Anthropic Principle, World Ensemble, Design," *American Philosophical Quarterly* 19, no. 2 (1982): 141-51; and his book-length treatment *Universes* (London: Routledge, 1989).

[22]Richard Swinburne, "The Argument from the Fine-Tuning of the Universe," appendix to *The Existence of God,* rev. ed. (Oxford: Clarendon, 1991), p. 322.

[23]Ibid., p. 320 n. 31.

can count as evidence for theism.[24]

Swinburne would agree with other proponents of what has been termed a "new-style natural theology"[25] that design arguments have inevitable limitations and cannot in themselves constitute airtight arguments for theism. It has been recognized, for example, from the time of David Hume that design arguments taken by themselves cannot demonstrate the existence of one, infinitely perfect, personal God.[26] Nevertheless, design arguments have value within the total range of evidence that counts in favor of Christian theism. The intellectually justified inference that the universe's fine-tuning is the product of intelligent design can be seen as part of a larger "web of belief" that connects many different strands of human experience and that undergirds a cumulative case for Christian belief.[27]

In conclusion, then, the hypothesis of divine design is to be preferred as the most plausible explanation of the remarkable fine-tuning of the universe. The anthropic principle, understood by some as merely a tautology or trivial truth, is worthy of serious philosophical and theological analysis because it brings attention to a comprehensive body of physical and cosmological data that call for explanation. While it is an overstatement to claim that the anthropic principle represents the "great unnoticed revolution of late-twentieth-century thought" and the overthrow of the "random universe," it nevertheless is to be welcomed as powerfully reintroducing the issue of teleology and design into modern philosophy and philosophy of science.

---

[24] As argued by Swinburne, "Argument from the Fine-Tuning," p. 291: "On our total evidence theism is more probable than not. . . . The experience of so many men in their moments of religious vision corroborates what nature and history shows to be quite likely—that there is a God who made and sustains man and the universe."

[25] According to physicist John Polkinghorne, this type of natural theology is more modest in its ambitions than traditional natural theology, seeking "insight" rather than logical demonstration; it aims to be not a rival to science but a "comradely discipline" complementing science's search for an understanding of the natural world (John Polkinghorne, "Contemporary Interactions Between Science and Theology," *Modern Believing* 36, no. 4 [1995]: 33). Polkinghorne includes Ian Barbour, Arthur Peacocke, Paul Davies and himself among the proponents of this approach.

[26] Such criticisms were made by David Hume in his *Dialogues on Natural Religion* (1776). A modern critical edition of this text may be found in *The Natural History of Religion and Dialogues Concerning Natural Religion,* ed. John Valdimer Price (Oxford: Clarendon, 1976). See also on this point Kenneth T. Gallagher, "Remarks on the Argument from Design," *Review of Metaphysics* 48, no. 1 (1994): 30.

[27] Such an approach to religious epistemology is argued by William P. Alston in *Perceiving God: The Epistemology of Religious Experience* (Ithaca, N.Y.: Cornell University Press, 1991). Cf. p. 306: "Though no single strand is sufficient to keep the faith secure, when combined into a rope they all together have strength to do the job."

9

The Search for Extraterrestrial Intelligence & the Christian Doctrine of Redemption

*I*n August 1996 scientists at the NASA Space Center in Houston, Texas, made a dramatic announcement of the discovery of what they believed to be evidence of primitive life on early Mars.[1] The Martian meteorite ALH84001, recovered in Antarctica, contained microscopic carbonate globules that resembled bacteria found on earth. Although many in the scientific community considered the evidence inconclusive,[2] the announcement sparked a new surge of popular and scientific interest in the search for extraterrestrial life and intelligence.

A number of authors have suggested that the discovery of intelligent extra-

---

[1]David S. MacKay et al., "Search for Past Life on Mars: Possible Relic Biogenic Activity in Martian Meteorite ALH84001," *Science* 273 (August 16, 1996): 924-30.
[2]Cf. Monica Grady, Ian Wright and Colin Pillinger, "Opening a Martian Can of Worms?" *Nature* 382 (August 15, 1996): 575-76.

terrestrial beings[3] would have momentous consequences for human beings' view of themselves and their place in the universe. Noted philosopher and historian of science Ernan McMullin of Notre Dame University has expressed surprise that this issue has not received more attention from theologians. In light of the new vistas of thought opened up by the discoveries of twentieth-century astronomy, McMullin believes that "a religion which is unable to find a place for extraterrestrial persons in its view of God and the universe might find it difficult to command terrestrial assent in the days to come."

The theological issues potentially at stake are enormous: "Could one still take the Christian doctrines of incarnation and redemption seriously if there were millions of developed civilizations dotted throughout the universe?" McMullin pointedly asks. He clearly sees that the possibility of extraterrestrial intelligence inevitably raises questions about the uniqueness and finality of the person and work of Christ and the Christian scheme of redemption revealed in the Bible. If extraterrestrial beings do exist elsewhere in the universe and are alienated from God, how are they related—or are they in any way related—to the "once for all" incarnation and atoning death of Christ in the New Testament? Would Jesus Christ need to become incarnate again and die again to secure their redemption? According to McMullin, "theologians have been silent on these issues, no doubt feeling that the problems of earth are more than enough to occupy them."[4]

The issues being raised here are speculative but not entirely hypothetical. To date there have been over one hundred projects related to what is now called SETI (search for extraterrestrial intelligence), in many different countries, with sophisticated scientific instrumentation.[5] Thus far none of these projects has found any evidence of intelligent life elsewhere in the universe.

Despite the null results of SETI projects to date, the theological issues posed are still worth exploring. Stanley Jaki, another noted historian, is surely

---

[3]In this discussion "extraterrestrial intelligence" will refer to any *embodied,* intelligent beings other than *Homo sapiens* that might exist elsewhere in the universe. The existence of other *spiritual* intelligences referred to in the Bible (angels, demons, principalities, powers and so forth) is assumed.

[4]Ernan McMullin, "Persons in the Universe," *Zygon* 15, no. 1 (March 1980): 69, 88. Actually it is incorrect to say that "theologians have been silent on these issues." McMullin seems to be unaware of the evidence presented in the later studies of Steven J. Dick and Michael J. Crowe (see note 7) that shows that these and related issues have been discussed by Christian theologians since the third century A.D.

[5]Woodruff T. Sullivan, "Alone in the Universe?" *Nature* 380 (March 21, 1996): 211.

correct in claiming that the Christian theist has the intellectual freedom to look at the question of extraterrestrial intelligence as a "truly open question." No one has the right to prescribe to God a priori "to create intellects everywhere or to limit his power to do so."[6] Both possibilities would be consistent with divine omnipotence and the revealed character of God.

Regardless of the empirical results of present and future SETI projects, the questions raised by McMullin and others are worth pursuing as theological "thought experiments" that may yield new and fruitful perspectives on familiar biblical doctrines. The central purpose of this chapter will be to argue, after reviewing some of the history of prior discussions, that the cosmic Christology of Colossians 1:15-20 is sufficiently expansive to encompass the redemption of any intelligent beings that could exist elsewhere in the universe.

Extraterrestrial Life: Premodern Discussions

While the term "extraterrestrial life" originated in the twentieth century, the concept of "other worlds" or "a plurality of worlds" dates back to the ancient Greeks.[7] Atomist Democritus (c.460-370 B.C.) speculated on the existence of a plurality of worlds. In the fourth century B.C. Epicurus asserted the existence of an infinity of worlds. Based on his atomistic philosophy, Epicurus hypothesized that the motions of an infinity of atoms would produce an unlimited number of worlds. Roman Stoic philosopher Lucretius was also a pluralist. In his treatise *De rerum naturae* he postulated the existence of other worlds based on the idea of the uniformity of nature and a "principle of plenitude": what is *possible* will be realized somewhere; other worlds are possible; consequently we would expect their instantiation. The principle of plenitude was destined to play an influential role in speculations about other worlds and extraterrestrial life down to the present day.

Arrayed against these pluralistic conjectures was the formidable opinion of Aristotle, who in his treatise *De caelo* argued for the existence of only one world. Just as a circle can have only one center and one circum-

[6]Stanley L. Jaki, *Cosmos and Creator* (Edinburgh: Scottish Academic Press, 1980), p. 125.
[7]For the following references I am indebted to the fine historical studies by Steven J. Dick, *Plurality of Worlds: The Origins of the Extraterrestrial Life Debate from Democritus to Kant* (Cambridge: Cambridge University Press, 1982), and Michael J. Crowe, *The Extraterrestrial Life Debate, 1750-1900* (Cambridge: Cambridge University Press, 1986). In the context of early Greek discussions "worlds" *(cosmoi)* referred to a system involving an earth, planets and fixed stars; the issue of extraterrestrial *intelligent life* was rarely if ever considered.

ference, he argued, so the universe must have only one center if it is to be an ordered whole.[8]

Since the idea of a plurality of worlds was associated with the materialistic philosophies of the Greek atomists, it is not surprising that early Christian writers opposed such conjectures. Pluralism was rejected by Hippolytus of Rome (third century) and by Eusebius of Caesarea (c. 260-c. 340).[9] In book 11 of the *City of God* Augustine rejects the speculations of Epicurus in these matters.[10] The atomistic philosophies of Democritus and Epicurus were seen as inconsistent with the biblical doctrines of creation and divine providence and as essentially atheistic in character.

During the Middle Ages the writings of Aristotle became more readily available in Europe through the translations of the Arabic philosophers. Scholastic theologians such as Albertus Magnus and his most famous student, Thomas Aquinas, discussed the question of the existence of other worlds in the light of Aristotle's arguments. Albertus went as far as to say that the issue of the plurality of worlds was "one of the most wondrous and noble questions in Nature" but, in agreement with Aristotle, rejected the actual existence of other *cosmoi.*[11]

In the *Summa Theologica* Aquinas considers "whether there is only one world." Appealing to the divine omnipotence, Aquinas argues that hypothetically God could have created many worlds as an expression of his power: "He could create many, since His power is not limited to the creation of one world." Nevertheless, in actuality God has chosen to create only one world. "The very order of things created by God shows the unity of the world," according to Aquinas. "Whatever things come from God, have relations of order to each other. . . . Hence it must be that all things should belong to one world."[12] While Aquinas's reasoning is not transparent here, he appears to reflect something of the "one circle/one center" thinking of Aristotle. The orderly processes of nature, Aquinas believes, reflect the one God and imply that the creation is one unified cosmos

---

[8]Aristotle *De caelo* 1.8.277a.

[9]Hippolytus *Philosophumena* 1; Eusebius *Praeparatio evangelica* 15. These references are found in Grant McColley, "The Seventeenth-Century Doctrine of a Plurality of Worlds," *Annals of Science* 1 (1936): 393. McColley includes a helpful review of ancient and medieval opinion.

[10]Augustine *City of God* 11.5.

[11]Cited in Crowe, *Extraterrestrial Life Debate,* p. 552.

[12]Aquinas *Summa Theologica* 1.q47.a3; trans. Fathers of the English Dominican Province (London: R. & T. Washbourne, 1912-1913), p. 260.

rather than a set of unrelated worlds.[13]

Elsewhere in the *Summa* Aquinas addresses the question "whether it was necessary for the restoration of the human race that the Word of God should become incarnate." For Aquinas this question was raised by prior scholastic debates rather than by the issue of other worlds, but as will be seen below, this question of the *necessity of the incarnation* has considerable relevance to the issue of extraterrestrial intelligences. Aquinas concludes that the incarnation was not necessary in an absolute sense, "for God of His omnipotent power could have restored human nature in many other ways." (These "other ways" are not specified.) But the incarnation was necessary in a relative sense, in that it was fitting and useful to humankind. The incarnation of the Son of God was necessary in this relative sense to strengthen our faith, hope and love and to aid our fuller participation in the divine life.[14] While he was not directly addressing the issue, it seems clear that Aquinas would have given a negative answer to the question, would Christ have to become incarnate again in some other world in order to redeem a fallen race of alien beings? God's "omnipotent power" could restore them in "many other ways."

William Vorilong (d. 1464), whose commentary on the *Sentences* of Peter Abelard was frequently quoted in the Middle Ages, was apparently the first Christian theologian to explicitly relate the issue of other worlds to the doctrines of original sin and the atonement. Vorilong is not going beyond his contemporaries when he suggests that God in his omnipotence could actually have made an infinity of worlds. Vorilong goes further, however, when he states that other beings on these worlds, if they existed, though created by God, would not share Adam's fallen nature. And as to the question "whether Christ by dying on this earth could redeem the inhabitants of another world," Vorilong answers that "he is able to do this even if the worlds were infinite, but it would not be fitting for him to go into another world that he must die again."[15] For Vorilong, the already accomplished incarnation and death of Christ on earth are sufficient to provide for the redemption of any beings that might exist in other worlds.

---

[13]Similar ideas appear to be at work in contemporary discussions of SETI and the origins of life, when it is commonly assumed that the laws of physics and chemistry would be the same throughout the universe.

[14]Aquinas *Summa Theologica* 3.q1.a2 (p. 6).

[15]Cited by Grant McColley and H. W. Miller, "Saint Bonaventure, Francis Mayron, William Vorilong and the Doctrine of a Plurality of Worlds," *Speculum* 12 (1937): 388.

In the sixteenth century the Lutheran Reformer Phillip Melanchthon reflects awareness of the issues raised by the new Copernican astronomy. In his *Initia Doctrina Physica* (1567) he asserts that if there were other worlds, Christ would not die and rise again there. Melanchthon appears to believe that to accept the actual existence of a plurality of worlds would be inconsistent with the Christian doctrine of the atonement.[16]

The Modern Period: Enlightenment to the Nineteenth Century

Subsequent to the epochal discoveries of Galileo in the seventeenth century, the Christian church was faced with the challenge of incorporating an enlarged view of the universe into its worldview and biblical interpretation. One critic of Christianity who was not slow to see these challenges and who attempted to use the new science for his own polemical purposes was Thomas Paine, the radical activist and pamphleteer who was involved in both the American and French revolutions. His widely read book *The Age of Reason* (1794) was one of the most vehement attacks on the Christian religion and the Bible published up to that time. In Paine's mind, the vast universe discovered by the astronomers showed how outmoded was the biblical picture:

> Though it is not a direct article of the Christian system, that this world is the whole of the habitable creation, yet it is so worked up . . . from what is called the Mosaic account of the Creation, the story of Eve and the apple . . . that to believe that God created a plurality of worlds, at least as numerous as what we call stars, renders the Christian system of faith at once little and ridiculous, and scatters it in the mind like feathers in the air. The two beliefs cannot be held together in the same mind, and he who thinks that he believes both has thought but little of either.[17]

Paine was throwing down the gauntlet to Christian believers. In his view one could believe in either an expanded universe with many worlds or the traditional biblical cosmology, but not both at the same time. Paine's challenge was to be taken up in various ways by Christian apologists in the nineteenth century.

---

[16]McColley, "Seventeenth-Century Doctrine," p. 413. The views of the heterodox Roman Catholic monk Giordano Bruno (1548-1600), who advocated an infinite universe containing an infinite number of worlds, are discussed in John Hedley Brooke, *Science and Religion: Some Historical Perspectives* (Cambridge: Cambridge University Press, 1991), pp. 39-40, 73-74.

[17]Thomas Paine, *The Age of Reason*, in *The Complete writings of Thomas Paine*, ed. Philip S. Foner (New York: Citadel, 1945), pp. 498-99.

During the 1800s a number of prominent clergymen and scientists debated the issue of life on other worlds and its theological implications. A popular pastor and preacher of the Free Church of Scotland, Thomas Chalmers, preached a series of sermons later published under the title *Astronomical Discourses* (1817). Chalmers was not sure if there were other fallen beings elsewhere in the universe. He suggested, however, that just as the effects of the cross on earth were not diminished by time, so these effects might also extend outward in space to other planets. For all we know, Chalmers mused, "the plan of redemption may have its influences and its bearings on those creatures of God who people other regions."[18]

Distinguished Scottish scientist David Brewster (1781-1868) agreed with Chalmers. In his book *More Worlds Than One* (1854) he saw no reason that the "force of the atonement" should diminish with distance or not extend "to the planetary races in the past . . . and to the planetary races in the future" (pp. 149-50).

Scottish Presbyterian scholar William Leitch (1818-1864), a graduate of Glasgow University, moved to Canada in 1860 to become the principal of Queen's College, Kingston. In his book of 1862, *God's Glory in the Heavens,* Leitch surveyed the astronomical discoveries known at the time and reflected discerningly on "the religious questions to which they give rise" (p. v). Leitch ruled out the idea of multiple incarnations for Christ, believing that such would be inconsistent with Scripture, which declares that "he will forever bear his human nature." Leitch also believed that Scripture does not support the idea that the atonement might extend to other races of fallen beings. He seemed to imply, in effect, that redemption is required only by earthlings (p. 329).

The Twentieth Century's Scientific Discussions
Since the nineteenth century the extraterrestrial life debate has been dominated by scientists rather than by philosophers and theologians as in earlier centuries. The current dominance of scientific categories reflects not only the general secularization of educated thought in much of the West since the Enlightenment but a number of specific intellectual developments and scientific discoveries as well. The widespread acceptance of the Darwinian para-

---

[18]These references from nineteenth-century writers are found in Crowe, *Extraterrestrial Life Debate*, pp. 187, 305, 452.

digm in biology, the astronomical discoveries of Edwin Hubble and others which dramatically enlarged the known universe, the discovery of the structure of the DNA molecule by Francis Crick and James Watson, the synthesis of prebiotic molecules by Harold Urey and others, and the new tools of radio astronomy all contributed to a belief held by significant numbers of scientists that life exists elsewhere in the universe and that it is worthwhile to search for signs of it.[19]

Scientific opinion has been highly divided on the question of the actual existence of extraterrestrial intelligence. Some physicists and astronomers (e.g., Carl Sagan, Paul Davies) are very optimistic in this regard, while most evolutionary biologists (e.g., Theodosius Dobzhansky, Ernst Mayr, Stephen Jay Gould) are quite skeptical, believing that the emergence of intelligent life on earth was an extremely improbable event, unlikely to have been duplicated elsewhere in the universe.

An "ETI optimist" such as Davies bases his beliefs not only on the premise that the laws of physics and chemistry are uniform throughout the universe but also on the hypothesis that matter may have "self-organizing" properties that make the emergence of life likely elsewhere in the cosmos.[20] Such optimistic assessments about the likelihood of intelligent life are rejected by many biologists, astronomers and physicists. Astronomer Brandon Carter, who coined the term "anthropic principle," believes that "civilizations comparable with our

---

[19]Discussions of the extraterrestrial life debate, focusing on scientific considerations, include Paul Davies, *Are We Alone?* (London: Penguin, 1995); Jean Heidmann, *Extraterrestrial Intelligence,* trans. Storm Dunlop (Cambridge: Cambridge University Press, 1995); Edward Regis Jr., ed., *Extraterrestrials: Science and Alien Intelligence* (Cambridge: Cambridge University Press, 1985).

[20]For Davies, see *Are We Alone?* and also Paul Davies, *The Cosmic Blueprint* (London: William Heinemann, 1987). On the notion of matter as "self-organizing," Davies has followed the ideas of Stuart Kauffman, *The Origins of Order: Self-Organization and Selection in Evolution* (Oxford: Oxford University Press, 1993). For other writers who are optimistic concerning ETI, see I. S. Shklovskii and Carl Sagan, *Intelligent Life in the Universe* (San Francisco: Holden-Day, 1966), a cooperative book by Sagan and a Soviet astronomer; Carl Sagan, *The Cosmic Connection: An Extraterrestrial Perspective* (London: Hodder & Stoughton, 1973); Philip Morrison, John Billingham and John Wolfe, eds., *The Search for Extraterrestrial Intelligence* (New York: Dover Publications, 1979), "prepared for the National Aeronautics and Space Administration," recommending NASA support for SETI; G. F. R. Ellis and G. B. Brundit, "Life in the Infinite Universe," *Quarterly Journal of the Royal Astronomical Society* 20 (1979): 37-41, arguing that an infinite, unbounded universe would make it probable that there would be infinitely many worlds with intelligent beings; Francis Jackson and Patrick Moore, *Life in the universe* (London: Routledge & Kegan Paul, 1987), cautiously suggesting it is "probable" that there are many other planets in the universe with "carbon-based organisms."

own are likely to be exceedingly rare" and the chances of being able to communicate with any alien intelligences exceedingly remote.[21] An evolutionary paleontologist such as Stephen Jay Gould would deny any notion of matter's "self-organizing" tendencies and would see the actual evolutionary pathway leading to *Homo sapiens* as completely fortuitous and unlikely to be repeated in any other "roll of the evolutionary dice."[22] Astronomer Fred Hoyle has argued that the emergence of life on earth is so improbable that the first seeds of life must have been brought to earth from elsewhere in the galaxy by a meteorite or a comet.[23] Astronomers John D. Barrow and Frank Tipler examine the evidence and conclude that "it is very likely that we are the only intelligent species now existing in our galaxy."[24]

The fact that there are such great divergences of opinion within the scientific community about the likelihood of the existence of extraterrestrial intelligence suggests that in this field speculations and hypotheses are "underdetermined by the data."[25] Here I do not attempt to resolve the scientific arguments, but proceed with a "thought experiment" addressing the theological issues arising.

The Twentieth Century's Theological Discussions

Compared to the nineteenth and earlier centuries, relatively little theological attention has recently been given to the possible implications of intelligent life

---

[21]Brandon Carter, "The Anthropic Principle and Its Implications for Biological Evolution," *Philosophical Transactions of the Royal Society of London* A310 (1983): 354. As the term was first used, "anthropic principle" called attention to the fact that the emergence of intelligent life on earth (or anywhere else in the universe) was sensitively dependent on the values of certain fundamental constants of nature, such as the strength of the gravitational force, the charge on the electron, the "strong" nuclear force and so on. Were these values different from their present ones, life presumably would not have emerged.

[22]Stephen Jay Gould, *Wonderful Life* (New York: W. W. Norton, 1989).

[23]Fred Hoyle, *The Intelligent Universe* (London: Michael Joseph, 1983). Francis Crick, the codiscoverer of the structure of the DNA molecule, in his *Life Itself: Its Origin and Nature* (London: MacDonald, 1981), puts forward as an apparently serious suggestion the "directed panspermia" hypothesis: microorganisms were sent to earth in unmanned spaceships by a higher civilization. Crick admits that the evidence is thin and the chain of reasoning very tenuous, so that we must "allow our imagination a free hand" (p. 117).

[24]John D. Barrow and Frank J. Tipler, *The Anthropic Cosmological Principle* (Oxford: Oxford University Press, 1986), p. 576; see all of chap. 9, "Argument Against the Existence of Extraterrestrial Life."

[25]As Sullivan has noted, "it is indeed sobering that, after almost four decades of scientific investigation into extraterrestrial life, the field of exobiology (or bioastronomy) thrives despite its inability to demonstrate that its subject matter even exists" ("Alone in the Universe?" p. 211).

elsewhere in the universe. This is not entirely surprising, since for the last hundred years or so a great amount of the church's energies have been spent in responding to the intellectual challenges posed by the ideas of Charles Darwin, Karl Marx and Sigmund Freud; the historical criticism of the Bible; growing awareness of world religions and religious pluralism; and the sociological impact of industrialization, urbanization, population growth, changing sexual mores and two world wars. Theologians indeed have had enough problems on earth to deflect their attention from extraterrestrial concerns!

One of the exceptions to this general lack of interest in ETI is represented by a 1952 book by Oxford mathematician E. A. Milne, *Modern Cosmology and the Christian Idea of God.* The ideas in this book were first presented as the Cadbury Lectures at the University of Birmingham in 1950. Milne does not engage in an extended analysis of the theological issues raised by modern cosmology, but he does note that some Christians have felt a difficulty with the concept of a vast universe with a possibly infinite number of planets, especially in relation to the biblical teaching concerning the incarnation. Was the incarnation of which the New Testament speaks a unique event, "or has it been re-enacted on each of a countless number of planets?" Milne's answer is that a Christian would "recoil in horror from such a conclusion." One could not imagine "the Son of God suffering vicariously on each of a myriad of planets."[26]

Milne asserts that the incarnation and atonement must be unique historical events but does not give biblical arguments for his conclusion. He suggests that a scenario involving multiple incarnations and atonements can be avoided if we suppose that our planet is unique. Then what of the possibility of other intelligent beings on other planets that might be in need of redemption? He admits that we "are in deep waters here, in a sea of great mysteries," but suggests that the new technology of radio astronomy may provide an answer. It may be possible one day to establish radio communication with other beings in the universe, transmit the knowledge of Christian redemption to them, and so "the re-enactment of the tragedy of the crucifixion in other planets would be unnecessary."[27]

In his Bampton Lectures of 1956, published under the title *Christian Theol-*

---

[26]E. A. Milne, *Modern Cosmology and the Christian Idea of God* (Oxford: Clarendon, 1952), p. 153.
[27]Ibid., pp. 153-54.

ogy and Natural Science, E. L. Mascall responds directly to some of Milne's theological points. If for Milne the crucifixion of Christ is an event of unrelieved horror, how can we tolerate the idea of God's ordaining it even once? On the other hand, if the horror is not unrelieved "but is changed into victory and glory, why cannot the change happen again elsewhere?"[28]

Mascall concludes somewhat tentatively that there are no conclusive theological reasons to exclude other incarnations and atonements. If the incarnation involved no diminution in deity, why could not the Son of God, in principle, assume other created natures? For Mascall, there would seem to be no compelling reason that "other finite rational natures should not be united to that person too."[29] This raises the somewhat bizarre image not of the historic God-man but of a bionic Redeemer who unites to his divine nature not only the nature of *Homo sapiens* but the natures of many other sentient, embodied creatures as well.

Mascall admits that the entire subject is very speculative and that the relationship of other beings to God in creation and redemption may be so different as to not require an incarnation at all. Nevertheless, he sees considerable value in such speculations. "Theological principles tend to become torpid for lack of exercise," he writes, "and there is much to be said for giving them now and then a scamper in a field where the paths are few and the boundaries are undefined."[30]

In 1958 C. S. Lewis published an article, "Religion and Rocketry," in which he reflected on the theological significance of the existence of intelligent life on other planets.[31] Lewis was skeptical that such beings actually existed; even if they did, he believed their discovery would not have much lasting impact on Christian theology. Nevertheless, Lewis was of the opinion that if there were such spiritual intelligences, and if they were fallen, it might be conceivable that God would provide for their redemption in some way other than through the incarnation and atonement provided by Christ in earthly history. He speculated that Romans 8:19-23, where the apostle Paul looks forward to the redemption of the whole creation, implies that the

---

[28] E. L. Mascall, *Christian Theology and Natural Science* (London: Longmans, Green, 1956), p. 39.

[29] Ibid., p. 41.

[30] Ibid., p. 45.

[31] C. S. Lewis, "Religion and Rocketry," in *Fern-Seed and Elephants: And Other Essays on Christianity,* ed. Walter Hooper (London: Fontana, 1975), pp. 86-95. This essay was originally published under the title "Will We Lose God in Outer Space?" *Christian Herald* 81 (April 1958).

redemption of humankind might have cosmic meaning for other fallen races.[32] Lewis, however, did not relate his speculations to specific texts in the New Testament dealing with the incarnation and the atonement. He seemed to be more concerned with practical issues than with the theoretical problems that could arise from the discovery of intelligent life elsewhere in the universe. Lewis was concerned that humans, with their long history of exploiting one another, might also be tempted to exploit and abuse other creatures that might exist elsewhere in the universe.[33]

A Constructive Proposal: Colossians 1:15-20 and Cosmic Redemption

Having surveyed some of the history of theological and scientific speculation on the subject of extraterrestrial intelligence, one would be inclined to agree with Mascall's judgment that this subject's "paths are few and [its] boundaries . . . undefined." In this final section of the chapter I present a proposal that attempts to give some of these "paths and boundaries" greater definition by calling attention to a New Testament text that has received inadequate attention in this debate: Colossians 1:15-20. I believe that the Christology of Colossians is sufficiently vast in scope to provide a basis for the redemption of fallen beings anywhere in the universe, without the need for any additional incarnations or atonements.

For the purposes of this discussion Paul's authorship of Colossians is assumed, and no attempt is made to choose between the various reconstructions by New Testament scholars of the particular heresies that are reflected in the epistle.[34] My proposal does not depend on any one position the reader

---

[32]Lewis, "Religion and Rocketry," p. 90.

[33]Ibid., p. 92.

[34]For discussion of the authorship, dating and setting of Colossians the following commentaries may be consulted: Peter T. O'Brien, *Colossians, Philemon* (Waco, Tex.: Word, 1982); Markus Barth and Helmut Blanke, *Colossians: A New Translation with Introduction and Commentary,* Anchor Bible, trans. Astrid B. Beck (New York: Doubleday, 1994); Murray J. Harris, *Colossians and Philemon* (Grand Rapids, Mich.: Eerdmans, 1991); Eduard Lohse, *A Commentary on the Epistles to the Colossians and to Philemon,* trans. William J. Poehlmann and Robert J. Karris (Philadelphia: Fortress, 1971); J. B. Lightfoot, *Saint Paul's Epistles to the Colossians and to Philemon* (London: Macmillan, 1897). Detailed discussions concerning the nature of the Colossian heresy are also found in Thomas J. Sappington, *Revelation and Redemption at Colossae* (Sheffield, U.K.: Sheffield Academic Press, 1991; "ascetic-mystical piety" in Jewish apocalypticism); Richard E. DeMaris, *The Colossian Controversy: Wisdom in Dispute at Colossae* (Sheffield, U.K.: Sheffield Academic Press, 1994; Hellenistic Jewish interpretations of Jewish tradition heavily influenced by the Greek philosophy of Middle Platonism); Clinton E. Arnold, *The Colossian Syncretism: The Interface Between Christianity and Folk Belief at Colossae*

might wish to adopt on matters of authorship and setting.

It is evident that in the christological hymn of Colossians 1:15-20 redemption is cosmic in scope.[35] The fact that in the space of six verses there are seven occurrences of "all," "all things" or "everything" is a clear indication that the redemptive effects of the atoning death of Christ are not limited to humanity but extend in some way to the entire created universe. The apostle stresses in the most emphatic way the absolute supremacy of Christ in every realm of space, time and human experience. This supremacy of Christ is asserted in creation (vv. 15-16), providence (v. 17), incarnation (v. 19), reconciliation (v. 20), resurrection (v. 18) and the church (v.18).

Christ is supreme over the entire created order, since he is the image (*eikon;* cf. Heb 1:3) of the invisible God, the outward manifestation of the divine glory and nature, the "firstborn" *(prototokos)* of all creation (v. 15). As the firstborn Son has preeminence in the family order, so Christ has preeminence in the order of creation. His supremacy extends not only over the visible things of the physical universe but over the invisible order of spiritual intelligences as well. All things whatsoever—from quarks to archangels—were created by him and for him; Christ is both the efficient and the final cause of the entire created order (cf. Jn 1:3; 1 Cor 8:6).[36]

Christ is preeminent in the order of divine providence (Col 1:17). Not only did Christ create all things; in him "all things hold together." For the apostle Paul, the Redeemer is also the "Sustainer and Unifier of the Universe."[37] The laws of physics and chemistry which give order and coherence to the material creation are not autonomous principles but expressions of the divine will manifested in and executed through Christ. This providential sustaining action by

---

(Tübingen, Germany: J. C. B. Mohr/Paul Siebeck, 1995; a syncretistic combination of elements of Christianity and folk religions of Asia Minor).

[35]Most New Testament scholars believe that this passage is rooted in an early Christian hymn that was taken over and modified by the apostle. For discussion of the relationship of this material to other elements of early Christian tradition, see John G. Gibbs, *Creation and Redemption: A Study in Pauline Theology* (Leiden, Netherlands: E. J. Brill, 1971), pp. 92-114. For helpful insights on the matter of the "cosmic scope of redemption" in Paul's Christology, I am indebted to John G. Gibbs, "The Cosmic Scope of Redemption According to Paul," *Biblica* 56 (1975): 13-29; and John G. Gibbs, "Pauline Cosmic Christology and Ecological Crisis," *Journal of Biblical Literature* 90 (1971): 466-79.

[36]Gibbs calls attention to the fact that the relating of creation and redemption in the Colossian christological hymn is consistent with the epistolary context (cf. Col 1:6, 21, 23; 2:9-10; 3:10) and other texts in Paul's letters (Rom 8:21-22; 10:6-7; 1 Cor 1:24; 2 Cor 4:4; 5:19) (Gibbs, "Cosmic Scope of Redemption," p. 21).

[37]O'Brien, *Colossians, Philemon,* p. 48.

the Son of God continues moment by moment in the present; without it the universe would be subject to dissolution and nonbeing. Excluded here is any thought of a deistic "watchmaker universe" created by God in the past and then abandoned to its own devices. The divine Son of God is not only transcendent in authority over the entire created order but also present *immanently* within each moment of time and every physical process and entity.

In the Colossian hymn the supremacy of Christ is manifested in both his preexistent and existent states.[38] In his incarnation "all the fullness" (*pan to pleroma*, v. 19) of the divine essence was embodied in the person of Christ.[39] This apostolic assertion of the unqualified deity of Jesus Christ was in later centuries to find classic creedal formulation in the Nicene (*homoousios*, "same nature") and Chalcedonian statements ("fully God, fully man"). The complete supremacy of the Redeemer in his historical career has also been manifested in his resurrection ("firstborn from the dead," Col 1:18) and subsequent exaltation to be head of the church (also v. 18).

The supremacy of Christ in creation, providence and incarnation finds its goal and climax in his atoning death on the cross, through which God has achieved his purpose "to reconcile all things" (*apokatallaksai ta panta*, v. 20) to himself. That the impact of this reconciling death is not limited to the terrestrial world of humanity is made clear by the further reference in the verse to "all things, whether things on earth or things in heaven."[40] This cosmic redemption has been achieved in principle, in an objective sense, through the

---

[38]For a study of the pre-existence of Christ in recent scholarship, see R. G. Hamerton-Kelly, *Preexistence, Wisdom and the Son of Man*, SNTS Monograph Series 21 (Cambridge: Cambridge University Press, 1973).

[39]At this point an observation could be made with respect to the reference to the incarnation by the writer of Hebrews in Hebrews 2:14, "he too shared in their humanity." This text could be understood as asserting not an *absolute* necessity for an incarnation to achieve redemption but rather as emphasizing that because Christ and his people share in flesh and blood, Christ is a merciful and faithful high priest who can sympathize with his people, having suffered and been tempted as they (Heb 2:17-18).

[40]The commentators are quite agreed on the cosmic scope of the reconciliation spoken of in this verse. So, for example, Lightfoot, *Saint Paul's Epistles*, p. 158: "The whole universe of things, material as well as spiritual, shall be restored to harmony with God"; Arnold, *Colossian Syncretism*, p. 269: "Christ's death is the basis for this restoration of harmony throughout heaven and earth"; Lohse, *Commentary on the Epistles*, p. 59 n. 202: "the author of Col utilizes the concept of a reconciliation which encompasses the whole of the universe." This is consistent with the thought of Ephesians 1:10: it is the divine purpose to bring everything in heaven and on earth into a unity in Christ. Lohse also notes (*Commentary on the Epistles*, p. 60 n. 205) that this cosmic reconciliation of heaven and earth is quite the opposite of Gnostic concepts, for which the reconciliation of the material world with the heavenly would be unthinkable.

one historic event of the shedding of Christ's blood on the cross (v. 20), though the full effects of this act will not be manifested until the end of history. The reconciliation of all things spoken of here probably has a broader sense that includes the pacification or subjugation of rebellious powers, rather than the more usual sense of the restoration of friendly relations between God and his redeemed people. Such a notion of "pacification," as P. T. O'Brien has noted, "was not strange to those living in the Mediterranean region under Roman rule of the first century A.D."[41]

It now remains to make some applications of Paul's cosmic Christology to the question of possibly existent extraterrestrial beings who could be alienated from God. What can be said about their possible redemption in the light of Colossians 1:15-20?

It seems clear that the references to "all things" in this passage are so comprehensive in scope as to include any extraterrestrial intelligent beings that may exist elsewhere in the universe.[42] Within the framework of the apostle's Christology, such beings would be understood as being created by the preexistent Christ (Col 1:16), ultimately for the purpose of manifesting his divine glory and authority (cf. v. 16), being maintained in their moment-by-moment existence by Christ (v. 17), and being reconciled (or pacified, subjugated) to God through the blood of Christ shed on the cross (v. 20). This one, completed event on earth (the cross) has a redemptive impact that is not limited to the human, terrestrial sphere but in fact extends throughout the universe, bringing back into relationship with God *all things* on earth or in heaven.

If the question arose regarding how more specifically the relationship of Christ's atoning work to the "reconciliation" of any alienated extraterrestrials might be understood, an extension of the concept of "federal headship" in traditional Reformed covenant theology could provide an appropriate framework. In the Westminster Confession of Faith (1647), for example, chapter 8

---

[41]O'Brien, *Colossians and Philemon,* p. 56. So also F. F. Bruce: With respect to the rebellious spiritual powers, "reconciliation applied to them means more of what is understood as pacification, the imposing of peace, something brought about by conquest. There is thus a close association between the portrayal of Christ as Reconciler in the Christ hymn [Col. 1:15-20] and the portrayal of Christ as Conqueror elsewhere [2:15] in the letter" (F. F. Bruce, "Christ as Conqueror and Reconciler," *Bibliotheca Sacra* 141 [1984]: 293).

[42]One would have to qualify the statement of Rodney Clapp in "Extraterrestrial Intelligence and Christian Wonder," *Christianity Today* 27, no. 7 (1983): 10: "The Bible concerns the human species, and we need not apologize that it addresses 'only' humans." In light of Colossians 1:15-20 it would be more accurate to say that while the biblical doctrine of reconciliation is primarily concerned with humans, it is not limited exclusively to humans.

speaks of "Christ the Mediator," stating that Christ in his sacrifice of himself "fully satisfied the justice of his Father, and purchased . . . reconciliation . . . for all those whom the Father hath given him." The Confession further states that the redemptive benefits of the death of Christ were not limited by time but were "communicated unto the elect, in all ages successively from the beginning of the world."[43] If the atonement can be understood as not being limited by time, it can just as readily be understood as not being limited by space or distance. Christ assumed in the incarnation a true and complete human nature that he might represent humankind as the covenant head of a redeemed people (Rom 5:12-21; 1 Cor 15:45-49). By extension, it could be postulated that God designated the human nature of *Homo sapiens* to represent the nature of all sentient, embodied beings. God is free in his sovereignty to impute the merits of the death of Christ not only to elect humans but to any "elect" beings whatsoever.[44]

The conclusion of this argument, then, is that the Christology of Colossians 1:15-20 makes it unnecessary to postulate additional incarnations or atonements in order to conceptualize the possible reconciliation of any alienated extraterrestrials elsewhere in the universe. The once-for-all incarnation and death of Christ on the cross has already provided the basis for such a reconciliation (vv. 19-20). This conclusion is consistent with the earlier opinions of Aquinas, Vorilong, Chalmers and Milne but is based on a more developed exegetical argument from biblical theology.

Finally, it can be seen that this line of argument addresses the challenge to Christian theology posed over two centuries ago by Thomas Paine. The author of *The Age of Reason* concluded incorrectly that modern discoveries of the universe's vast dimensions made the biblical scheme of redemption outmoded and untenable. Had Paine given closer attention to the capacious Christology and cosmology of Colossians 1:15-20, he would have discovered there a cosmic redemption, an atonement by Christ in which God had chosen "to reconcile to himself *all things*, whether . . . on earth . . . or in heaven, by making peace through his blood, shed on the cross." In modern cosmology, to be sure, the earth no longer occupies a central place spatially. But spiritually, in a post-Hubble universe, when that enlarged universe is viewed in the light of Paul's

---

[43]Westminster Confession of Faith (1647) 8.5-6; in Philip Schaff, ed., *The Creeds of the Evangelical Protestant Churches* (London: Hodder & Stoughton, 1877), p. 621.

[44]Neither this hypothesis nor the prior discussion of Colossians 1:20 should be construed as an argument for universalism or "universal salvation."

cosmic Christology, the place of *Homo sapiens* is if anything more central, since the picture of God's redemptive purposes is seen to be painted on a breathtakingly larger canvas.

10

Cosmic Endgame

Theological Reflections on
Recent Scientific Speculations
on the Ultimate Fate of the Universe

I hope with these lectures," stated Freeman Dyson, a physicist at the Institute for Advanced Study in Princeton, New Jersey, "to hasten the arrival of the day when eschatology, the study of the end of the universe, will be a respectable scientific discipline and not merely a branch of theology."[1] In a seminal and far-ranging set of speculative lectures originally delivered at New York University in 1978, Dyson set out to challenge the prevailing pessimism of scientific opinion concerning the ultimate fate of the physical universe. Boldly extrapolating the known laws of physics into the most remote

---

[1]Freeman J. Dyson, "Time Without End: Physics and Biology in an Open Universe," *Reviews of Modern Physics* 51, no. 3 (1979): 447. For a more recent attempt to project the long-term future of an open universe, see Fred C. Adams and Gregory Laughlin, "A Dying Universe: The Long-Term Fate and Evolution of Astrophysical Objects," *Reviews of Modern Physics* 69 (1997): 337-72. A popular version of the latter article may be found in *Sky and Telescope* 96, no. 2 (August 1998): 32-39. Unlike Dyson, however, Adams and Laughlin remain agnostic on the question whether life and sentience could survive in the far distant future of such an open universe.

reaches of time, he challenged the dominant view that "we have only the choice of being fried in a closed universe or frozen in an open one."[2] Some form of intelligent "life"—perhaps only in the form of a computer-chip-like structure—might be able to continue to exist in the outer darkness and extreme coldness of an unendingly expanding universe, long after *Homo sapiens* and other forms of carbon-based life had perished from the cosmos. Making no apologies for mixing "philosophical speculations with mathematical equations," Dyson boldly disregarded the traditional scientific reluctance to mix scientific analysis with questions of the ultimate purpose and meaning of life.

Dyson was, in effect, issuing an invitation to faith communities to engage in a conversation that would relate religious understandings of the end of the universe to the new scientific "eschatologies." This paper will attempt to reflect theologically on recent scientific attempts like that of Dyson to avoid the pessimistic conclusions about the fate of the universe that have dominated the scientific community since the development of modern thermodynamics and its notion of the "heat death" of the universe. This chapter will attempt to assess the intellectual challenges and the apologetic opportunities for the church's witness in the face of these scientific eschatologies.

The Rise of Modern Scientific Eschatologies

The development of the discipline of thermodynamics in the nineteenth century gave rise to scientific speculations about the ultimate fate of the universe that have continued down to the present day. In a public lecture delivered in 1854 titled "On the Interaction of Natural Forces," Hermann Helmholtz, professor of physics at the University of Berlin, reflected on the implications of the second law of thermodynamics for the very long-term prospects of the human race. The second law, which came to be recognized as one of the fundamental principles of physics, states that in any closed physical system, the amount of energy available for useful work decreases over time. Or stated another way, the amount of *entropy* or disorder in a system tends to increase over time.[3] The useful energy in physical systems inevitably tends to dissipate

---

[2]Ibid., p. 448.

[3]For general introductions to thermodynamics and the second law, see Hans C. Ohanian, *Physics* (New York: W. W. Norton, 1985), pp. 520-25; George B. Arfken et al., *University Physics* (New York: Academic Press, 1984), pp. 444-58; and C. J. Adkins, *An Introduction to Thermal Physics* (Cambridge: Cambridge University Press, 1987). For a more advanced treatment, see Mark W.

or run down, just as a clock, once wound up, will eventually run down. Helm-holtz and other physicists recognized that the universe as a whole is "running down": eventually, over the vast reaches of cosmic time, the sun and all the stars will have exhausted their fuel, and the cosmos will face the unending darkness and cold of the "heat death" of the universe.

According to Helmholtz, "inexorable laws of mechanics" indicate that the store of available energy in the universe must finally be exhausted. The second law of thermodynamics permits the human race "a long but not an endless existence; it threatens us with a day of judgment, the dawn of which is still happily obscured." Eventually the inescapable working of the laws of physics will force the human race to perish and give way to "new and more complete forms, as the lizards and the mammoth have given place to us."[4]

As the nineteenth century progressed, the pessimistic conclusions of the physicists began to influence leaders in other scientific disciplines. Charles Darwin, for example, had, on the basis of his evolutionary views, come to expect greater perfection and progress for the human race over time. The implications of the second law, however, challenged this optimism in a funda-mental way. For Darwin it was an "intolerable thought" that the human race and all sentient beings were inevitably "doomed to complete annihilation" after long-continued ages of slow progress. In his autobiography, begun in 1876 but not first published until 1887, Darwin admitted that it seemed a sci-entific inevitability that "the sun with all the planets will in time grow too cold for life." To those who had a strong faith in the immortality of the human soul, such a prospect might not appear to be so dreadful, but he could not number himself among that company.[5]

In the early decades of the twentieth century the implications of thermody-

Zemansky, *Heat and Thermodynamics,* 5th ed. (New York: McGraw-Hill, 1968), chap. 9, "Entropy," pp. 214-50. A readable discussion of thermodynamics for a general audience, with helpful insights on historical and philosophical dimensions of the subject, is provided by Martin Goldstein and Inge F. Goldstein, *The Refrigerator and the Universe: Understanding the Laws of Energy* (Cambridge, Mass.: Harvard University Press, 1993).

[4]Hermann Helmholtz, *Popular Lectures on Scientific Subjects,* trans. E. Atkinson (London: Long-mans, Green, 1884), pp. 170-71. It was not widely recognized in the nineteenth century, but the second law implied a finite age for the universe: if the available energy was indeed running down, it could not have been running down *forever.* For the attempts of British physicist William Thompson (Lord Kelvin) to use the principles of thermodynamics to calculate an absolute date for the age of the earth, see Joe D. Burchfield, *Lord Kelvin and the Age of the Earth* (Chicago: University of Chicago Press, 1990).

[5]Charles Darwin, *The Autobiography of Charles Darwin, 1809-1882,* ed. Nora Barlow (London: Collins, 1958), p. 92.

namics were communicated to the general public by British astronomers Arthur Eddington and James Jeans. In his Gifford Lectures of 1927, Eddington, professor of astronomy at Cambridge, spoke about the "running down of the universe." "Whoever wishes for a universe which can continue indefinitely in activity," he stated, "must lead a crusade against the second law of thermodynamics." The final fate of the universe, according to Eddington, was a state of "chaotic changelessness." In his view such a fate, while certainly a gloomy prospect, was to be preferred to suggestions that the universe might undergo endless cycles of expansion and collapse. "I would feel more content that the universe, . . . having achieved whatever may be achieved, lapse back into chaotic changelessness, than that its purpose be banalised by continual repetition." To Eddington it seemed "rather stupid to be doing the same thing over and over again."[6] It is worth noting that Eddington's discussion of the second law led him to address questions of meaning and purpose that had generally been excluded from scientific discourse by the positivistic philosophies of science of the nineteenth century.

In a series of popular lectures later published under the title *The Universe Around Us,* Sir James Jeans discussed questions of "beginnings and endings" and the long-term implications of the second law. "Energy cannot run downhill forever," he noted, "And so the universe cannot go on forever. . . . The active life of the universe must cease." In the very far distant future, the result will be "a dead, although possibly warm universe—a 'heat death.' Such is the teaching of modern thermodynamics." In spite of this gloomy conclusion, Jeans was surprisingly optimistic about the prospects of the human race prior to the final end: "a day of almost unthinkable length stretches before us with unimaginable opportunities for accomplishment."[7] For this British astronomer, the ultimately pessimistic implications of thermodynamics were evidently mitigated by a nearer-term optimism growing out of a faith in the powers of modern science and technology.

One of the best-known twentieth-century responses to the gloomy message of thermodynamics is an often-quoted passage in Bertrand Russell's *Why I Am Not a Christian.* Russell summarized the implications of modern science as he understood it for the human future in this way:

---

[6]A. S. Eddington, *The Nature of the Physical World* (Cambridge: Cambridge University Press, 1928), p. 86.
[7]James Jeans, *The Universe Around Us* (Cambridge: Cambridge University Press, 1929), p. 320.

> That man is the product of causes which had no prevision of the end they were achieving; that his origin, his growth, his hopes and fears, his loves and his beliefs, are but the outcome of accidental collocation of atoms; that no fire, no heroism, no intensity of thought and feeling, can preserve an individual life beyond the grave; that all the labors of the ages, all the devotion, all the inspiration, all the noonday brightness of human genius, are destined to extinction in the vast death of the solar system, and the whole temple of Man's achievement must inevitably be buried beneath the debris of a universe in ruins—all these things, if not quite beyond dispute, are yet so nearly certain that no philosophy which rejects them can hope to stand. . . . Only on the firm foundations of unyielding despair, can the soul's habitation henceforth be safely built.

Despite this eloquent expression of scientific and philosophic despair, Russell went on to say that in practice this gloomy scenario would have little impact on the average person's everyday life. No one really worries much about the fate of the universe millions of years into the future; such considerations merely lead you to "turn your attention to other things."[8] It seems for Russell that the only way that modern persons can cope with the gloomy truth that human life must inevitably die out is to live in what psychologists would call a permanent state of avoidance and denial.

Later in the twentieth century the tradition of what might be called "thermodynamic pessimism" was expressed in the writing of the Nobel Prize-winning American physicist Steven Weinberg. In his widely read book of 1977, *The First Three Minutes: a Modern View of the Origin of the Universe,* Weinberg brought to the attention of the general public modern science's attempts to apply methods of elementary particle physics to understanding the universe's development in the very first minutes after the big bang. At the end of this book Weinberg offered personal reflections on the human meaning of the current scientific picture of the origins of the universe and its ultimate fate. It is "almost irresistible," he noted, for human beings to believe that we have a special place in the universe and that human life is not just some "farcical outcome of a chain of accidents reaching back to the first three minutes." It is not easy for human beings to come to grips with the scientific picture of an earth that is just a "tiny part of an overwhelmingly hostile universe" and the prospect that the present universe "faces a future extinction of endless cold or

---

[8]The passage from Russell is quoted in John D. Barrow and Frank J. Tipler, *The Anthropic Cosmological Principle* (Oxford: Clarendon, 1986), p. 167.

intolerable heat." The inevitably gloomy conclusion of this analysis, according to Weinberg, in a much-quoted statement, is that "the more the universe seems comprehensible, the more it also seems pointless."[9]

Weinberg's response to such a scenario differs from Bertrand Russell's strategy of avoidance and denial. There may be no comfort in the results of modern science, but perhaps people may find some solace in the process of research itself. For Weinberg, the very attempt to understand the universe lifts human life above the level of farce and meaninglessness and "gives it some of the grace of tragedy."[10] Human life may have no enduring purpose or meaning, but perhaps it can have the stoical dignity of an honest and scientifically informed self-awareness.

Recent Expressions of Cosmic Optimism

During the final two decades of the twentieth century there were several notable attempts by physicists to challenge the dominant "thermodynamic pessimism" stemming from the nineteenth century.[11] The pioneering effort in this regard was the above-cited series of lectures delivered in 1978 at New York University by Freeman Dyson. Dyson set himself the task of answering the question whether intelligent life can continue to exist indefinitely in an "open" universe that continues to expand and cool forever. In order to proceed with his calculations Dyson had to make a number of assumptions. He predicated an "open" universe, that is, a universe in which the total mass of the cosmos is insufficient to halt through gravitational attraction the expansion begun at the big bang. Dyson had already come to the conclusion that if the universe were "closed," that is, if the cosmic expansion will ultimately halt and the universe finally collapse upon itself in a "big crunch," then life cannot exist forever. In such a case, he reluctantly conceded, "we have no escape from frying." No matter how far the human race might try to burrow itself into the earth to shield itself from the "ever increasing fury" of the

---

[9]Steven Weinberg, *The First Three Minutes* (London: Andre Deutsch, 1977), p. 154.

[10]Ibid., p. 155.

[11]Dyson, "Time Without End"; and Barrow and Tipler, *Anthropic Cosmological Principle*. These technical treatments, together with related issues, are discussed in more popular form in Jamal N. Islam, *The Ultimate Fate of the Universe* (Cambridge: Cambridge University Press, 1983); Frank Close, *End: Cosmic Catastrophe and the Fate of the Universe* (London: Simon & Schuster, 1988); Paul Davies, *The Last Three Minutes: Conjectures About the Fate of the Universe* (London: Weidenfeld & Nicolson, 1994); and Frank J. Tipler, *The Physics of Immortality* (London: Weidenfeld & Nicolson, 1994).

background radiation, we could "only postpone by a few million years our miserable end."[12]

Dyson also assumed (1) that the laws of physics do not change over time and (2) that the relevant laws of physics are already adequately known. With regard to the latter assumption, Dyson was, of course, incorporating the principles of quantum mechanics and discoveries in cosmology such as the evidence for the big bang that were not known by the nineteenth-century thermodynamicists. To make such assumptions seemed reasonable enough, and without them the calculations could hardly proceed. Dyson freely admitted the highly speculative nature of his investigation but argued that it is nevertheless intellectually worthwhile to explore the consequences of known physical laws "as far as we can reach into the past or the future," because such extrapolations of known laws into new territory can lead to the asking of important new questions.[13]

Dyson began his investigation by studying the physical processes that would occur in an expanding universe over very long periods of time. He concluded that in about 10^{14} years all the stars will have exhausted their hydrogen fuel and burned out, finally reaching a cold, dark state as white dwarfs, neutron stars or black holes. After 10^{64} years black holes will have "evaporated" by the emission of heat radiation by the Hawking process. After 10^{65} years, because of a quantum-mechanical effect known as "barrier penetration" (or "quantum tunneling"), the molecules in all remaining solid objects will have moved and rearranged themselves in somewhat random fashion, behaving like the molecules in a liquid, flowing into diffuse, spherical shapes under the influence of gravity. After the incredibly long period of $10^{1,500}$ years, because of nuclear processes, all elements will have decayed or fused into iron. Finally, in the most remote imaginable future, depending on the minimum mass required to form a black hole, all matter will have disappeared into radiation or else last forever in the form of microscopic grains of iron dust.[14]

Having explored the nature of physical processes far into the remotest

---

[12]Dyson, "Time Without End," p. 448. Evidence reported in 2001 appears to indicate that the expansion of the universe is accelerating rather than decelerating and that the universe is indeed open, destined to expand forever: R. Cowen, "Starry Data Support Revved-Up Cosmos," *Science News* 159 (2001): 196.

[13]Dyson, "Time Without End," pp. 449-50.

[14]These results, and others, together with Dyson's detailed calculations and assumptions are found in ibid., pp. 450-53.

future, Dyson turned to the question of the continuance of intelligent life under the extremely cold and dark conditions of an ever-expanding open universe. What forms of sentient life might be able to persist long after *Homo sapiens* and other forms of carbon-based life had become extinct? Answering such a question, of course, involves making certain assumptions about the nature and definition of "life." For the purposes of his calculations, Dyson assumed that the basis of consciousness is not a particular type of matter but rather a particular type of complex *structure,* and that a computer or computerlike structure (such as an organized dust cloud) could be sentient and so considered "alive." Dyson admitted that neither of these assumptions can be known to be true given our present state of knowledge. Proceeding under these assumptions, however, he envisioned a distant future when life would have evolved away from flesh and blood and become embodied in something like a cloud, "a large assemblage of dust grains carrying positive and negative charges, organizing itself and communicating with itself by means of electromagnetic forces."[15]

Having made these assumptions, Dyson proceeded with calculations concerning the energy requirements of such a form of life. This life form would need to maintain an internal temperature greater than that of universal background radiation as the universe continued to expand, and it would need to continue to radiate waste heat into space. He further postulated that the life form would adopt a strategy of "hibernation" in order to conserve energy, with increasingly long periods of "sleep" alternating with shorter and shorter cycles of "wakefulness" as the universe continued to cool and expand into outer darkness. Dyson then calculated that a life form with a cognitive complexity equivalent to that of the present human species could maintain itself forever, needing only about as much energy as the sun radiates in eight hours.[16] By using the technology of analog rather than digital computers, this life cloud

---

[15]Ibid., p. 454. Dyson's discussion of biological processes, from which the following quotations and calculations are drawn, is found on pp. 453-57. It is significant that Dyson works with a rather minimalist model of sentient life, one based on computers and information processing. Of the two processes that biologists would consider essential to the definition of life—metabolism and replication—Dyson focuses only on the former and essentially ignores the latter. His calculations are concerned to show that some future life form might be able to store and metabolize energy indefinitely, without the necessity of reproducing itself.

[16]Dyson deals only with the amount of energy presumably needed to support the life form and does not deal with the "detailed architectural problems" of what physical structures and mechanisms might be able to actually capture this energy from the environment, store it and then use it metabolically.

could enjoy a memory and subjective experience of "endlessly growing capacity." Dyson cheerfully concluded that he had demonstrated the possibility of "a universe of life surviving forever . . . growing without limit in richness and complexity."[17]

Dyson's optimistic vision of the universe's distant future contrasts sharply with the pessimism of Steven Weinberg and the nineteenth-century thermodynamicists. Just how plausible is such a scenario? Apart from strictly quantitative considerations of energy requirements, at the level of "quality of life" considerations the Dyson scenario would seem to leave much to be desired. He assumes that a computer or computerlike structure such as a dust cloud could be sentient; he does not discuss the question whether such a being would also experience the emotional and affective states that we consider essential to a genuine human existence. The human brain—the most complex entity in the known universe—supports such affective states, but could a computer chip or dust cloud maintain the level of internal complexity needed for endless eons of time under the extreme conditions of cold that Dyson envisions? One might easily imagine a "person-in-the-street" reaction to this vision of a computer-chip existence in the outer darkness of a world forever approaching the coldness of absolute zero: "If that's the best that Dyson has to offer, then I don't want it. I would prefer a normal human life—and death—to the 'life everlasting' of the physicists." Indeed, Dyson's vision of the remote future seems to bear more resemblance to the endless cryopreservation of a human body in a persistent vegetative state or to the "outer darkness" of the gospel tradition than to the "abundant life" and "life everlasting" of the Christian eschatological hope.

Such qualitative issues aside, however, Dyson's intellectually daring analysis is worthy of the most serious consideration on its own quantitative terms. Even at this level the proposal appears to be seriously if not fatally flawed. Dyson had admitted that his analysis proceeded with the assumptions that (1) the proton does not decay and (2) black holes of arbitrarily small mass cannot exist.[18] If *either* of these assumptions turns out to be untrue, then matter is unstable, all material objects would disappear leaving only radiation, and the

---

[17]Ibid., p. 459. Dyson also offers calculations (pp. 457-59) that presumably show that such life forms could continue to communicate with each other across the vast reaches of space in an ever-expanding universe, but these calculations will not be considered in the present discussion.
[18]Ibid., pp. 450, 453.

stable structures necessary for life would be impossible.[19]

Furthermore—and this appears to be a fatal flaw in the Dyson proposal—it seems that in his vision of the remotest future the Princeton physicist has failed to adequately take into account a degenerative process that he himself has recognized. As previously noted, on the time scale of $T = 10^{65}$ years, because of the quantum-mechanical effect of barrier penetration, every solid object behaves like a liquid, flowing into a spherical shape like a liquid, its molecules diffusing like the molecules in a water droplet.[20] This means that any physical object—including Dyson's computerlike "life form"—will have its internal structure disorganized, given enough time. To restore the internal order and structure necessary for sentient life would require the expenditure of additional amounts of energy that have not been factored into Dyson's calculations.[21] How could this additional energy be captured, stored and processed in an environment that is approaching absolute zero in temperature?

Furthermore, the life form continues to dissipate waste heat into space even when it "hibernates" in its "sleeping" state. The energy stored by the life form is finite. Even though Dyson's model is based on a "subjective time" experienced by the life form which *seems,* due to a slowed metabolism, to go on forever, in real time the physical processes of the second law of thermodynamics and the degenerative effects of quantum-mechanical barrier penetration continue to operate. A finite store of internal energy that continues to be dissipated into space cannot forever support metabolism in real time; nor can an increasingly dilute store of energy in an ever-expanding space be effectively captured to repair the degenerative forces that inevitably destroy the life form's internal structure. The consequence of this analysis is that Dyson's proposal ultimately fails: the "hibernation" strategy is finally defeated by the inexorable, degenerative effects of the laws of thermodynamics and quantum

---

[19]As of 1998, empirical evidence concerning the stability or decay of the proton was inconclusive. Strictly speaking, if the proton does decay with an expected lifetime on the order of 10^{31} years, as predicted by Grand Unification Theories, not *all* matter would cease to exist: there would still be a plasmalike cosmos consisting of electrons, positrons, neutrinos and photons. Nevertheless, it is difficult to imagine a world in which the stable structures necessary for sentient life could be maintained with such components. In such a case there is the additional difficulty of preventing the electrons and positrons from annihilating one another in bursts of radiation.

[20]Dyson, "Time Without End," p. 452.

[21]This criticism is also raised in an important article by Steven Frautschi, "Entropy in an Expanding Universe," *Science* 217, no. 4560 (August 13, 1982): 599. At the time of writing Frautschi was a professor of physics at Cal Tech in Pasadena.

mechanics. There is no longer sufficient energy available to support even the most minimal level of metabolic activity. Dyson's life form, after the longest eons of a "virtual-reality" existence, finally expires in the heat death and outer darkness of an ever-expanding universe.

Another scientific "eschatology" was presented in John D. Barrow and Frank J. Tipler's *The Anthropic Cosmological Principle*,[22] a major contribution to discussions of the issues of design in the universe and extraterrestrial life. In chapter ten of their book these authors address the question of "the future of the universe." They recognize that the generally prevailing understanding of the implications of the modern scientific worldview is that humankind is an "insignificant accident lost in the immensity of the Cosmos," an "extremely fortuitous accident" unlikely to have occurred elsewhere in the visible universe, and that over the very longest reaches of time "*Homo sapiens* must eventually become extinct."[23]

Barrow and Tipler develop a scenario concerning the ultimate fate of life in a closed universe, one that will finally collapse upon itself in a "big crunch."[24] *Homo sapiens* may be inevitably doomed, but these authors believe that from a behavioral point of view intelligent *machines* can be regarded as persons and that under certain conditions they might be able to survive "forever" under the extreme conditions near the "Final State." These intelligent machines (plasma-like computers?) would be our descendants, transmitting the values of the human race into an arbitrarily distant future.[25]

In a scenario where the boundary between science fact and science fiction becomes very blurred, Barrow and Tipler picture life beginning its expansion

---

[22]See note 8 above. This same general point of view regarding the ultimate fate of the universe is presented in a somewhat more popular form in Frank J. Tipler's highly speculative *The Physics of Immortality: Modern Cosmology, God and the Resurrection of the Dead* (New York: Doubleday, 1994).

[23]Barrow and Tipler, *Anthropic Cosmological Principle*, pp. 613, 615.

[24]Prior to the late 1990s astronomers generally believed that available evidence was insufficient to decide the question whether the universe is closed or open. In one more recent discussion of this issue, on the basis of their reading of evidence from the Hubble space telescope, Carolyn Collins Petersen and John C. Brandt conclude that it is somewhat more likely that "we are constrained to live in [an open] universe that is expanding forever" (Petersen and Brandt, *Hubble Vision: Astronomy with the Hubble Space Telescope* [Cambridge: Cambridge University Press, 1995], p. 229). Cf. evidence reported in 1998 which also appears to favor an open universe, cited in note 12 above. Astronomers now generally believe that the rate of cosmic expansion is actually *accelerating:* see Jeremiah P. Ostriker and Paul J. Steinhart, "The Quintessential Universe," *Scientific American* 284 (January 2001): 46-55.

[25]Barrow and Tipler, *Anthropic Cosmological Principle*, p. 615.

from earth and proceeding to colonize outer space, ultimately encompassing the entire universe, even affecting the dynamic evolution of the cosmos itself. More and more information is processed at ever-faster rates as the universe begins to collapse and to approach the final big-crunch singularity. In terms of *subjective* time experienced by the intelligent machines, it seems that time lasts forever. Before the final Götterdamerung-like collapse is reached, these machines attain what Barrow and Tipler call the "Omega Point," where life has gained control of all matter, has expanded into all universes that are logically possible and will have stored an infinite amount of information—including every bit of information that it is logically possible to know. With life's having achieved these godlike attributes, Barrow and Tipler modestly conclude that "this is the end."[26]

This emphatically Promethean vision of an aggressively expanding life contrasts starkly with Dyson's minimalist vision of hibernating life hanging on by the slenderest of threads in an ever-expanding, cold, dark universe. How much scientific plausibility does the Barrow-Tipler scenario have?

One reviewer of Barrow and Tipler's work, astronomer and physicist William Press of Harvard's Center for Astrophysics, acknowledges the book's considerable and valuable scientific and historical exposition but also points to its serious weaknesses. There is a distressing amount of "mathematical flim-flam," according to Press, "of precise results in a manner designed to mislead less-mathematical readers," leading them to jump to the authors' nonmathematical conclusions.[27] Like an inverted pyramid, the conclusions of Barrow and Tipler all too often represent very broad and sweeping generalizations supported by a rather narrow base of empirical data.

Another reviewer, Fred W. Hallberg, has pointed out that the Barrow-Tipler scenario is based on a chain of nine assumptions, each of which is quite debatable on empirical grounds. Some of these assumptions are that life and consciousness are inherently expansive and would want to colonize the universe; that computers preprogrammed to replicate themselves could actually be built; that digital computers could actually be conscious beings; that there would be a continuous upward trend in disposable income for future intelligent beings to afford the project of intergalactic colonization;

---

[26]Ibid., pp. 675-77: the end of their book, and the end (final state) of life in the universe.
[27]William H. Press, "A Place for Teleology?" *Nature* 320 (March 27, 1986): 315.

that future life could actually be embodied in the form of plasmas or energy fields rather than the molecular structures of the present; that these beings could actually maintain their metabolisms by using exotic sources of gravitational energy as the universe approached its final fiery collapse.[28] Not one of these assumptions is known to be true, and if even *one* of them were false, then the entire Barrow-Tipler scenario of life in the remotest future would collapse.

One of the critical assumptions made by Barrow and Tipler is that life could in fact maintain itself under the conditions of extreme heat that would characterize the universe approaching the final state. One is led to agree with the simple conclusion of Jamal Islam, that there "is very little hope for life of any kind surviving the big crunch in a closed universe."[29] This critical assumption has been subjected to a devastating critique by G. F. R. Ellis and D. H. Coule. There is simply no known physical theory that can support the idea that the complex hierarchical structures necessary for life (or a computer) could be maintained under the intense conditions prevailing near the final state. Any such structures would be torn apart by intense background radiation in a fraction of a second; any computerlike structure would be burned up, torn apart and melted down into its component parts. The complex structures needed for life could not avoid being buffeted "by photons, electrons, positrons, quarks, and heavier particles at MeV [millions of electron volts] energies and beyond."[30] The Barrow-Tipler scenario inevitably fails as "life" is vaporized in the unspeakable heat of a universe in its final collapse.

---

[28]Fred W. Hallberg, "Barrow and Tipler's Anthropic Cosmological Principle," *Zygon* 23, no. 2 (1988): 147-51. Hallberg points out that Barrow and Tipler seem to be inspired by the evolutionary speculations of the French Jesuit Pierre Teilhard de Chardin, *The Phenomenon of Man* (1959): Teilhard envisions life moving toward an "Omega Point" of higher cosmic consciousness. The Barrow-Tipler thesis is also severely criticized by W. R. Stoeger and G. F. R. Ellis, "A Response to Tipler's Omega-Point Theory" (Frank J. Tipler, *The Physics of Immortality* [New York: Doubleday, 1994], a further extension of the Barrow-Tipler position of 1986), *Science and Christian Belief* 7, no. 2 (1995): 163-72: in terms of its major elements, the theory "is not testable even in principle, either scientifically or theologically—certainly not relative to its key conclusions" (p. 167).

[29]Islam, *Ultimate Fate of the Universe,* p. 114. Islam also raises the perceptive question, "Can intelligent beings survive indefinitely the social conflicts . . . that beset [modern] society?" (p. 134). The Barrow-Tipler thesis seems to naively expect that beings in the far distant future will not be afflicted with the wars, violence, crime and other socially destructive behaviors that have plagued all known societies from the dawn of history.

[30]G. F. R. Ellis and D. H. Coule, "Life at the End of the Universe?" *General Relativity and Gravitation* 26, no. 7 (1994): 738.

Some Concluding Theological Reflections

This analysis has shown, then, that at the end of the day, the attempts by Dyson, Barrow and Tipler to overcome the "thermodynamic pessimism" of the nineteenth century do not succeed. The inexorable working of the laws of physics, when extrapolated into the most remote reaches of time, provides no reasonable hope that sentient life can exist forever. Steven Weinberg's 1977 conclusion seems substantially correct: the final destiny of intelligent life[31] is to be "fried" in a closed universe or frozen in an open one. Despite the revolutionary scientific discoveries that have occurred since the nineteenth century—special and general relativity, quantum mechanics, the expanding universe of big-bang cosmology—the fundamental scientific outlook is still the same; thermodynamic pessimism finally prevails.[32]

From a theological perspective, recent scientific eschatologies are significant even though they are not convincing on purely scientific grounds. The work of Dyson, Barrow and Tipler could be seen as expressions at a particular historical period dominated by the scientific imagination of the perennial human search for transcendence. From the perspective of Christian theology, it is to be expected that human beings made in the image of God will seek in any culture and historical epoch to transcend the determinisms of circumstance and the iron necessities of physical law. Centuries ago St. Augustine expressed this irrepressible desire for transcendence, an implication of humankind's creation as *imago Dei,* in the well-known words of his *Confessions:* "Thou hast made us for Thyself, and our heart is restless until it rests in Thee."[33] The search for a scientifically based immortality is one form that the human quest for transcendence can take at the present stage of history.

Further, the unsuccessful attempts by Dyson, Tipler and Barrow to establish secular versions of eternal life provide yet another illustration of the wisdom of seeing the relationship of science and Christian faith as involving *complementarity* rather than competition or dominance. That is to say, science and Christian faith inhabit a common universe and claim to know realities

---

[31] Apart, of course, from the possibility of divine intervention—a possibility not entertained from Steven Weinberg's naturalistic standpoint.

[32] This is also the conclusion of Martin and Inge Goldstein, *Refrigerator and the Universe,* p. 388: "So it appears that in spite of the new insights of quantum mechanics and relativity, the grim inference for the future drawn from the second law in the nineteenth century is not far wrong."

[33] Augustine, *Confessions,* trans. Vernon J. Bourke (Washington, D.C.: Catholic University of America Press, 1953), 1.1.

beyond the self, but know their respective realities through different methods and languages and for quite different purposes.[34] In notable turning points in the history of science, such as the Galileo affair in the seventeenth century[35] and the development of modern geology in the late eighteenth and early nineteenth centuries,[36] Christian theologians went beyond the bounds of their proper competence when they attempted to substitute biblical exegesis for empirical research or to impose traditional interpretations of biblical texts regarding natural matters on scientists. If church leaders were tempted to engage in "cognitive imperialism" in the centuries when Christendom was socially dominant, perhaps the opposite danger is more real today. The natural sciences are now cognitively dominant in most areas of modern industrialized societies, and religion plays a more marginal role in shaping public life than it did in previous centuries.[37] Dyson, Barrow and Tipler appear to be overstepping proper boundaries when they attempt to use the methods of physics to argue for conclusions that are metaphysical and religious in nature. The history of the science-religion relationship indicates that both disciplines are best served when theologians do not attempt to derive empirical results from their religious texts and when physicists do not presume to settle issues of value, meaning and purpose by the scientific method.

Finally, it might be suggested that these secular eschatologies provide the church with a useful point of contact for communication of the Christian mes-

---

[34]For a helpful discussion of various ways of understanding the relationship between religion and the natural sciences, see Ian G. Barbour, *Religion in an Age of Science* (London: SCM Press, 1990), esp. pp. 3-92, "Ways of Relating Science and Religion."

[35]Jerome J. Langford, *Galileo, Science and the Church,* 3rd ed. (Ann Arbor: University of Michigan Press, 1992) provides a cogent analysis of the historical, scientific and political dimensions of this pivotal controversy. The best analysis of the important role of presuppositions concerning biblical interpretation and theology is found in Richard J. Blackwell, *Galileo, Bellarmine and the Bible* (Notre Dame, Ind.: University of Notre Dame Press, 1991).

[36]Valuable articles by Davis A. Young, "Scripture in the Hands of the Geologists," *Westminster Theological Journal* 49 (1987): 1-34 and 257-304, document the misguided attempts by some Christian workers during the early years of geology to derive geological data directly from the texts of Scripture. It would seem that the "creation science" movement today is repeating the errors of the past by continuing to treat biblical texts as (potentially) primary sources for strictly scientific conclusions. The most comprehensive scholarly account of the history and development of the modern "creation science" movement is provided by Ronald L. Numbers, *The Creationists: The Evolution of Scientific Creationism* (Berkeley: University of California Press, 1992).

[37]The thesis of the "privatization" of religion in modern industrial societies has been developed in various ways by Peter Berger, *The Sacred Canopy: A Sociological Theory of Religion* (Garden City, N.Y.: Doubleday, 1969), and David F. Wells, *God In The Wasteland: The Reality of Truth in a World of Fading Dreams* (Grand Rapids, Mich.: Eerdmans, 1994).

sage in a scientific age.[38] The grim conclusions of physics are complemented by the biblical witness that attests that "God *alone* has immortality" (1 Tim 6:16)[39]—all created beings and all forms of life are perishable and doomed to extinction unless God freely wills, through grace, to bestow on these creatures everlasting life. If, however, the human species is to find ultimate hope[40] of unending life in the face of the history of species extinction on planet earth, that hope cannot be realistically supplied by the laws of physics. In the face of the pessimism and ultimate hopelessness implied by the inexorable laws of thermodynamics, Christian faith can point modern persons to the resurrection of Jesus Christ, in which God has redemptively transcended the forces of disintegration and death and "brought life and immortality to light through the gospel" (2 Tim 1:10). For Christian faith, the grim prospects of the universe's heat death are transcended by the omnipotent power of God attested in the resurrection and by the hope of a cosmos that will finally be transformed and liberated from its bondage to decay (Rom 8:21-22; Rev 21:1).

---

[38]The concept of a "point of contact" in the culture for the Christian message has been discussed, for example, by Helmut Thielicke, *The Evangelical Faith: v. I: Prolegomena: The Relation of Theology to Modern Thought Forms,* trans. Geoffrey W. Bromiley (Grand Rapids, Mich.: Eerdmans, 1974), pp. 39, 139, 144ff. See also the discussion in a previous theological era by Paul Tillich of his "method of correlation" ("The method of correlation explains the contents of the Christian faith through existential questions and theological answers in mutual interdependence") and "apologetic theology" ("Apologetic theology . . . answers the question implied in the 'situation' in the power of the eternal message, and with the means provided by the situation whose questions it answers") in Paul Tillich, *Systematic Theology: Three Volumes in One* (Chicago: University of Chicago Press, 1967), 1:6, 60.

[39]The fossil record shows that in the history of life on earth, extinction is the rule and not the exception (David M. Raup, *Extinction: Bad Genes or Bad Luck?* [New York: W. W. Norton, 1991]). The average life span of a species in the fossil record is on the order of four million years.

[40]In recent Protestant theology the theme of hope has been most systematically developed by Jürgen Moltmann, *Theology of Hope: On the Ground and the Implications of a Christian Eschatology,* trans. James W. Leitch (London: SCM Press, 1967). For Moltmann hope is "the foundation and the mainspring of theological thinking as such," and the resurrection of Christ is not only a "consolation in a life . . . doomed to die, but it is God's contradiction of suffering and death" (pp. 19, 21). In a secular context, the importance of a future hope as a critical factor in the experience of many who survived the Nazi death camps is documented in the fascinating work of Viennese psychiatrist Viktor E. Frankl, *Man's Search for Meaning: An Introduction to Logotherapy* (Boston: Beacon, 1962). The story of how the Christian church and its message provided a sense of hope to many pagans amidst the growing pessimism of late antiquity is documented in E. R. Dodds, *Pagan and Christian in an Age of Anxiety* (Cambridge: Cambridge University Press, 1965), focusing on the period from Marcus Aurelius to Constantine.

Epilogue

In his 1871 inaugural lecture at the University of Cambridge the great physicist James Clerk Maxwell, expressing a mood prevalent at the time, suggested that about the only real work left to scientists would be to measure the fundamental constants of nature to a few more decimal places. Maxwell could not have anticipated the explosion of scientific discoveries in the century to come—atomic radiation, quantum theory, special and general relativity, the big bang—that were to fundamentally alter the way we understand the universe. The frontiers of science expanded beyond the wildest dreams of nineteenth-century scientists. Philosophers and theologians are still struggling to understand the implications of these discoveries. The twenty-first century promises to be no less filled with paradigm-shattering discoveries. This collection of essays has been a modest attempt to reflect on some of the more important scientific discoveries of the twentieth century in the light of Christian faith.

Participants in today's science and religion dialogue are fortunate to be working in a new climate of intellectual openness that has largely moved beyond the "warfare" or "conflict" model popularized in the nineteenth century by John Draper, *A History of the Conflict Between Science and Religion* (1874) and Andrew Dickson White, *A History of the Warfare of Science with Theology and Christendom* (1896). While not denying the reality of conflict in this history, especially in the controversies surrounding Galileo and Darwin, historians of science now underscore the complex and richly nuanced nature of the science-religion relationship, stressing the vital contributions of a Christian worldview to the rise of modern science, and the broad variety of ways the Christian community responded to new scientific discoveries. Scientist-theologians such as John Polkinghorne and Arthur Peacocke emphasize the *complementary* ways of knowing the world represented by science and religion and advocate "new-style natural theologies" that seek not to "prove" the existence of God but to show the coherence of faith and scientific knowledge within the multiple dimensions of human experience.

Other broader cultural trends have added to the new interest in more positive forms of the science-religion dialogue. The mushroom clouds of Hiroshima and Nagasaki underscored the realization in the minds of many that modern physics could supply the knowledge to build an atomic bomb but could not supply the ethical principles to govern its use. The Human Genome Project and genetic research raise questions such as, Should we clone human beings—if we are able? Such questions cannot be answered by the scientific method. Reflective scientists, who realize that science gives humankind enormous power over nature but not the moral principles to govern that power, have as a result been more open to conversations with ethicists and theologians on such matters.

In more recent years the science-religion conversation has been complicated by postmodern/feminist attacks on the objectivity of science. From this point of view, modern science, largely the province of white European and American males, is not an objective, value-free enterprise but a socially constructed one that has been used to oppress women, non-Western cultures and the earth. While not denying the socially located nature of science, this collection of essays has been written from the point of view that science does indeed give valid though not exhaustive truth about the world and thus should be defended and appreciated by Christians and other faith communities.

If there is an overarching message to emerge from these essays, perhaps it is a message of *humility*. Some of the more important scientific discoveries of the twentieth century pointed to the fundamental limits humanity faces in its efforts to know and control the world. The special theory of relativity implies that human beings cannot transmit messages to one another faster than the speed of light; the laws of physics place a fundamental "speed limit" on our ability to communicate. In quantum mechanics, the Heisenberg uncertainty principle teaches that our knowledge of subatomic reality is inherently limited: we can never know simultaneously, with unlimited precision, both the momentum and the location of a given subatomic particle.

The work of logician Kurt Gödel demonstrated that all complex mathematical systems are themselves inherently incomplete. Discoveries in the field of chaos theory have shown that our ability to predict the future states of complex physical systems (such as the weather) is inherently limited. The Enlightenment dream of a perfectly predictable clockwork universe has been shattered by deeper scientific understandings of how the world really works. A big-bang universe, now believed to be accelerating in its rate of expansion, humbles us as we contemplate its vastness and complexity.

The message of humility implied by these scientific discoveries is deeply consistent with the message of faith. Humanity has a fundamental need of humility in the face of an Infinite God and the vastness of the universe. The frontiers of science can, for a believer, truly become frontiers of faith. It is indeed an exciting time to ponder God's universe in the light of a biblical and Christian faith.

Bibliography

Chapter 1: Genesis 1:1 and Big Bang Cosmology

Anderson, Bernard W., ed. *Creation in the Old Testament*. Philadelphia: Fortress, 1984.

Aquinas, Thomas. *Summa Theologica*. Translated by Fathers of the English Dominican Province. London: R. & G. Washbourne, 1912.

————. *Summa Contra Gentiles,* book 2, *Creation*. Translated by James F. Anderson. Notre Dame, Ind.: University of Notre Dame Press, 1975.

Aristotle. *On the Heavens*. Translated by W. K. C. Guthrie. Loeb Classical Library. Cambridge, Mass.: Harvard University Press, 1939.

Atkatz, David, and Heinz Pagels. "Origin of the Universe as a Quantum Tunneling Event." *Physical Review* D25, no. 8 (1982): 2065-73.

Augustine. *Confessions*. Translated by W. Watts. Cambridge, Mass.: Harvard University Press, 1946.

Barbour, Ian G. *Religion in an Age of Science*. London: SCM Press, 1990.

Barrow, John D. *Theories of Everything: The Quest for Ultimate Explanation*. Oxford: Clarendon, 1991.

————, and Joseph Silk. *The Left Hand of Creation: The Origin and Evolution of the Expanding Universe*. London: Heinemann, 1983.

Barth, Karl. *Church Dogmatics* 3/1. The Doctrine of Creation. Translated by J. W. Edwards, O. Bussey and H. Knight. Edinburgh: T & T Clark, 1958.

Blacker, Carmen, and Michael Loewe, eds. *Ancient Cosmologies*. London: George Allen & Unwin, 1975.

Bondi, Herman, and Thomas Gold. "The Steady-State Theory of the Expanding Universe." *Monthly Notices of the Royal Astronomical Society* 108 (1948): 252-70.

Brout, R., et al. "The Creation of the Universe as a Quantum Phenomenon." *Annals of Physics* 115 (1978): 78-106.

Brunner, Emil. *The Christian Doctrine of Creation and Redemption*. Translated by Olive Wyon. London: Lutterworth, 1952.

Bultmann, Rudolf. *Jesus Christ and Mythology*. New York: Charles Scribner's Sons, 1958.

Cassuto, Umberto. *A Commentary on the Book of Genesis,* part 1. Jerusalem: Magnes,

1961.

Copan, Paul. "Is *Creatio ex Nihilo* a Post-biblical Invention? An Examination of Gerhard May's Proposal." *Trinity Journal* 17, n.s. (1996): 77-93.

Craig, William Lane, and Quentin Smith. *Theism, Atheism and Big Bang Cosmology.* Oxford: Clarendon, 1993.

Dalley, Stephanie. *Myths from Mesopotamia: Creation, the Flood, Gilgamesh and Others.* New York: Oxford University Press, 1989.

Davies, Paul. *God and the New Physics.* London: J. M. Dent & Sons, 1983.

————. *The Last Three Minutes: Conjectures About the Ultimate Fate of the Universe.* London: Weidenfeld & Nicolson, 1994.

De Vega, H. J., and N. Sanchez. *String Theory, Quantum Cosmology and Quantum Gravity.* Singapore: World Scientific Publishing, 1987.

Dicke, R. H., et al. "Cosmic Black-Body Radiation." *Astrophysical Journal* 142 (1965): 414-19.

Drees, Willem. *Beyond the Big Bang: Quantum Cosmologies and God.* LaSalle, Ill.: Open Court, 1990.

Eichrodt, Walther. *Theology of the Old Testament,* vol. 2. London: SCM Press, 1967.

Ehrhardt, Arnold. *The Beginning: A Study in the Greek Philosophical Approach to the Concept of Creation from Anaximander to St. John.* Manchester, U.K.: Manchester University Press, 1968.

Feldman, Seymour. "Creation in Philosophy." In *Encyclopedia Judaica* 5:1066. Jerusalem: Keter, 1972.

Freedman, H., and Maurice Simon, trans. *Midrash Rabbah: Genesis 1.* London: Soncino, 1939.

Gilkey, Langdon. "Cosmology, Ontology and the Travail of Biblical Language." *Journal of Religion* 41 (1961): 194-205.

Gribbin, John. *In Search of the Big Bang: Quantum Physics and Cosmology.* London: Heinemann, 1986.

Hahm, David E. *The Origins of Stoic Cosmology.* Columbus: Ohio State University Press, 1977.

Hartle, J. B., and Stephen W. Hawking. "Wave Function of the Universe." *Physical Review* D (1983): 2960-75.

Hasel, Gerhard F. "Recent Translations of Genesis 1:1: A Critical Look." *Bible Translator* 22, no. 4 (October 1971): 154-67.

————. "The Polemic Nature of the Genesis Cosmology." *Evangelical Quarterly* 46 (1974): 81-102.

Hawking, Stephen W. *A Brief History of Time: From the Big Bang to Black Holes.* London: Bantam, 1988.

————. "The Quantum Theory of the Universe." In *Intersections Between Elementary Particle Physics and Cosmology,* edited by Tsvi Piran and Steven Weinberg, pp. 711-97. Philadelphia: World Scientific Publishing, 1986.

————, and Roger Penrose. "The Singularities of Gravitational Collapse and Cosmology." *Proceedings of the Royal Society of London* A314 (1970): 529-48.

Heidel, Alexander. *The Babylonian Genesis: The Story of Creation.* Chicago: University of Chicago Press, 1951.

Hirsch, Edward. "In the Beginning: A New Translation of the Hebrew Bible." *Religious Studies News* 11, no. 1 (February 1996): 1.

Horgan, John. "Particle Metaphysics." *Scientific American* 270, no. 2 (February 1994): 70-78.

Hoyle, Fred. "A New Model for the Expanding Universe." *Monthly Notices of the Royal Astronomical Society* 108 (1948): 372-82.

Humbert, P. "Trois notes sur Genese I." In *Interpretationes ad Vetus Testamentum*, pp. 85-96. Oslo: Fabritius & Sonner, 1955.

Isham, C. J. "Creation of the Universe as a Quantum Process." In *Physics, Philosophy and Theology: A Common Quest for Understanding*, edited by Robert J. Russell, William R. Stoeger and George V. Coyne, pp. 375-405. Vatican City: Vatican Observatory, 1988.

Jaki, Stanley L. *God and the Cosmologists.* Edinburgh: Scottish Academic Press, 1989.

Josephus. *Josephus,* vol. 4. Translated by Henry Thackeray. Loeb Classical Library. Cambridge, Mass.: Harvard University Press, 1930.

Kant, Immanuel. *Critique of Pure Reason.* Translated by Norman Kemp Smith. London: Macmillan, 1963.

Lambert, W. G. "A New Look at the Babylonian Background of Genesis." *Journal of Theological Studies* 16 (1965): 287-300.

Lightman, Alan. *Ancient Light: Our Changing View of the Universe.* Cambridge, Mass.: Harvard University Press, 1991.

———, and Roberta Brewer. *Origins: The Lives and Worlds of Modern Cosmologists.* Cambridge, Mass.: Harvard University Press, 1990.

Lindberg, David C. *The Beginnings of Western Science.* Chicago: University of Chicago Press, 1992.

———, and Ronald L. Numbers, eds. *God and Nature: Historical Essays on the Encounter Between Christianity and Science.* Berkeley: University of California Press, 1986.

Linde, A. D. *Inflation and Quantum Cosmology.* New York: Academic Press, 1990.

Lindley, David. *The End of Physics: The Myth of a Unified Theory.* New York: Basic-Books, 1993.

Longair, Malcolm S. *Our Evolving Universe.* Cambridge: Cambridge University Press, 1996.

May, Gerhard. *Creatio ex Nihilo: The Doctrine of "Creation out of Nothing" in Early Christian Thought.* Edinburgh: T & T Clark, 1994.

Mukerjee, Madhusree. "Explaining Everything." *Scientific American* 274, no. 1 (January 1996): 72-78.

Murphy, Nancey. *Theology in the Age of Scientific Reasoning.* Ithaca, N.Y.: Cornell University Press, 1990.

Narlikar, Jayant V. *Introduction to Cosmology.* 2nd ed. Cambridge: Cambridge University Press, 1993.

O'Flaherty, Wendy Doniger. *Hindu Myths: A Sourcebook Translated from the Sanskrit.* New York: Penguin, 1975.

Pagels, Heinz R. *Perfect Symmetry: The Search for the Beginning of Time.* London: Michael Joseph, 1985.

Pannenberg, Wolfhart. *Theology and the Philosophy of Science.* Translated by Francis McDonagh. London: Darton, Longman & Todd, 1976.

Peacocke, Arthur R., ed. *The Sciences and Theology in the Twentieth Century.* Stocksfield, U.K.: Oriel, 1981.

Penzias, A. A., and R. W. Wilson. "A Measurement of Excess Antenna Temperature at 4080 Mc/s." *Astrophysical Journal* 142 (1965): 419-21.

Philo. *Philo,* vol. 1. Translated by F. H. Colson and G. H. Whitaker. Loeb Classical Library. Cambridge, Mass.: Harvard University Press, 1929.

Plato. *Timaeus.* In *Plato,* vol. 9. Translated by R. G. Bury. Loeb Classical Library. Cambridge, Mass.: Harvard University Press, 1929.

Polkinghorne, John. "Contemporary Interactions Between Science and Theology." *Modern Believing* 36, no. 4 (October 1995): 33-38.

Rabinowitz, Louis. "Rabbinic View of Creation." In *Encyclopedia Judaica* 5:1063. Jerusalem: Keter, 1972.

Rad, Gerhard von. *Genesis: A Commentary.* Translated by John H. Marks. London: SCM Press, 1961.

Roos, Matts. *Introduction to Cosmology.* New York: John Wiley & Sons, 1994.

Sarna, Nahum. *Understanding Genesis.* New York: Schocken, 1970.

Silk, Joseph. *The Big Bang.* New York: W. H. Freeman, 1989.

Skinner, John. *A Critical and Exegetical Commentary on Genesis.* 2nd ed. Edinburgh: T & T Clark, 1930.

Speiser, E. A. *Genesis.* Anchor Bible. Garden City, N.Y.: Doubleday, 1964.

Tanner, Norman P., ed. *Decrees of the Ecumenical Councils.* Vol. 1, *Nicaea I to Lateran V.* London: Sheed & Ward, 1990.

Tillich, Paul. *Systematic Theology,* vol. 1. London: Nisbet, 1951.

Trefil, James S. *The Moment of Creation: Big Bang Physics from Before the First Millisecond to the Present Universe.* New York: Macmillan, 1984.

Tryon, Edward P. "Is the Universe a Vacuum Fluctuation?" *Nature* 264 (December 14, 1973): 396-97.

Tsumura, David T. *The Earth and the Waters in Genesis 1 and 2: A Linguistic Investigation.* Sheffield, U.K.: Sheffield Academic Press, 1989.

Urbach, Ephraim. *The Sages: Their Concepts and Beliefs.* Translated by Israel Abrahams. Jerusalem: Magnes, 1979.

Vawter, Bruce. *On Genesis: A New Reading.* London: Geoffrey Chapman, 1977.

Vilenkin, Alexander. "Creation of Universes from Nothing." *Physics Letters* B117 (1982): 25-28.

Waltke, Bruce K. "The Creation Account in Genesis 1:1-3." *Bibliotheca Sacra* 132 (1975): 216-28.

Weinberg, Steven. *Dreams of a Final Theory.* London: Hutchinson Radius, 1993.

Wenham, Gordon. *Genesis 1-15*. Waco, Tex.: Word, 1987.

Westermann, Claus. *Genesis 1-11: A Commentary.* Translated by John J. Scullion. London: SPCK, 1984.

Wolfson, Harry A. *Philo: Foundations of Religious Philosophy.* Cambridge, Mass.: Harvard University Press, 1947.

Young, Davis A. "Scripture in the Hands of the Geologists." *Westminster Theological Journal* 49 (1987): 1-34, 257-304.

Yourgrau, Wolfgang, and Allen D. Beck, eds. *Cosmology, History and Theology.* New York: Plenum, 1977.

Zel'dovich, Ya B., and I. D. Novikov. *The Structure and Evolution of the Universe.* Translated by Leslie Fishbone. Chicago: University of Chicago Press, 1983.

Chapter 2: Quantum Indeterminacy and the Omniscience of God

Aquinas, Thomas. *Summa Theologiae.* Vol. 4, *Knowledge in God.* Blackfriars ed. Translated by Thomas Gornall. New York: McGraw-Hill, 1964.

Augustine. *Confessions.* Translated by W. Watts. Cambridge, Mass.: Harvard University Press, 1946.

Barbour, Ian G. *Religion in an Age of Science.* London: SCM Press, 1990.

Craig, William Lane. *Divine Foreknowledge and Human Freedom: The Coherence of Theism—Omniscience.* Leiden, Netherlands: E. J. Brill, 1991.

———. *The Problem of Divine Foreknowledge of Future Contingents from Aristotle to Suarez.* Leiden, Netherlands: E. J. Brill, 1988.

———, and Quentin Smith. *Theism, Atheism and Big Bang Cosmology.* Oxford: Clarendon, 1993.

Cushing, James T., and Ernan McMullin, eds. *Philosophical Consequences of Quantum Theory: Reflections on Bell's Theorem.* Notre Dame, Ind.: University of Notre Dame Press, 1989.

Davies, P. C. W. *The Ghost in the Atom.* Cambridge: Cambridge University Press, 1985.

D'Espagnat, Bernard. *Conceptual Foundations of Quantum Mechanics.* Menlo Park, Calif.: W. A. Benjamin, 1971.

——— "The Quantum Theory and Reality." *Scientific American* 241 (1979): 128-40.

———. *Reality and the Physicist: Knowledge, Duration and the Quantum World.* Cambridge: Cambridge University Press, 1989.

Gale, Richard M. *On the Nature and Existence of God.* Cambridge: Cambridge University Press, 1991.

Garrigou-Lagrange, R. *God: His Existence and Nature.* Translated by Dom Bede Rose. St. Louis: B. Herder, 1934.

Glanz, James. "Measurements Are the Only Reality, Say Quantum Tests." *Science* 270 (1995): 1439-40.

Grunbaum, Adolf. *Philosophical Problems of Space and Time.* Dordrecht, Netherlands: D. Reidel, 1973.

Hasker, William. *God, Time and Knowledge.* Ithaca, N.Y.: Cornell University Press,

1989.

Herbert, Nick. *Quantum Reality: Beyond the New Physics.* London: Rider, 1985.

Honner, John. *The Description of Nature: Niels Bohr and the Philosophy of Quantum Physics.* Oxford: Clarendon, 1987.

Jammer, Max. *The Philosophy of Quantum Mechanics.* New York: John Wiley & Sons, 1974.

Kvanvig, Jonathan L. *The Possibility of an All-Knowing God.* London: Macmillan, 1986.

Molina, Luis. *On Foreknowledge.* Translated by Alfred J. Freddoso. Ithaca, N.Y.: Cornell University Press, 1988.

Morris, Thomas V., ed. *The Concept of God.* Oxford: Oxford University Press, 1987.

Omnes, Roland. *The Interpretation of Quantum Mechanics.* Princeton, N.J.: Princeton University Press, 1994.

Owen, H. P. *Christian Theism: A Study of Its Basic Principles.* Edinburgh: T&T Clark, 1984.

Padgett, Alan G. "God and Time: Toward a New Doctrine of Divine Timeless Eternity." *Religious Studies* 25 (1989): 209-15.

Peacocke, Arthur. *Theology for a Scientific Age.* 2nd ed. London: SCM Press, 1993.

Pearcey, Nancy R., and Charles B. Thaxton. *The Soul of Science: Christian Faith and Natural Philosophy.* Wheaton, Ill.: Crossway, 1994.

Peres, Asher. *Quantum Theory: Concepts and Methods.* Dordrecht, Netherlands: Kluwer Academic, 1993.

Pike, Nelson. *God and Timelessness.* London: Routledge & Kegan Paul, 1970.

Plantinga, Alvin. *The Nature of Necessity.* Oxford: Clarendon, 1974.

Polkinghorne, John C. *The Quantum World.* London: Longman, 1984.

Pollard, William G. *Chance and Providence: God's Action in a World Governed by Scientific Law.* New York: Charles Scribner's Sons, 1958.

Reichenbach, Hans. *The Philosophy of Space and Time.* Translated by Maria Reichenbach and John Freund. New York: Dover, 1958.

Rohrlich, Fritz. "Facing Quantum Mechanical Reality." *Science* 221 (1983): 1251-55.

Russell, Robert John, Nancey Murphy and Arthur Peacocke, eds. *Chaos and Complexity: Scientific Perspectives on Divine Action.* Vatican City: Vatican Observatory, 1995.

Sklar, Lawrence. *Space, Time and Spacetime.* Berkeley: University of California Press, 1974.

Thomas, Owen C., ed. *God's Activity in the World: The Contemporary Problem.* Chico, Calif.: Scholars Press, 1983.

Torrance, Thomas F. *Space, Time and Incarnation.* Oxford: Oxford University Press, 1969.

─────. *Space, Time and Resurrection.* Edinburgh: Handsell, 1976.

Ward, Keith. *Rational Theology and the Creativity of God.* Oxford: Basil Blackwell, 1982.

Wheeler, John Archibald, and Woiciech H. Zurek, eds. *Quantum Theory and Measure-*

ment. Princeton, N.J.: Princeton University Press, 1983.

Whitrow, G. J. *The Natural Philosophy of Time.* London: Thomas Nelson & Sons, 1961.

Chapter 3: The "Copenhagen" Interpretation of Quantum Mechanics and "Delayed-Choice" Experiments

Armstrong, Brian G. *Calvinism and the Amyraut Heresy: Protestant Scholasticism and Humanism in Seventeenth-Century France.* Madison: University of Wisconsin Press, 1969.

Barth, Karl. *Church Dogmatics.* 2/2, *The Doctrine of God.* Translated and edited by Geoffrey W. Bromiley and Thomas F. Torrance. Edinburgh: T & T Clark, 1957.

Calvin, John. *Concerning the Eternal Predestination of God.* Translated by J. K. S. Reid. London: James Clarke, 1961.

———. *Institutes of the Christian Religion.* Translated by John Allen. Philadelphia: Presbyterian Board of Christian Education, 1936.

Davies, P. C. W., and J. R. Brown. *The Ghost in the Atom: A Discussion of the Mysteries of Quantum Physics.* Cambridge: Cambridge University Press, 1986.

D'Espagnat, Bernard. *Foundations of Quantum Mechanics.* 2nd ed. Reading, Mass.: W. A. Benjamin, 1976.

Edwards, David. *Christian England.* Rev. ed. 3 vols. London: Collins, 1989.

Glanz, James. "Measurements Are the Only Reality, Say Quantum Tests." *Science* 270 (December 1, 1995): 1439-40.

Grunbaum, Adolf. *Philosophical Problems of Space and Time.* Dordrecht, Netherlands: D. Reidel, 1973.

Hellmuth, Thomas, et al. "Delayed-Choice Experiments in Quantum Interference." *Physical Review* A35, no. 6 (March 1987): 2532-40.

Herbert, Nick. *Quantum Reality: Beyond the New Physics.* London: Rider, 1985.

Herzog, T. J., et al. "Complementarity and the Quantum Eraser." *Physical Review Letters* 75 (1995): 3034-37.

Hodge, Charles. *Romans.* 1835; reprint Wheaton, Ill.: Crossway, 1993.

Honner, John. *The Description of Nature: Niels Bohr and the Philosophy of Quantum Physics.* Oxford: Clarendon, 1987.

Jammer, Max. *The Philosophy of Quantum Mechanics.* New York: Wiley, 1974.

Jewett, Paul K. *Election and Predestination.* Grand Rapids, Mich.: Eerdmans, 1985.

Kendall, R. T. *Calvin and English Calvinism to 1649.* Oxford: Oxford University Press, 1979.

Kwiat, P. G., et al. "Observations of a 'Quantum Eraser': A Revival of Coherence in a Two-Photon Interference Experiment." *Physical Review* A45 (1992): 7729-39.

Leenhardt, Franz J. *The Epistle to the Romans.* Translated by Harold Knight. London: Lutterworth, 1961.

Marlow, A. R., ed. *Mathematical Foundations of Quantum Theory.* New York: Academic Press, 1978.

Muller, Richard A. *Christ and the Decree: Christology and Predestination in Reformed*

Theology from Calvin to Perkins. Durham, N.C.: Labyrinth, 1986.

Nicole, Roger. *Moyse Amyraut: A Bibliography with Special Reference to the Controversy on Universal Grace.* New York: Garland, 1981.

Reichenbach, Hans. *The Philosophy of Space and Time.* Translated by Maria Reichenbach and John Freund. New York: Dover, 1958.

Russell, R. J., William Stoeger and George V. Coyne, eds. *Physics, Philosophy and Theology: A Common Quest for Understanding.* Vatican City: Vatican Observatory, 1988.

Schaff, Philip. *The Creeds of Christendom.* 4th ed. New York: Harper & Brothers, 1884.

Torrance, James B. "Strengths and Weaknesses of the Westminster Theology." In *The Westminster Confession in the Church Today,* edited by Alasdair I. C. Herron, pp. 40-53. Edinburgh: St. Andrews Press, 1982.

Torrance, Thomas F. *Space, Time and Incarnation.* Oxford: Oxford University Press, 1969.

———. *Space, Time and Resurrection.* Edinburgh: Handsell, 1976.

———. *Theological Science.* London: Oxford University Press, 1969.

Watson, Andrew. " 'Eraser' Rubs Out Information to Reveal Light's Dual Nature." *Science* 270 (November 10, 1995): 913-14.

Weber, Otto. *Foundations of Dogmatics,* vol. 2. Translated by Darrell L. Gruder. Grand Rapids, Mich.: Eerdmans, 1983.

Wheeler, John A., and Wojciech H. Zurek, eds. *Quantum Theory and Measurement.* Princeton, N.J.: Princeton University Press, 1983.

Whitrow, G. J. *The Natural Philosophy of Time.* London: Thomas Nelson and Sons, 1961.

Chapter 4: Theological Reflections on Chaos Theory

Aquinas, Thomas. *Summa Contra Gentiles.* Book 3, *Providence.* Translated by Vernon J. Bourke. Notre Dame, Ind.: University of Notre Dame Press, 1975.

Bartholemew, D. J. *God of Chance.* London: SCM Press, 1984.

Berry, M. V., et al. "Dynamical Chaos." *Proceedings of the Royal Society* A413 (1987): 1-199.

Chandler, Stuart. "When the World Falls Apart: Methodology for Employing Chaos and Emptiness as Theological Constructs." *Harvard Theological Review* 85 (1992): 467-91.

Crutchfield, James, et al. "Chaos." *Scientific American* 255, no. 6 (December 1986): 38-49.

Dalley, Stephanie. *Myths from Mesopotamia: Creation, the Flood, Gilgamesh and Others.* New York: Oxford University Press, 1989.

Davies, Paul. *The Cosmic Blueprint.* London: Unwin Hyman, 1989.

Dawkins, Richard. *The Blind Watchmaker.* Harlow, U.K.: Longman, 1986.

Ditto, William, and Louis Pecora. "Mastering Chaos." *Scientific American* 269, no. 2 (August 1993): 62-83.

Geach, Peter. *Providence and Evil.* Cambridge: Cambridge University Press, 1977.

Gleick, James. *Chaos: Making a New Science.* London: Abacus, 1993.

Gould, Stephen Jay. *Wonderful Life.* New York: W. W. Norton, 1989.

Hefner, Philip. "God and Chaos: The Demiurge Versus the Urgrund." *Zygon* 19, no. 4 (1984): 469-85.

Heidel, Alexander. *The Babylonian Genesis: The Story of Creation.* Chicago: University of Chicago Press, 1951.

Hodge, Charles. *What Is Darwinism?* New York: Scribner, Armstrong, 1874.

Houghton, J. T. "New Ideas of Chaos in Physics." *Science and Christian Belief* 1 (1989): 41-51.

Kim, Jong Hyun, and John Stringer, eds. *Applied Chaos.* New York: John Wiley & Sons, 1992.

Laplace, Pierre-Simon. *Philosophical Essay on Probabilities.* Translated from 5th French ed. of 1825 by Andrew I. Dole. New York: Springer-Verlag, 1995.

Laskar, Jacques. "Large-Scale Chaos in the Solar System and Planetological Consequences." *Sciences de la terre et des planetes* (Paris), series 2a, 322, no. 3, item 163.

Lichtenberg, A. J., and M. A. Lieberman. *Regular and Stochastic Motion.* New York: Springer-Verlag, 1983.

Lighthill, James. "The Recently Recognized Failure of Predictability in Newtonian Dynamics." *Proceedings of the Royal Society of London* A407 (1986): 35-50.

Lorenz, Edward N. "Deterministic Nonperiodic Flow." *Journal of the Atmospheric Sciences* 20 (1963): 130-41.

Mackay, Donald M. *Science, Chance and Providence.* Oxford: Oxford University Press, 1978.

Mandelbrot, Bernard. *The Fractal Geometry of Nature.* New York: W. H. Freeman, 1977.

May, Robert M., "Simple Mathematical Models with Very Complicated Dynamics." *Nature* 261 (1976): 459-67.

Monod, Jacques. *Chance and Necessity.* London: Collins, 1972.

Moon, Francis C. *Chaotic and Fractal Dynamics: An Introduction for Applied Scientists and Engineers.* New York: John Wiley & Sons, 1992.

Moore, James R. *The Post-Darwinian Controversies.* Cambridge: Cambridge University Press, 1979.

Peacocke, Arthur. *Theology for a Scientific Age.* London: SCM Press, 1993.

Plato. *Timaeus.* In *Plato,* vol. 9. Translated by R. G. Bury. Cambridge, Mass.: Harvard University Press, 1929.

Pollard, William G. *Chance and Providence: God's Action in a World Governed by Scientific Law.* London: Faber and Faber, 1958.

Prigogine, Ilya. *Order out of Chaos: Man's New Dialogue with Nature.* New York: Bantam, 1984.

Quine, W. V. O. "Two Dogmas of Empiricism." *Philosophical Review* 40 (1951): 20-43.

———, and J. S. Ullian. *The Web of Belief.* 2nd ed. New York: Random House, 1978.

Ruelle, David. *Chance and Chaos.* London: Penguin, 1993.

Russell, Robert John, Nancey Murphy and Arthur R. Peacocke, eds. *Chaos and Complexity: Scientific Perspectives on Divine Action.* Vatican City: Vatican Observatory, 1995.

Stewart, Ian. *Does God Play Dice? The Mathematics of Chaos.* Oxford: Basil Blackwell, 1989.

Stines, J. W. "Time, Chaos Theory and the Thought of Michael Polanyi." *Perspectives on Science and Christian Faith* 44 (1992): 220-27.

Swinburne, Richard. *The Existence of God.* Rev. ed. Oxford: Clarendon, 1979; 1991.

Torrance, Thomas F. "God and the Contingent World." *Zygon* 14, no. 4 (1979): 329-38.

Westermann, Claus. *Genesis 1-11: A Commentary.* Translated by John J. Scullion. London: SPCK, 1984.

Chapter 5: Does Gödel's Proof Have Theological Implications?

Alston, William P. *Perceiving God: The Epistemology of Religious Experience.* Ithaca, N.Y.: Cornell University Press, 1991.

Craig, William Lane. *Divine Foreknowledge and Human Freedom: The Coherence of Theism—Omniscience.* Leiden, Netherlands: E. J. Brill, 1991.

Cundy, H. Martyn. "Gödel's Theorem in Perspective." *Science and Christian Belief* 3, no. 1 (April 1991): 35-49.

Cultand, Nigel J. "What Does Gödel Tell Us?" *Science and Christian Belief* 3, no. 1 (1991): 51-55.

Davis, Philip J., and Reuben Hersh. *Descartes' Dream: The World According to Mathematics.* New York: Harcourt Brace Jovanovich, 1986.

Ellington, Mark. *The Integrity of Biblical Narrative: Story in Theology and Proclamation.* Minneapolis: Fortress, 1990.

Gensler, Harry J. *Gödel's Theorem Simplified.* Lanham, Md.: University Press of America, 1984.

Gödel, Kurt. *Collected Works.* Edited by Solomon Feferman. Oxford: Clarendon, 1986.

———. "Über formal unentscheidbare Satze der *Principia mathematica* und verwandter Systeme I." *Monatshefte für Mathematik und Physik* 38 (1931): 173-98.

Good, I. J. "Gödel's Theorem Is a Red Herring." *British Journal for the Philosophy of Science* 19 (1969): 357-58.

Grim, Patrick. "Logic and the Limits of Knowledge and Truth." *Nous* 22 (1988): 341-67.

Hauerwas, Stanley, and Gregory L. Jones, eds. *Why Narrative? Readings in Narrative Theology.* Grand Rapids, Mich.: Eerdmans, 1989.

Heijenoort, J. Van. "Gödel's Theorem." In *Encyclopedia of Philosophy,* edited by Paul Edwards, 3:348-57. New York: Macmillan, 1967.

Heppe, Heinrich. *Reformed Dogmatics, Set Out and Illustrated from the Sources.* Edited by Ernst Bizer; translated by G. T. Thomson. London: Allen & Unwin, 1950.

Hodge, Charles. *Systematic Theology.* 3 vols. New York: Charles Scribner, 1878.

Hofstadter, Douglas R. *Gödel, Escher, Bach.* New York: Basic Books, 1979.

Kadvany, John. "Reflections on the Legacy of Kurt Gödel: Mathematics, Skepticism,

Postmodernism." *Philosophical Forum* 20, no. 3 (1989):161-81.

Kleene, Stephen Cole. *Introduction to Metamathematics.* Amsterdam: North-Holland, 1952.

Lindbeck, George. *The Nature of Doctrine: Religion and Theology.* London: SPCK, 1984.

Lucas, J. R. "Minds, Machines and Gödel." *Philosophy* 36 (1961): 112-27.

————. *The Freedom of the Will.* Oxford: Clarendon, 1970.

Murphy, Nancey. "Scientific Realism and Postmodern Philosophy." *British Journal for the Philosophy of Science* 41 (1990): 291-303.

————. "Postmodern Non-relativism: Imre Lakatos, Theo Meyering and Alasdair MacIntyre." *Philosophical Forum* 27, no. 1 (1995): 37-53.

Nagel, Ernest, and James R. Newman. *Gödel's Proof.* London: Routledge and Kegan Paul, 1959.

Swinburne, Richard. *The Coherence of Theism.* Oxford: Clarendon, 1977.

Toulmin, Stephen. *Cosmopolis.* New York: Free Press, 1990.

Wang, Hao. "Some Facts about Kurt Gödel." *Journal of Symbolic Logic* 43, no. 3 (1981): 653-59.

————. *Reflections on Kurt Gödel.* Cambridge, Mass.: MIT Press, 1987.

Wilder, Raymond J. *Introduction to the Foundations of Mathematics.* New York: John Wiley & Sons, 1952.

Chapter 6: Is "Progressive Creation" Still a Helpful Concept?

Ahlberg, Per E., Jennifer A. Clack and Ervins Luksevics. "Rapid Braincase Evolution Between *Panderichthys* and the Earliest Tetrapods." *Nature* 381 (May 2, 1996): 61-63.

Berry, R. J. "Creation and the Environment." *Science and Christian Belief* 7 (1995): 21-43.

Boardman, Richard S., ed. *Fossil Invertebrates.* London: Blackwell Scientific, 1987.

Burns, George W., and Paul J. Bottino. *The Science of Genetics.* 6th ed. New York: Macmillan, 1989.

Cairns-Smith, A. G. *Genetic Takeover and the Mineral Origins of Life.* Cambridge: Cambridge University Press, 1982.

————. *Seven Clues to the Origin of Life.* Cambridge: Cambridge University Press, 1985.

Carroll, Robert L. "Revealing the Patterns of Macroevolution." *Nature* 381 (May 2, 1996): 19-20.

————. *Vertebrate Paleontology and Evolution.* New York: W. H. Freeman, 1988.

Clarkson, E. N. K. *Invertebrate Paleontology and Evolution.* 2nd ed. London: Allen & Unwin, 1986.

Colbert, Edwin H., and Michael Morales. *Evolution of the Vertebrates: A History of the Backboned Animals Through Time.* 4th ed. New York: John Wiley & Sons, 1991.

Crick, Francis. *Life Itself: Its Origin and Nature.* London: Macdonald, 1981.

Crimes, Peter T. "The Period of Evolutionary Failure and the Dawn of Evolutionary

Success: The Record of Biotic Changes Across the Precambrian-Cambrian Boundary." In *The Paleobiology of Trace Fossils,* edited by Stephen K. Donovan, pp. 105-33. New York: John Wiley & Sons, 1994.

Day, Michael H. *Guide to Fossil Man.* 4th ed. Chicago: University of Chicago Press, 1986.

Dyson, Freeman. *Origins of Life.* Cambridge: Cambridge University Press, 1985.

Eicher, Don L., and A. Lee McAlester. *History of the Earth.* Englewood Cliffs, N.J.: Prentice-Hall, 1980.

Eigen, Manfred. *Steps Toward Life: A Perspective on Evolution.* Translated by Paul Woolley. Oxford: Oxford University Press, 1992.

─────, et al. "The Origin of Genetic Information." *Scientific American* 244, no. 4 (April 1981): 78-94.

Eldredge, Niles. *Time Frames: The Rethinking of Darwinian Evolution and the Theory of Punctuated Equilibria.* London: Heinemann, 1986.

Ferris, James P., et al. "Synthesis of Long Prebiotic Oligomers on Mineral Surfaces." *Nature* 381 (May 2, 1996): 59-61.

Forty, Richard. *Fossils: The Key to the Past.* London: Heinemann, 1982.

Futuyma, Douglas J. *Evolutionary Biology.* 2nd ed. Sunderland, Mass.: Sinauer Associates, 1986.

Gould, Stephen Jay. *Ontogeny and Phylogeny.* Cambridge, Mass.: Harvard University Press, 1977.

Haas, John W., Jr. "The Christian View of Science and Scripture: A Retrospective Look." *Journal of the American Scientific Affiliation* 31 (1979): 117.

Hasel, Gerhard F. "The Polemic Nature of the Genesis Cosmology." *Evangelical Quarterly* 46 (1974): 81-102.

Hoffman, Antoni. *Arguments on Evolution: A Paleontologist's Perspective.* New York: Oxford University Press, 1989.

Jenkins, John B. *Genetics.* Boston: Houghton Mifflin, 1975.

Kemp, T. S. *Mammal-Like Reptiles and the Origin of Mammals.* London: Academic Press, 1982.

Klein, Richard G. *The Human Career: Human Biological and Cultural Origins.* Chicago: University of Chicago Press, 1989.

Levington, Jeffrey. *Genetics, Paleontology and Macroevolution.* Cambridge: Cambridge University Press, 1988.

Levi-Setti, Riccardo. *Trilobites: A Photographic Atlas.* Chicago: University of Chicago Press, 1975.

Lewin, Roger. *Human Evolution: An Illustrated Introduction.* 3rd ed. Boston: Blackwell Scientific, 1993.

Mayr, Ernst. *The Growth of Biological Thought: Diversity, Evolution and Inheritance.* Cambridge, Mass.: Harvard University Press, 1982.

Miller, Stanley L., and Leslie Orgel. *The Origins of Life on the Earth.* Englewood Cliffs, N.J.: Prentice-Hall, 1974.

Morris, Henry, and Gary Parker. *What Is Creation Science?* El Cajon, Calif.: Master

Books, 1987.

Numbers, Ronald L. *The Creationists: The Evolution of Scientific Creationism.* Berkeley: University of California Press, 1992.

Oparin, A. I. *The Origin of Life on the Earth.* 3rd ed. Translated by Ann Synge. Edinburgh: Oliver and Boyd, 1957.

Orgel, Leslie E. "The Origin of Life on the Earth." *Scientific American* 271, no. 4 (October 1994): 53-61.

Packer, J. I. *"Fundamentalism" and the Word of God.* London: InterVarsity Fellowship, 1958.

Ramm, Bernard. *The Christian View of Science and Scripture.* Grand Rapids, Mich.: Eerdmans, 1954.

Reader, John. *Missing Links: The Hunt for Earliest Man.* New York: Penguin, 1988.

Ridley, Mark. *Evolution.* Boston: Blackwell Scientific, 1993.

Ringgren, Helmer. *"bara."* In *Theological Dictionary of the Old Testament,* edited by G. Johannes Botterweck and Helmer Ringgren, translated by John T. Willis, 2:242-49. Grand Rapids, Mich.: Eerdmans, 1975.

Schmalhausen, I. I. *The Origin of the Terrestrial Vertebrates.* Translated by Leon Kelso. New York: Academic Press, 1968.

Simpson, George Gaylord. *The Major Features of Evolution.* New York: Columbia University Press, 1953.

Stanley, Steven M. *The New Evolutionary Timetable: Fossils, Genes and the Origin of Species.* New York: Basic Books, 1981.

Stearn, Colin W., and Robert L. Carroll. *Paleontology: The Record of Life.* New York: John Wiley & Sons, 1989.

Stent, Gunther. *Molecular Genetics: An Introductory Narrative.* San Francisco: W. H. Freeman, 1971.

Suzuki, David, and Peter Knudston. *Genetics: The Clash Between the New Genetics and Human Values.* Cambridge, Mass.: Harvard University Press, 1989.

Tattersall, Ian. *The Fossil Trail.* New York: Oxford University Press, 1995.

Van Till, Howard J. "Basil, Augustine and the Doctrine of Creation's Functional Integrity." *Science and Christian Belief* 8, no. 1 (1996): 21-38.

———. *The Fourth Day: What the Bible and the Heavens Are Telling Us About the Creation.* Grand Rapids, Mich.: Eerdmans, 1986.

Waltke, Bruce K. "The Creation Account in Genesis 1:1-3: Part 1, Introduction to Biblical Cosmogony." *Bibliotheca Sacra* 132 (1975): 25-36.

Watson, James D. *The Double Helix: A Personal Account of the Discovery of the Structure of DNA.* Edited by Gunther S. Stent. London: Weidenfeld and Nicolson, 1981.

Weatherall, D. J. *The New Genetics and Clinical Practice.* 3rd ed. Oxford: Oxford University Press, 1991.

Wenham, Gordon. *Genesis 1-15.* Waco, Tex.: Word, 1987.

Westermann, Claus. *Genesis 1-11: A Commentary.* Translated by John J. Scullion. London: SPCK, 1984.

Whitcomb, John C., Jr., and Henry M. Morris. *The Genesis Flood: The Biblical Record and Its Scientific Implications.* Philadelphia: Presbyterian & Reformed, 1961.

Whittington, H. B. *Trilobites.* Woodbridge, U.K.: Boydell, 1992.

Wills, Christopher. *The Wisdom of the Genes: New Pathways in Evolution.* New York: Basic Books, 1989.

Young, David. *The Discovery of Evolution.* Cambridge: Cambridge University Press, 1992.

Chapter 8: The Anthropic Principle—or "Designer Universe"?

Alston, William P. *Perceiving God: The Epistemology of Religious Experience.* Ithaca, N.Y.: Cornell University Press, 1991.

Barrow, John D., and Frank J. Tipler. *The Anthropic Cosmological Principle.* Oxford: Clarendon, 1986.

Carr, B. J., and M. J. Rees. "The Anthropic Principle and the Structure of the Physical World." *Nature* 278 (1979): 605-12.

Carter, Brandon. "The Anthropic Principle and Its Implications for Biological Evolution." *Philosophical Transactions of the Royal Society of London* A310 (1983): 347-63.

Craig, William Lane. "Barrow and Tipler on the Anthropic Principle vs. Divine Design." *British Journal for the Philosophy of Science* 39 (1988): 389-95.

Crowe, Michael J. *The Extraterrestrial Life Debate, 1750-1900.* Cambridge: Cambridge University Press, 1986.

Davies, Paul. *The Mind of God: Science and the Search for Ultimate Meaning.* London: Simon & Schuster, 1992.

Dick, Steven J. *Plurality of Worlds: The Origins of the Extraterrestrial Life Debate from Democritus to Kant.* Cambridge: Cambridge University Press, 1982.

Dicke, R. H. "Dirac's Cosmology and Mach's Principle." *Nature* 192 (1961): 440-41.

Dirac, P. A. M. "The Cosmological Constant." *Nature* 139 (1937): 323-24.

Dyson, Freeman. *Disturbing the Universe.* New York: Harper & Row, 1979.

Earman, John. "The SAP Also Rises: A Critical Examination of the Anthropic Principle." *American Philosophical Quarterly* 24, no. 4 (1987): 307-16.

Everett, Hugh. " 'Relative State' Formulation of Quantum Mechanics." *Reviews of Modern Physics* 29 (1957): 454-62.

Gallagher, Kenneth T. "Remarks on the Argument from Design." *Review of Metaphysics* 48, no. 1 (1994): 19-31.

Glynn, Patrick. "Beyond the Death of God." *National Review,* May 6, 1966, pp. 28-32.

Hume, David. *Dialogues Concerning Natural Religion.* Edited by John Valdimer. Oxford: Clarendon, 1976.

Leslie, John. "Anthropic Principle, World Ensemble, Design." *American Philosophical Quarterly* 19, no. 2 (1982): 141-51.

————. "How to Draw Conclusions from a Fine-Tuned Universe." In *Physics, Philosophy and Theology: A Common Quest for Understanding,* edited by Robert John Russell, William Stoeger Jr. and George V. Coyne,. pp. 297-311. Vatican City: Vatican Observatory, 1988.

————. *Universes.* London: Routledge, 1989.

Polkinghorne, John. "Contemporary Interactions Between Science and Theology." *Modern Believing* 36, no. 4 (1995): 33-38.

————. *One World: The Interaction of Science and Theology.* London: SPCK, 1986.

Swinburne, Richard. "The Argument from the Fine-Tuning of the Universe." Appendix to *The Existence of God,* rev. ed. Oxford: Clarendon, 1979.

Wilson, Patrick A. "What Is the Explanandum of the Anthropic Principle?" *American Philosophical Quarterly* 28, no. 2 (1991): 167-73.

Zycynski, Joseph M. "The Weak Anthropic Principle and the Design Argument." *Zygon* 31, no. 1 (1996): 115-30.

Chapter 9: The Search for Extraterrestrial Intelligence & the Christian Doctrine of Redemption

Aquinas, Thomas. *Summa Theologica,* part 1. Translated by Fathers of the English Dominican Province. London: R. & T. Washbourne, 1912.

Arnold, Clinton E. *The Colossian Syncretism: The Interface Between Christianity and Folk Belief at Colossae.* Tübingen: J. C. B. Mohr, 1995.

Barrow, John D., and Frank J. Tipler. *The Anthropic Cosmological Principle.* Oxford: Oxford University Press, 1986.

Barth, Markus, and Helmut Blanke. *Colossians: A New Translation with Introduction and Commentary.* Translated by Astrid B. Beck. New York: Doubleday, 1994.

Brooke, John Hedley. *Science and Religion: Some Historical Perspectives.* Cambridge: Cambridge University Press, 1991.

Bruce, F. F. "Christ as Conqueror and Reconciler." *Bibliotheca Sacra* 141 (1984): 291-302.

Carter, Brandon. "The Anthropic Principle and Its Implications for Biological Evolution." *Philosophical Transactions of the Royal Society of London* A310 (1983): 347-63.

Clapp, Rodney. "Extraterrestrial Intelligence and Christian Wonder." *Christianity Today* 27, no. 7 (1983): 10.

Crick, Francis. *Life Itself: Its Origin and Nature.* London: MacDonald, 1981.

Davies, Paul. *Are We Alone?* London: Penguin, 1995.

————. *The Cosmic Blueprint.* London: William Heinemann, 1987.

DeMaris, Richard E. *The Colossian Controversy: Wisdom in Dispute at Colossae.* Sheffield, U.K.: Sheffield Academic Press, 1994.

Dick, Steven J. *Plurality of Worlds: The Origins of the Extraterrestrial Life Debate from Democritus to Kant.* Cambridge: Cambridge University Press, 1982.

Ellis, G. F. R., and G. B. Brundit. "Life in the Infinite Universe." *Quarterly Journal of the Royal Astronomical Society* 20 (1979): 37-41.

Gibbs, John G. "The Cosmic Scope of Redemption According to Paul." *Biblica* 56 (1975): 13-29.

————. *Creation and Redemption: A Study in Pauline Theology.* Leiden, Netherlands: E. J. Brill, 1971.

————. "Pauline Cosmic Christology and Ecological Crisis." *Journal of Biblical Literature* 90 (1971): 466-79.

Gould, Stephen Jay. *Wonderful Life.* New York: W. W. Norton, 1989.

Grady, Monica, Ian Wright and Colin Pillinger. "Opening a Martian Can of Worms?" *Nature* 382 (August 15, 1996): 575-76.

Hamerton-Kelly, R. G. *Pre-existence, Wisdom and the Son of Man.* SNTS Monograph Series 21. Cambridge: Cambridge University Press, 1973.

Harris, Murray J. *Colossians and Philemon.* Grand Rapids, Mich.: Eerdmans, 1991.

Heidmann, Jean. *Extraterrestrial Intelligence.* Translated by Storm Dunlop. Cambridge: Cambridge University Press, 1995.

Hoyle, Fred. *The Intelligent Universe.* London: Michael Joseph, 1983.

Jackson, Francis, and Patrick Moore. *Life in the Universe.* London: Routledge & Kegan Paul, 1987.

Jaki, Stanley L. *Cosmos and Creator.* Edinburgh: Scottish Academic Press, 1980.

Kauffman, Stuart. *The Origins of Order: Self-Organization and Selection in Evolution.* Oxford: Oxford University Press, 1993.

Lewis, C. S. "Religion and Rocketry." In *Fern-Seed and Elephants: And Other Essays on Christianity,* edited by Walter Hooper, pp. 86-95. London: Fontana, 1975

Lightfoot, J. B. *Saint Paul's Epistles to the Colossians and to Philemon.* London: Macmillan, 1897.

Lohse, Eduard. *A Commentary on the Epistles to the Colossians and to Philemon.* Translated by William J. Poehlmann and Robert J. Karris. Philadelphia: Fortress, 1971.

MacKay, David S., et al. "Search for Past Life on Mars: Possible Relic Biogenic Activity in Martian Meteorite ALH84001." *Science* 273 (August 16, 1996): 924-30.

Mascall, E. L. *Christian Theology and Natural Science.* London: Longmans, Green, 1956.

McColley, Grant. "The Seventeenth Century Doctrine of a Plurality of Worlds." *Annals of Science* 1 (1936): 385-430.

McColley, Grant, and H. W. Miller. "Saint Bonaventure, Francis Mayron, William Vorilong and the Doctrine of a Plurality of Worlds." *Speculum* 12 (1937): 386-89.

McMullin, Ernan. "Persons in the Universe." *Zygon* 15, no. 1 (March 1980): 69-89.

Milne, E. A. *Modern Cosmology and the Christian Idea of God.* Oxford: Clarendon, 1952.

Morrison, Philip, John Billingham and John Wolfe, eds. *The Search for Extraterrestrial Intelligence.* New York: Dover, 1979.

O'Brien, Peter T. *Colossians, Philemon.* Waco, Tex.: Word, 1982.

Paine, Thomas. *The Complete Writings of Thomas Paine.* Edited by Philip S. Foner. New York: Citadel, 1945.

Regis, Edward, Jr. *Extraterrestrials: Science and Alien Intelligence.* Cambridge: Cambridge University Press, 1985.

Sagan, Carl. *The Cosmic Connection: An Extraterrestrial Perspective.* London: Hodder & Stoughton, 1973.

Sappington, Thomas J. *Revelation and Redemption at Colossae*. Sheffield, U.K.: Sheffield Academic Press, 1991.

Schaff, Philip. *The Creeds of the Evangelical Protestant Churches*. London: Hodder & Stoughton, 1877.

Shklovski, I. S., and Carl Sagan. *Intelligent Life in the Universe*. San Francisco: Holden-Day, 1966.

Sullivan, Woodruff T. "Alone in the Universe?" *Nature* 380 (March 21, 1996): 211.

Chapter 10: Cosmic Endgame

Adkins, C. J. *An Introduction to Thermal Physics*. Cambridge: Cambridge University Press, 1987.

Arfken, George B., et al. *University Physics*. New York: Academic Press, 1984.

Augustine. *Confessions*. Translated by Vernon J. Bourke. Washington, D.C.: Catholic University of America Press, 1953.

Barbour, Ian G. *Religion in an Age of Science*. London: SCM Press, 1990.

Barrow, John D., and Frank J. Tipler. *The Anthropic Cosmological Principle*. Oxford: Clarendon, 1986.

Berger, Peter. *The Sacred Canopy: A Sociological Theory of Religion*. Garden City, N.Y.: Doubleday, 1969.

Blackwell, Richard J. *Galileo, Bellarmine and the Bible*. Notre Dame, Ind.: University of Notre Dame Press, 1991.

Burchfield, Joe D. *Lord Kelvin and the Age of the Earth*. Chicago: University of Chicago Press, 1975.

Close, Frank. *End: Cosmic Catastrophe and the Fate of the Universe*. London: Simon & Schuster, 1988.

Darwin, Charles. *The Autobiography of Charles Darwin, 1809-1882*. Edited by Nora Barlow. London: Collins, 1958.

Davies, Paul. *The Last Three Minutes: Conjectures About the Fate of the Universe*. London: Weidenfeld & Nicolson, 1994.

Dodds, E. R. *Pagan and Christian in an Age of Anxiety*. Cambridge: Cambridge University Press, 1965.

Dyson, Freeman J. "Time Without End: Physics and Biology in an Open Universe." *Reviews of Modern Physics* 51, no. 3 (1979): 447-60.

Eddington, A. S. *The Nature of the Physical World*. Cambridge: Cambridge University Press, 1928.

Ellis, G. F. R., and D. H. Coule. "Life at the End of the Universe?" *General Relativity and Gravitation* 26:7 (1994): 731-39.

Frankl, Viktor E. *Man's Search for Meaning: An Introduction to Logotherapy*. Boston: Beacon, 1962.

Frautschi, Steven. "Entropy in an Expanding Universe." *Science* 217, no. 4560 (1982): 593-99.

Goldstein, Martin, and Inge Goldstein. *The Refrigerator and the Universe: Understanding the Laws of Energy*. Cambridge, Mass.: Harvard University Press, 1993.

Hallberg, Fred W. "Barrow and Tipler's Anthropic Cosmological Principle." *Zygon* 23:2 (June 1988): 139-57.

Helmholtz, Hermann. *Popular Lectures on Scientific Subjects.* Translated by E. Atkinson. London: Longmans, Green, 1884.

Islam, Jamal N. *The Ultimate Fate of the Universe.* Cambridge: Cambridge University Press, 1983.

Jeans, James. *The Universe Around Us.* Cambridge: Cambridge Cambridge University Press, 1929.

Langford, Jerome J. *Galileo, Science and the Church.* 3rd ed. Ann Arbor: University of Michigan Press, 1992.

Moltmann, Jürgen. *Theology of Hope: On the Ground and the Implications of a Christian Eschatology.* Translated by James W. Leitch. London: SCM Press, 1967.

Numbers, Ronald L. *The Creationists: The Evolution of Scientific Creationism.* Berkeley: University of California Press, 1992.

Ohanian, Hans C. *Physics.* New York: W. W. Norton, 1985.

Petersen, Carolyn Collins, and John C. Brandt. *Hubble Vision: Astronomy with the Hubble Space Telescope.* Cambridge: Cambridge University Press, 1995.

Press, William H. "A Place for Teleology?" *Nature* 320 (March 27, 1986): 315-16.

Stoeger, W. R., and G. F. R. Ellis. "A Response to Tipler's Omega-Point Theory." *Science and Christian Belief* 7, no. 2 (1995): 163-72.

Thielicke, Helmut. *The Evangelical Faith.* Vol. 1, *Prolegomena: The Relation of Theology to Modern Thought Forms.* Translated by Geoffrey W. Bromiley. Grand Rapids, Mich.: Eerdmans, 1974.

Tillich, Paul. *Systematic Theology.* Chicago: University of Chicago Press, 1967.

Tipler, Frank J. *The Physics of Immortality: Modern Cosmology, God and the Resurrection of the Dead.* New York: Doubleday, 1994.

Weinberg, Steven. *The First Three Minutes.* London: Andre Deutsch, 1977.

Wells, David F. *God in the Wasteland: The Reality of Truth in a World of Fading Dreams.* Grand Rapids, Mich.: Eerdmans, 1994.

Young, Davis A. "Scripture in the Hands of the Geologists." *Westminster Theological Journal* 49 (1987): 1-34; 257-304.

Zemansky, Mark W. *Heat and Thermodynamics.* 5th ed. New York: McGraw-Hill, 1968.

Subject and Name Index

Abelard, Peter, 145
Abrahams, Israel, 20
Adams, Fred C., 159
Adkins, C. J., 160
Ahlberg, Per, 120
Albertus Magnus, 144
Allen, John, 60
Alston, William P., 100, 139
Amyraut, Moyse, 69
Anderson, Bernard, 13, 17
Anderson, James F., 23
Anselm, 45
Aquila, 19, 20
Aquinas, Thomas, 22, 42-44, 46, 47, 49, 50-54, 85, 107, 144, 145, 156
Arfken, George B., 160
Aristotle, 14, 42, 86, 89, 90, 97, 116, 143, 144
Arminius, James, 53, 58, 68, 69
Armstrong, Brian G., 69
Arnold, Clinton E., 152, 154
Atkatz, David, 31
Atkinson, E., 161
Augustine, 14, 20, 22, 42, 47, 48, 53, 106, 144, 172
Aurelius, Marcus, 174
Australopithecines, 122
Austro-Hungarian Empire, 90
Bampton Lectures, 150
Barbour, Ian G., 13, 14, 15, 39, 139, 173
Barlow, Nora, 161
Barrow, John D., 27, 34, 131, 132, 136, 138, 149, 163, 164, 169-173
Barth, Karl, 13, 59, 67,
107, 109
Barth, Markus, 152
Bartholemew, D. J., 78, 84
Bathsheba, 86
Beck, Allen D., 29
Beck, Astric B., 152
Belgic Confession, 65
Bell, John, 40
Berger, Peter, 173
Berkouwer, G. C., 108
Berlin, University of, 160
Berry, M. V., 74
Berry, R. J., 116
Berdyaev, Nicolas, 78
Billingham, John, 148
Birmingham, University of, 150
Blacker, Carmen, 24
Blackwell, Richard J., 173
Blanke, Helmut, 152
Boardman, Richard S., 124
Boethius, 42, 44, 45, 49, 50
Bohr, Neils, 38, 49, 60-62
Bondi, Hermann, 24, 27, 28
Boole, George, 93
Boston Theological Institute, 103
Botterweck, G. Johannes, 116
Bottino, Paul J., 117
Bourke, Vernon J., 85, 172
Brahma, 25
Brandt, John C., 169
Brent, 31
Brewer, Roberta, 27, 33
Brewster, David, 147
Brno, Czechoslovakia, 90
Bromiley, Geoffrey W., 49, 59, 107, 109, 174
Brooke, John Hedley, 146
Brout, R., 31
Brown, J. R., 60, 62
Brown, Warren S., 104
Bruce, F. F., 155
Brundit, G. B., 148
Brunner, Emil, 13
Bruno, Giordano, 146
Brussels, Univervsity of, 31
Bultmann, Rudolf, 12, 13
Burns George W., 117
Bury, R. G., 23, 86
Bussey, O., 13
Cadbury Lectures, 150
Cairns, David, 107
Cairns-Smith, A. G., 126
Calvin, John, 53, 54, 58, 60, 65, 69, 70, 85, 106
Cambridge, University of, 162, 175
Carnegie-Mellon University, 106
Carr, B. J., 129, 135
Carroll, Robert L., 118-120
Carter, Brandon, 131, 148, 149
Cassuto, Umberto, 17
Castro, Tony, 9
Center for Theology and the Natural Sciences, 78
Chalmers, David J., 104
Chalmers, Thomas, 147, 156
Chandler, Stuart, 78
de Chardin, Pierre Teilhard, 171
Chicago, University of, 124
Childs, Brevard, 98
Churchland, Paul M., 104
Clack, Jennifer A., 120
Clapp, Rodney, 155
Clark, Andy, 104
Clarkson, E. N. K., 123, 124
Clement (of Alexandria), 21, 106
Clines, D. J. A., 108
Colbert, Edwin H., 120, 121
Colson, F. H., 19
Constantine, 174
Copen, Paul, 19
Copenhagen School, 8, 57, 60-62, 65, 66,
68
Copernicus, Nicolaus, 131, 146
Coule, D. H., 171
Cowen, R., 165
Coyne, George V., 33, 61, 138
Craig, William Lane, 34, 42, 45-47, 53, 55, 95, 133, 137, 138
Crevier, Daniel, 103, 105, 106
Crick, Frances, 117, 125, 148, 149
Crimes, T. Peter, 123
Crowe, Michael J., 136, 142-44, 147
Crutchfield, James, 74, 76, 79, 80, 82, 83
Cultand, Nigel J., 101
Cundy, H. Martyn, 91, 96
Cushing, James T., 40
D'Espagnat, Bernard, 38, 40, 63
Dalley, Stephanie, 18, 86
Dartmouth University, 105, 106
Darwin, Charles, 83, 118, 130, 147, 149, 161, 175
David, King, 86
Davids, P. H., 110
Davies, Paul C., 28, 29, 34, 35, 38, 60, 62, 74, 82, 83, 137-139, 148, 164
Davis, Philip J., 99
Dawkins, Richard, 85, 112
Day, Michael H., 122
de Vega, H. J., 34
"Deep Blue" computer, 104, 106
DeMaris, Richard E., 152
Democritus, 143, 144
Dennett, Daniel C., 104
Descartes, René, 99, 100, 109, 124
Dick, Steven J., 136, 142, 143
Dicke, Robert H., 28, 130

Dirac, P. A. M., 130
Ditto, William, 74
Dobzhansky, Theodo-
sius, 148
Dodds, E. R., 174
Donaldson, James, 21
Donovan, Stephen K.,
123
Dort, Synod of, 58, 59,
65
Draper, John W., 36,
175
Drees, Willem, 12
Dreyfus, Herbert, 104
Dunlop, Storm, 148
Dyson, Freeman, 125,
129, 132, 133, 159,
160, 164, 170, 172,
173
Earman, John, 137
von Eckardt, Barbara,
104
Écoles Normales,
Paris, 81
Eddington, Arthur, 162
Ediacara Hills, Austra-
lia, 123
Edinburgh, University
of, 123
Edwards, David L., 67
Edwards, J. W., 13
Edwards, Paul, 91
Ehrhardt, Arnold, 24
Eicher, Don L., 122
Eichrodt, Walther, 17,
18
Eigen, Manfred, 125,
126
Einstein, Albert, 15,
28, 47, 60, 63, 77,
82, 91, 101, 110
Eldredge, Niles, 118,
119
Ellingson, Mark, 98
Ellis, G. F. R., 148,
171
Elwell, Walter A., 110
Enuma Elish, 17, 18,
86
Epicurus, 143, 144
Euclid, 76, 90-93, 101,
135
Eusebius of Caesarea,
144
Everett, Hugh, 136
Farmer, Doyne, 79, 80
Fathers of the English

Dominican Prov-
ince, 22, 107, 144
Feferman, Solomon,
89, 90
Feldman, Seymour, 19
Ferris, James P., 126
First Vatican Council,
23
Fishbone, Leslie, 29
Foerst, Anne, 109
Ford, David F., 97, 98
Ford, Gerald, 91
Fortey, Richard, 123
Frankl, Viktor E., 174
Frautschi, Steven, 168
Freedman, H., 20
Freddoso, Alfred J.,
46, 50
Frei, Hans, 98
Freud, Sigmund, 150
Freund, John, 48, 63
Foner, Philip S., 146
Fourth Lateran Coun-
cil, 23
Fox, Everett, 16
Futuyma, Douglas J.,
117
Gale, Richard M., 45
Galileo, 14, 15, 39,
146, 173, 175
Gallagher, Kenneth T.,
139
Gallican Confession,
65
Gamaliel, Rabbi, 20
Garrigou-Lagrange,
Reginald, 44, 51
Geach, Peter, 77
Gensler, Harry J., 91,
92
Gibbs, John G., 153
Gifford Lectures, 162
Gilkey, Langdon, 13
Glanz, James, 40, 63
Gleick, James, 72, 75,
79, 82
Glynn, Patrick, 130
Gödel, Adele, 90
Gödel, Kurt, 8,35, 89-
96, 98, 100, 101,
176
Gold, Thomas, 24, 27,
28
Goldbach, Christian,
92
Goldstein, Inge F.,
161, 172

Goldstein, Martin,
161, 172
Good, I. J., 94
Gordon-Conwell, 7,9
Gornall, Thomas, 42
Gould, Stephen Jay,
85, 112, 117-119,
148, 149
Grady, Monica, 141
Gribbin, John, 32, 33
Grim, Patrick, 94, 95
Gruder, Darrell L., 59
97, 109
Grunbaum, Adolf, 48,
63
Gunkel, Hermann, 17,
18
Guthrie, W. K. C., 24
Haas, John W., 113
Hahm, David E., 25
Hallberg, Fred W.,
170, 171
Hamerton-Kelly, R.
G., 154
Harris, Murray J., 152
Harris, R. Laird, 116
Hartle, J. B., 32, 33, 34
Harvard Center for
Astrophysics, 170
Hasel, Gerhard F., 16,
17, 115
Hasker, William, 45
Hauerwas, Stanley, 98
Hawking, Stephen W.,
25, 26, 28, 32-35
Hefner, Philip, 78
Heidel, Alexander, 17,
18, 86
Heidmann, Jean, 148
Heijenoort, J. van, 91,
93, 98
Heisenberg, Werner,
38, 40, 81, 82
Hellmuth, Thomas, 60,
64
Helmholtz, Hermann,
160, 161
Heppe, Heinrich, 97
Heraclitus, 25
Herbert, Nick, 38, 60-
63
Hermogenes, 22
Herron, Alasdair I. C.,
66
Hersh, Reuben, 99
Herzog, T. J., 64
Hippolytus of Rome,

144
Hiroshima, Japan, 110,
176
Hirsch, Edward, 16
Hodge, Charles, 67,
84, 85, 96, 97
Hoffman, Antoni, 119
Hofstadter, Douglas
R., 91, 94
Homo erectus, 122
Homo habilis, 122
*Homo neanderthalen-
sis,* 122
Homo sapiens, 122
Honner, John, 49, 60
Hooper, Walter, 151
Horgan, John, 11, 30,
34
Houghton, J. T., 74,
78, 83
Hoyle, Fred, 24, 27,
149
Hubble, Edwin, 25,
26, 148, 157
Human Genome
Project, 110, 176
Hume, David, 130,
139
Humbert, P., 16, 17
Hunter College,
C.U.N.Y., 30
Huygens, 124
IBM, 106
Institute for Advanced
Study, 90, 91, 159
International Union of
Theoretical and
Applied Mechanics,
71
Irenaeus, 22, 106
Isham, C. J., 33
Islam, Jamal N., 164,
171
Jackson, Francis, 148
Jaki, Stanley, 29, 35,
142, 143
Jammer, Max, 38, 63
Jarvik, Erik, 119
Jeans, James, 162
Jeeves, Malcolm A.,
104
Jellema, Dirk W., 108
Jenkins, John B., 117
Jesus, 45, 66
Jewett, Paul K., 59
Jones, L. Gregory, 98
Jonsson, Gunnlaugur

A., 107, 108
Josephus, 20
Justin Martyr, 21
Kadvany, John, 98
Kant, Immanuel, 23, 130
Karris, Robert J., 152
Kasparov, Garry, 104, 106
Kaufmann, Stuart, 148
Kemp, T. S., 120, 121
Kendall, R. T., 59, 69
Kim, Jong Hyun, 74
Kittel, Gerhard, 49
Kleene, Stephen Cole, 93
Klein, Richard G., 122
Knight, H., 13
Knudston, Peter, 117
Kretzmann, Norman, 45
Kvanvig, Jonathan L., 45
Kwiat, P. G., 63
Lakatos, Imre, 99
Lake, Kirsopp, 21
Lambert, W.G., 18
Langford, Jerome J., 173
Laplace, Pierre-Simon, 81, 83
Laskar, Jacques, 81, 82
Laughlin, Gregory, 159
Leenhardt, Franz, 67
Leitch, James W., 174
Leitch, William, 147
Leslie, John, 34, 55, 133, 138
Levi-Sutti, Riccardo, 124
Levington, Jeffrey, 119
Levy, Steven, 104
Lewin, Roger, 122
Lewis, C. S., 151, 152
Lieberman, M. A., 74
Lichtenberg, A. J., 74
Lightfoot, J. B., 152, 154
Lighthill, James, 71, 73, 81
Lightman, Alan, 26-28, 33
Lindbeck, George, 97, 98
Lindberg, David C.,

25, 36, 111
Linde, A. D., 30, 136
Lindley, David, 35
Lloyd, G. E. R., 24
Loewe, Michael, 24
Lohse, Eduard, 152, 154
Longair, Malcolm S., 26
Lorenz, Edward, 72, 73
Los Alamos National Laboratory, 79
Lucas, J. R., 93, 94
Lucretius, 143
Luksevics, Ervins, 120
Luther, Martin, 107
Lyall, Francis, 110
MacIntyre, Alasdair, 99
MacKay, David S., 141
Mackay, Donald M., 77
Malony, H. Newton, 104
Mandelbrot, Bernard, 75, 76
Manhattan Project, 110
Marduk, 86
Marks, John H., 17
Marlow, A. R., 60
Marx, Karl, 150
Mascall, E. L., 151, 152
Massachusetts Institute of Technology, 72, 103, 105, 106
Maxwell, James Clerk, 175
May, Gerhard, 19
May, Robert, 74, 75
Mayr, Ernst, 117, 148
McAlester, A. Lee, 122
McColley, Grant, 144-146
McComiskey, Thomas E., 116
McDermott, Timothy, 43
McDonagh, Francis, 4
McFadden, Robert D., 104
McMullin, Ernan, 14, 40, 142, 143

Melanchthon, Phillip, 146
Meyering, Theo, 99
Miller, H. W., 145
Miller, Stanley, 124, 125
Milne, E. A., 150, 156
Minsky, Marvin, 105
Molina, Luis, 42, 45-47, 50, 51, 53, 95
Mohr, J. C. B., 153
Moltmann, Jürgen, 174
Monod, Jacques, 85
Moon, Francis C., 87
Moore, James R., 85
Moore, Patrick, 148
Morales, Michael, 120, 121
Moravec, Hans, 105, 106
Morris, Henry, 114, 127
Morris, Thomas V., 45
Morrison, Philip, 148
Moses, 19, 21
Mukerjee, Madhusree, 34
Muller, Richard A., 60
Murphey, Nancy, 14, 37, 79, 80, 99, 100, 104
Musculus, Wolfgang, 65
Nagasaki, Japan, 176
Nagel, Ernst, 91, 92, 93
Narlikar, Jayant V., 26, 33
NASA Self-Replicating Systems Concept Team, 103
NASA Space Center, Houston, 141
Neo-Platonists, 107
New York, University of, 159
Newman, James R., 91, 92, 93
Newton, Isaac, 15, 71-76, 80, 81, 82, 86
Nicole, Roger, 69
Noble, David F., 105, 106
Novikor, I. D., 29
Numbers, Ronald L., 36, 111, 113, 114,

173
O'Brien, Peter T., 152, 153, 155
O'Flaherty, Wendy Doniger, 25
Occam, William of, 137
Ohanian, Hans C., 160
Omnes, Roland, 38
Oparin, A. I., 125
Orgel, Leslie, 125, 126
Ostriker, Jeremiah P., 169
Owen, H. P., 45
Packer, J. I., 115
Padgett, Alan G., 50
Pagel, Heinz, 11, 31, 33-35
Paine, Thomas, 146
Pannenberg, Wolfhart, 14
Parker, Gary, 127
Parmenides, 49
Paine, Thomas, 156
Paul, apostle, 66, 109, 153, 157
Pauli Exclusion Principle, 132
Peacocke, Arthur, 8, 14, 15, 37-42, 47, 50, 53, 56, 79, 80, 84, 85, 139, 175
Pearcey, Nancy R., 38, 111
Pecora, Louis, 74
Penrose, Roger, 28, 104
Penzias, Arno, 26
Peres, Asher, 38
Peter Martyr, 65
Petersen, Carolyn Collins, 169
Phillips, Perry, 9
Philo, 19, 20
Pike, Nelson, 44, 45
Pillinger, Colin, 141
Pinker, Steven, 104
Piram, Tsvi, 25
Planck, Max, 33
Plantinga, Alvin, 45, 46
Plato, 19, 21, 23-25, 44, 50, 86, 107
Poehlmann, William J., 152
Polkinghorne, John, 7, 15, 38, 137, 139,

175
Pollard, William, 39, 77
Poincaré, Henri, 76
Polanyi, Michael, 78
Press, William, 170
Price, John Valdimer, 139
Prigogine, Ilya, 75, 77, 87
Princeton, University of, 168
Princeton Seminary, 84, 96
Protestant Scholastics, 97
Ptolemy, 14
Pythagoreans, 25
Queen's College, Kingston, 147
Quine, W. V. O., 100
Rabinowitz, Louis, 20
Ramm, Bernard, 8, 9, 113-115, 122, 124, 126, 127
Raup, David M., 174
Reader, John, 122
Rees, M. J., 129, 135
Regis, Edward, Jr., 148
Reichenbach, Hans, 48, 63
Reichenbach, Maria, 48, 63
Reid, J. K. S., 60
Richards, Jay Wesley, 136
Ridley, Mark, 117
Ringgren, Helmer, 116
Roberts, Alexander, 21
Rockefeller University, 31
Rohrlich, Fritz, 40
Roos, Matts, 26, 32
Rose, Dom Bede, 44
Royal Society of London, 71
Ruelle, David, 73
Russell, Bertrand, 93, 162, 163, 164
Russell, Robert J., 33, 37, 60, 61, 79, 80, 138
Sagan, Carl, 148
Sambursky, Shmuel, 25
Sanchez, N., 34
Sappington, Thomas

J., 152
Sarna, Nahum, 11, 16
Sasse, Hermann, 49
Schaff, Philip, 58, 156
Schmalhausen, I. I., 120
Scullion, John J., 17, 86, 115
Searle, John, 104
Septuagint, 19
van Seters, J., 110
SETI (Search for Extra-Terrestrial Intelligence), 142, 145, 148
Shannon, Claude, 105
Shklovskii, I. S., 148
Siberia, 90, 123
Silk, Joseph, 15, 26-29
Siebeck, Paul, 153
Simon, Maurice, 20
Simpson, George Gaylord, 112, 119
Skinner, John, 16
Sklar, Lawrence, 48
Smith, Norma Kemp, 23
Smith, Quentin, 34, 55
Socrates, 92
Solomonoff, Ray, 105
Sophists, 24
Speiser, E. A., 16
Spurgeon, Charles, 67
Stanford University, 106
Stanley, Steven M., 118
Stearn, Colin W., 118, 119
Steinhart, Paul J., 169
Stent, Gunther, 117
Stewart, Ian, 74
Stines, J. W., 78
Stoeger, William R., 33, 60, 138, 171
Stringer, John, 74
Stump, Eleonore, 45
Sullivan, Woodruff T., 142, 149
Suzuki, David, 117
Swinburne, Richard, 95, 100, 138, 139
Symmachus, 19
Taliaferro, Charles, 104
Tanner, Norman P., 23
Targum, 19

Tatian, 22
Tattersall, Ian, 122
Templeton, John, 7
Tertullian, 22
Thackeray, Henry, 20
Thaxton, Charles B., 38, 111
Theilecke, Helmut, 174
Theodotion, 19
Theophilus, 21
Thomas, Owen C., 39
Thompson, William Lord Kelvin, 16
Thomson, G. T., 97
Tiamat, 86
van Till, Howard J., 128
Tillich, Paul, 12, 13, 174
Tipler, Frank, 131, 132, 136, 138, 149, 163, 169, 173
Tommotian fauna, 123
Torrance, James B., 66
Torrance, Thomas F., 48, 50, 57, 59, 77, 78, 107, 109
Toulmin, Stephen, 99
Trefil, James S., 26, 35
Trinity College, 27
Tryon, Edward, 30
Tsumura, David, 18
Tufts University, 31
Turing, Alan, 105, 106
Ullian, J. S., 100
Urbach, Ephraim, 20
Urey, Harold, 148
Vawter, Bruce, 16
Vienna, University of, 90
Vilenkin, Alexander, 31, 32
von Rad, Gerhard, 17, 18
Vorilong, William, 145, 156
Vulgate, 19
Waltke, Bruce K., 17, 19, 115
Wang, Hao, 90
Ward, Keith, 54
Watson, Andrew, 63
Watson, James D., 117, 148
Watts, William, 20, 48
Weatherall, D. J., 117

Webb, Robert Alexander, 110
Weber, Otto, 59, 65, 70, 97, 109
Weinberg, Steven, 25, 35, 163, 164, 167, 172
Wells, David, 109
Wenham, Gordon, 17, 115
Westermann, Claus, 17, 86, 115
Westminster Confession, 54, 58, 59, 66, 85, 155-56
Wheeler, John Archibald, 38, 58, 60, 63, 64, 66, 68
White, Andrew Dickson, 36, 175
Whitehead, Alfred North, 44, 93
Whitcomb, John C., Jr., 114
Whitrow, G. J., 48, 63
Whittaker, G. H., 19
Whittington, H. B., 124
Wilder, Raymond L., 93
Willis, John T., 116
Wills, Christopher, 117
Wilson, Robert, 26
Wilson, Patrick A., 131
Wittgenstein, Ludwig, 97
Wolfe, John, 148
Wolfson, Harry, 20
Woolley, Paul, 126
Wright, George E., 13
Wright, Ian, 141
Wyon, Olive, 13
Yokohama, 90
Yougrau, Wolfgang, 29
Young, David, 117
Young, Davis, 14, 173
Zel'dovich, Ya B., 29
Zemansky, Mark W., 161
Zurek, Wojciech H., 38, 60
Zycinski, Joseph M., 132

Scripture Index

Genesis
1:1, 11, 12, 15, 16-19,
    21, 25, 36, 116
1:2, 15, 21
1:20-21, 127, 128
1:24, 128
1—11, 115

Numbers
11:31, 127

Genesis Rabbah
1:9, 20

1 Kings
6:6, 127

Job
38:4, 87

Psalms
19, 61
104:14, 127
104:24, 127
104:30, 117, 127
139:1-6, 46

Proverbs
8:23, 17

Isaiah
1:2, 109
40:21, 17

41:21-42, 45
44:6-8, 45
46:9-10, 17, 45

Jeremiah
3:19, 109

Ezekiel
18:33, 69

Wisdom of Solomon
11:17, 21

Hosea
11:1, 109

Amos
4:13, 116

2 Maccabees
7:28, 19,20

Matthew
10:29, 85

Mark
8:31, 45
9:31, 45
10:32-34, 45
14:13-15, 18-20, 27-
    30, 45

John
1:1, 21, 87
1:3, 21, 87, 153
3:16, 68, 69

Acts
13:48, 65
14:14-17, 61
17:22-26, 61

Romans
1:18-20, 61
4:17, 21
5:12-21, 156
8:15, 23, 109
8:19-23, 151, 174
9:4, 109
9:6-24, 65
9:18, 53
11:7, 23, 61, 66, 67,
    68

1 Corinthians
1:27-28, 65
8:6, 153
15:39, 128
15:45-49, 156

Galatians
4:5, 109

Ephesians
1:4, 58, 64, 65, 67, 68

1:5, 109

Colossians
1:16, 21
1:15-20, 87, 143, 152,
    153, 155, 156
1:17, 153
1:19-20, 9, 154, 155

1 Thessalonians
1:4-5, 65

1 Timothy
6:16

2 Timothy
1:9, 65
1:10, 174

Hebrews
1:3, 15, 153
11:3, 21

1 Peter
1:1-2, 65

2 Peter
3:9, 69

Revelation
4:11, 21
21:1, 174